The Magnificent Moisants

The Magnificent Moisants

Champions of Early Flight

Doris L. Rich

SMITHSONIAN INSTITUTION PRESS
Washington and London

Library of Congress Cataloging-in-Publication Data

Rich, Doris L.
    The magnificent Moisants : champions of early flight / Doris L. Rich.
        p.   cm.
    Includes bibliographical references and index.
    ISBN 1-56098-860-6
        1. Moisant family.   2. Air pilots—United States—Biography.   3. Stunt
flying—History.   4. Air shows—United States—History.   5. Aeronautics
—History.   6. Central America—Politics and government—1826–1951.
I. Title.
TL540.M554R53   1998
629.13′092′2—dc21
[B]   98-6876
                                                                                                    CIP

British Library Cataloguing-in-Publication Data available

Manufactured in the United States of America
05 04 03 02 01 00 99 98   5 4 3 2 1

For Henry and Laurie and their children
Larry, Beth, and Amy

CONTENTS

ACKNOWLEDGMENTS

Much of the material in this book came from the Smithsonian Institution's National Air and Space Museum library and archives, both in Washington, D.C., and at the Paul E. Garber Preservation, Restoration, and Storage Facility in Suitland, Maryland.

For their advice and assistance I thank Tim Cronen, Tom Crouch, Robert Dreesen, Phil Edwards, Dan Hagedorn, Kristine Kafke, Melissa Keiser, Paul McCutcheon, Brian Nicklas, Mary Pavlovich, Thomas F. Soapes, Pat Squire, Patricia Williams, and Larry Wilson.

Additional material came from special collections and archives at the following libraries and organizations: Library of Congress, National Archives, and Martin Luther King Memorial Library, all in Washington, D.C.; Alameda Free Public Library, Alameda, California; Bancroft Library, University of California at Berkeley; Branch County Library, Coldwater, Michigan; College Park Airport Museum, College Park, Maryland; Columbia University Oral History Collection, New York City; Eugene C. Barker Texas History Center, University of Texas, and the Collection Deposit Library, both in Austin; Family History Center, Bourbonnais, Illinois; Historic New Orleans Collection, Kemper and Leila Williams Foundation, New Orleans; Historical Society of Douglas County, Omaha, Nebraska; History of Aviation Collection, University of Texas at Richardson; Iroquois County Genealogy Society, Watseka, Illinois; Memphis Shelby County Public Library and Information Center, Memphis, Tennessee; Oakland Public Library, Oakland, California; San Diego Aerospace Museum, Balboa Park, San Diego; and Soper Library, Morgan State University, Baltimore.

Assisting me were Bob Adwers, Pamela Arceneux, Rota Burgers, Barbara Clark, Lynn Cutler, Verna and Harold Drake, Ralph L. Elder, Ray Fearing, Santiago A. Flores, Pat Fry, James R. Greenwood, Ann B. Haller, Kenneth Heger, Margaret Koyne, Patricia LaPointe, Norma Meier, Woodruff C. Minor, Terry O'Quinn, Larry Odoms, Larry Sall, and Christopher P. Schiff.

Information from correspondence came from Marie-Josèphe de Beauregard, Diana Estudillo, Giacinta Bradley Koontz, Edward L. Leiser, Lawrence Rich, Frank Strnad, and W. Ralph Wright.

I am grateful for the interview and other materials so generously given me by John A. Weyl, the Moisants' nephew who was at Santa Emilia on two occasions and in later years a frequent visitor at the home of his favorite aunt, Matilde, until her death in 1964; also to Richard de Wolf Kantner for permission to use the recorded recollections of his father, Harold Kantner; to Wesley R. Smith for reference material on aircraft; and to the late Henry Serrano Villard, aviation historian, who gave me encouragement when I most needed it.

Offering shelter during research travels were Margaret Stevens Bordwell, Donald C. and Daryl Ferguson, Lindsay and Berry Grant, A.J.M. and Mariam Hasan, Barbara Gault Hayes, Mary Cushman North, N. G. and Theresa Payne, and Deborah and Christopher Rich.

My thanks to Daniel H. Goodwin and Mark G. Hirsch of the Smithsonian Institution Press; to Therese D. Boyd, who has edited all of my books; and finally to Stanley Rich, my manager, agent, traveling companion, discerning critic, master of that infernal machine, the computer, and my husband for fifty wonderful years.

The Magnificent Moisants

1

THE SURROGATE FATHER

On the second day of January in 1862 at the baptismal font of St. John the Baptist Roman Catholic Church in L'Erable, Illinois, icy drops of water fell on the forehead of a day-old infant as the priest intoned, "Je te baptise au nom du Dieu Père, Dieu Fils et Dieu Saint Esprit, Charles Alfred Moisant." The child's parents were Medore Moisant and Josephine Fortier Moisant, both French-speaking immigrants from Canada. They had been married at the same church 11 months before the birth of this, the first of twelve children Josephine would bear. Medore (or Medose or Medard Moisant, or Moisan, depending on which priest, doctor, or census-taker was writing it down) was a 23-year-old farm laborer. Josephine was 21, the daughter of a farmer, Isaac Fortier, and Marie Locadie Bonse Fortier.

Although the Fortiers were landowners, there was no reason for them not to accept the young Moisant as a social equal and an acceptable husband for their daughter. The Moisant family name appears frequently in church records of the time, and the Moisants were active participants in the clannish community of French-speaking immigrant farmers who settled in Iroquois County. The Moisants and Fortiers, along with their neighbors in L'Erable and several nearby towns, comprised an enclave of French-speaking agriculturists who, though only 75 miles south of Chicago on the Illinois Central Railroad line, might well have been living on the European continent. It is unlikely Medore and Josephine knew or cared that in the year of their first child's birth Edwin Booth was in Chicago playing Romeo at the McVickers Theater to the Juliet of Mary McVickers, whose father owned the theater. Or that Booth and McVickers married soon after. Or even that Congress had passed the Homestead Act, granting settlers 160 acres of free public land to farm, improve, and eventually own. Medore would have jumped at the opportunity but for the fact that by the time the Homestead Act was passed, there was no free public land left in that part of Illinois.

In the decade following Charles Alfred's birth, in towns named Clifton, Beaverville, St. Anne, Manteno, and Kankakee, as well as in L'Erable, Moisants and Fortiers proliferated and thrived—brothers, sisters, aunts, uncles, cousins, nieces, and nephews of Medore and Josephine. It is not known how long Medore continued to work for a farmer named Joseph Tellier, but sometime in 1864 the young couple and their two children —a second son, Edward, was born in 1863—set up their own household on land Medore purchased from Josephine's father.

It was potentially fertile land along the Iroquois River. But springing as it had from a glacial lake 6,000 years earlier, the rich soil demanded constant care and cultivation. And it was brutally hard to get at, often almost strangled by a dense prairie-grass cover and the tangled and twisted network of grass roots just beneath. Years before the Moisants and the Fortiers claimed the land, the cattle of earlier immigrants did much to tame it, grazing on the thick prairie grass that was often tall enough to obscure both horse and rider. But much still remained to be done. Special breaking plows had to be developed to cut through and pulverize the grass roots. Even then, a costly system of drainage tiles had to be built and installed before the black, fertile earth could be planted.

Although small and slight like most of his fellow immigrants, Medore's stature was no measure of his energy and determination. He proved more than capable, not only developing his land into a profitable farm but becoming an exceptionally skilled carpenter at the same time. It may have been the need to provide for his growing family—a third son, Joseph Georges (George), was born in 1865—or it may have been simply that the farm itself was not enough to satisfy his ambition. But about the time George was born, Medore sold the farm and moved Josephine and the children to the nearest big town of Clifton (some seven miles to the northwest), where he had purchased two lots on Main Street, facing the railroad tracks on the north edge of the business district.

Medore and Josephine were to have nine more children. He continued to buy property along the Illinois-Indiana border south of Chicago and moved the family frequently as opportunity dictated, presumably farming in the summers and working in the winters as a carpenter on new rail stations being built to accommodate the continuing growth in the area.

They were, in fact, living in Chicago when a fourth son, Joseph Jean Baptiste (who later changed his name to John Bevins), was born April 25, 1870. By the time of the disastrous Chicago fire, which in 17 hours destroyed more than 17,000 houses and left 90,000 homeless in October 1871, the itinerant Moisants had moved back to Clifton. A page from the account book of that town's Taft and Gage Hardware Store includes the following entries:

> 30 August 1871 Medore Moisant
> 12 papers 6 oz tacks .72
> bolts .10
> 7 October 1871 Medier Moisant
> 1 grain scoop 1.75
> 23 February 1872 M. Moisant
> bal. on T. Kettle .40

Medore's original purchase of land in Clifton in 1865 had obviously proved financially successful. Over the next eight years he continued to buy both agricultural and commercial property closer and closer to Chicago in such towns as Chebanse, Beaverville, Papineau, and St. Anne in Kankakee County, where the first Moisant daughter, Ann Marguerite, was born in 1874. Four years later another daughter arrived, Matilde Josephine, born either on a farm outside Manteno, to which the family had moved in 1878, or, according to one family recollection, perhaps just across the border in Earl Park, Indiana. At any rate, the Manteno census of 1880 lists the Moisant family as Medore, farmer, 41; his wife Josephine, 39; and children George (no longer Joseph Georges), 14; John, 10; Annie, 6, and Matilde, 2. (When the census was taken, the oldest, Alfred, 19, was working for an uncle in Kankakee, and Edward, 17, was working elsewhere in the area.)

The 1880s were certainly busy years for the Moisants and probably difficult ones as well—especially for Josephine with her rapidly expanding family. By early 1881 they were living at 34th and Queens Streets in Chicago, where Medore's construction skills were no doubt in demand in a city still busy rebuilding itself from the fire. On April 3 that year Josephine gave birth to another daughter, unnamed on the birth certificate but listed as her tenth child. Almost exactly two years later, the family having moved again and now living at 39th and Bern, the last Moisant child, Louise, was born April 18, 1883. Since her birth certificate lists Louise as Josephine's twelfth child, this means that the previous child and four others born between Edward in 1863 and Matilde in 1877 or 1878 all failed to survive childhood.

Medore died in 1887, a few years short of 50. The strain of having to combine constant travel to construction work in and out of Chicago with continual oversight trips to his various farm and commercial properties along the Illinois-Indiana border no doubt contributed to his early demise. But he accomplished much in his abbreviated half century. He left his family if not rich at least comfortably provided for with income from both farm and real-estate holdings. He sired a dozen children, of whom seven survived into adulthood and at least three would accomplish even more—in areas and foreign countries, moreover, of which he himself could never have imagined.

Although the clannishness of rural French immigrant families was to survive as late as the 1940s when, according to one observer, "French-speaking high-school students would not socialize with any of the rest of us," the Moisant children escaped the cultural isolation that ensnared so many families like their own. Only Ann Marguerite would go on to college, but all would have a sound high school education. They spoke French at home but were totally bilingual. The experience of having lived not only on farms but also in the trade and meatpacking center of Chicago—a place so politically corrupt that Prince Otto von Bismarck, the Iron Chancellor of Germany, visited it in 1870 because, he said, he just had to see the "Boss City"—gave them a sophistication far beyond their years.

At Medore's death, 25-year-old Charles Alfred immediately took over as head of the family. Short, broadly built, a thatch of hair shadowing his wide brow and swarthy face, he sported a thick moustache and wore the three-piece wool suits of the rising young businessman he already was. Rejecting his father's advice to go to college and enter a profession, he had left home at 16 to work instead for an uncle in Kankakee who owned an ice business with 190 employees. His claim to have been named general manager after only three weeks on the job when his uncle took off for eight months in Europe may have been an exaggeration. But there is no doubt that Alfred J. Moisant—no one knew why he dropped the Charles and added the J—was an up-and-coming entrepreneur and salesman, not only of merchandise but of concepts and, above all, of himself as a dynamic and successful businessman.

Alfred had undoubtedly been to Chicago on his own after he went to work for his uncle and knew a great deal about that raucous city, whose society dictator was the jewel-laden Mrs. Potter Palmer, who kept a second mansion in Paris. And he no doubt approved rather than envied department-store magnate Marshall Field's expenditure of $75,000 to transform his house into a Japanese village for a "Mikado Ball" in honor of his son's seventeenth birthday. For by now he was as ambitious and "all-American" as any of his most chauvinistic contemporaries. But the one element of his immigrant background he refused to abandon was loyalty to family and clan. By virtue of not only seniority, but also of ambition and an innate sense of familial responsibility, Alfred reveled in his new role as unchallenged caretaker and decisionmaker of the Moisant family. A year after his father died he packed up the entire family—mother Josephine, Edward and his wife Mary, George, John, Ann Marguerite, Matilde, and Louise—and moved them to California.

The first appearance of the Moisant family names in California history is in the 1888 Alameda city directory, which records "Alfred J., commission merchant," "Edward, carpenter," "Mrs. J. [Josephine]," and "John B., student" residing at an unnumbered Alameda home at College Street near Monroe. Also living there were Edward's wife, Mary; their infant son, Clarence, and the three Moisant girls, Ann, Matilde, and Louise. George presumably was working and living elsewhere in the area.

Alameda and the Moisants were perfectly suited to each other. Despite the fact that Park Street, the main thoroughfare, was still muddy, rutted, and scarred by wagon tracks, Alameda was a thriving boom town whose population had tripled in the 1870s, doubled in the 1880s, and grew by half as much again in the 1890s. Just two years before Alfred and his family settled there, Alameda became the first city in California and only the second in the United States to operate its own electric plant. Buildings were being erected at an amazing rate—churches, schools, business blocks, and hundreds of homes. Most of Alameda's streets would be graded, curbed, and paved during the decade the Moisants lived there, although the very year they arrived a newspaper carrier complained indignantly about the daily hazards he faced of falling into open sewer trenches, or crashing into trees which "careless and thoughtless" people had felled without providing lanterns to warn of the danger.

The Moisants, too, prospered right along with Alameda. Young John and his three sisters felt perfectly at home in high school and would have been neither shunned nor slighted had they been overheard speaking French. More than 70 percent of Alameda high-schoolers in 1888 had at least one foreign-born parent. And whatever "Alfred J., commission merchant" was buying and selling it was obviously profitable. His arrival in Alameda began a decade of furious whirlwind activity during which Alfred himself—and his brothers by extension—could well have qualified as the prototype for the ultimate "rags-to-riches" Horatio Alger hero. Alfred claimed that within a year or two of arriving in California his "struggles were rewarded with ownership of a splendid farm in Alameda."

By 1890, two years after they had arrived in Alameda, the Moisants had moved into a second house on College Street, near Encinal, and the family name began to appear in the social columns of a local newspaper, the *Argus*. Spring and summer of that year appears to have been a particularly busy time for the younger Moisants. All duly recorded by the *Argus,* in the first week of March Annie returned to her College Street home to a surprise party given by her friends (possibly in honor of her sixteenth birthday); exactly one month later John, who was to turn 20 in a matter of weeks, was one of nine boys and eight girls invited to "a junior social gathering" at another girl's home for an evening of dancing, games, dinner, and "vocal selections"; and on July 5, "J. B. Moisant" was on the guest list of "a party of young people" treated to a Sunday yacht cruise around the harbor. Two months later, although mistakenly identified as Albert J., Alfred made his first appearance in the social column with a report that he was to leave July 19 "on a business trip to Central America." The commission merchant had apparently raised enough capital in California to enable him now to seek further profits abroad.

Alfred made that first trip alone. The next year he took John with him, leaving the country on August 5 and telling the *Argus* editor they owned land in Guatemala where they were going to establish coffee plantations. A lack of reliable ownership records and a marked penchant on the part of both men to exaggerate make it difficult to ascertain just how much property the Moisant brothers did own. While John spoke of plantations in Guatemala, Alfred claimed to have organized three large banks in Central America and acquired 40,000 acres of sugar and farm land and other property in El Salvador, Mexico, Nicaragua, and Honduras. On other occasions he spoke of owning two of the largest sugar and coffee ranches in El Salvador and of being the majority stockholder and founder of "the largest and most prosperous bank in the republic." Alfred attributed the family's success to "watchfulness and seizing opportunities." Of that there can be little doubt. Despite the fact that many of Alfred's claims were overstated, U.S. government records do confirm that by 1893 he had acquired at least 6,000 acres of land near Sonsonate, El Salvador. He also persuaded brothers George and Edward to assist him in developing the largest of his land holdings at Sonsonate.

Presumably keeping pace with Alfred's upward mobility, the Moisants in Alameda moved several times until, in 1895, they settled in a four-year-old Queen Anne house at 2708 Central Avenue. Here, while the Moisant men were busy in El Salvador, Josephine, with the aid of her daughter-in-law Mary, presided over a household of women and children. "Annie" and "Tillie," as they were referred to in the local newspaper, were both in high school, while Louise went to grade school with her nephew and niece, Clarence and Harriet, the children of Edward and Mary.

The Moisant children mingled easily with Alameda's other affluent families, joining in numerous parties and vacation trips to nearby resorts. This in a community where the average annual income was $2,000, and where the prevailing means of transport was the horse and buggy and a tandem bicycle cost as much as $300, or, as one critic put it, "as much as a horse and buggy to ride in fashion."

The same year the family settled into the Central Avenue house John Moisant returned from El Salvador to marry a 21-year-old neighbor, Edith F. Stanle, whose family was one of the most prominent in the city, the German-immigrant father being a federal government tax official in San Francisco and a past president of the Alameda Democratic Club. Despite the Stanle name, however, there was only one newspaper mention of the February 6 wedding, a brief paragraph in the next day's *Argus* stating that John had secured a marriage license. A possible explanation for such scant public notice of so prominent a family who were mentioned almost daily in both Alameda and San Francisco social columns is the fact that John applied for a passport only a month after the wedding and he was still in El Salvador on November 24 when Edith gave birth to a son, Stanlie, at her parents' residence. The marriage certificate, provided by John's nephew John A. Weyl, shows both Edith's parents as witnesses. They may have been the only, or among the very few, people present. Edith and her son joined John in Sonsonate three months after the birth and 13 months after the wedding. One year later, and shortly after her husband died, Edith's mother also went to Sonsonate with the avowed intention of staying. But after 11 months she returned to California without explanation, telling Alameda newsmen only that her son-in-law and family were all in good health—and then going to live with a son in San Francisco.

Weyl recalls Alfred telling him years later that during his first trip to El Salvador he became so enchanted with the beauty of the place that he vowed he would move his family there some day. And between 1896 and 1900 Alfred did just that, ordaining the gradual exit of most of the family from Alameda to "Santa Emilia," the plantation he and his brothers had been painstakingly putting together.

In a 1907 letter then–American Consul General in San Salvador William Lawrence Merry describes the Moisant property of Santa Emilia as

a hacienda . . . a beautiful and very fertile irrigated estate producing hard timber, sugar cane, cattle for beef and dairy purposes, corn, rice, etc. About 150 workmen are there employed and many reside on the place, this being encouraged by the Moisants. There are two American employees on the place, the engineer and sub-manager; all the remainder are natives. The profits annually average 100,000 silver and are increasing.

Merry's thumbnail description does scant justice to the expanse and beauty of the property. Eight miles inland from the port of Acajutla and only two or three more to Sonsonate, where the plantation's business office was located, Santa Emilia was large enough to have a stop all its own on the San Salvador–Acajutla rail line that ran 38 miles west from the capital to Sonsonate before jagging south to the sea. Crossed by two rivers, the plantation was so extensive that it required a full day to ride on horseback from one side to the other. Besides sugar cane there were cacao trees, small tropical evergreens bearing pods filled with seeds used to make cocoa and chocolate. The hacienda's main house was built of wood with a veranda reaching around three sides of the second story. A salon, dining room, and kitchen were on the ground floor with a front porch under the veranda. Behind the house was a smokehouse, mango, banana, and fig trees, and a vegetable garden. The sugar mill with its own generator was across the road, facing the main house, along with an office and row of small houses for employees, plantation workers, and their families. Although the government restricted the number of 150-pound bags a sugar grower could produce, the Moisants still had the third largest quota in El Salvador.

Sparked by Alfred's daring enterprise and ambition, Santa Emilia was the product of all four Moisant brothers. Edward, a gifted farmer, was plantation manager. He brought in good livestock from the United States—300 horses and pigs—and used 150 domestic oxen for pulling the "carrettas" or carts for hauling sugar cane. He also oversaw the vegetable gardens and fruit trees and cured meat in the smokehouse for the family's table. John was chief engineer and designer. Though constantly drawn away from the plantation by events and escapades he obviously found more appealing, he was nevertheless there long enough to create an irrigation system with water drawn from the Sonsonate River. He also built, into a cliffside by the river, a 15- by 22-foot swimming pool that the whole family could use as a retreat from the blistering heat of the dry season. And, two miles south of Acajutla, he and Edward dug beds for a salt works and installed a motor designed to pump saltwater from the ocean into the beds. George was treasurer, living not at the hacienda

but at the "Green House," a combination office and residence
on a corner of Main Street in Sonsonate.

The four Moisant brothers variously held joint and separate
interests. Along with Alfred, for example, John and Edward
were co-owners of the salt works, valued by the consulate general at $60,000. George and Edward owned several coffee plan-
tations. John acquired banking, ranch, and farm holdings
throughout Central America. But as majority stockholder of
Moisant Hermanos (Moisant Brothers) Sonsonate, the name
under which the hacienda was incorporated, Alfred was undis-
puted head of Santa Emilia, the base on which he built his ever-
expanding empire. At the turn of the century he founded the
Banco Nacional del Salvador with an authorized capital of $1
million. (Keeping 80 percent of the stock for himself he sold off
the rest to prominent San Salvador businessmen to enhance the
bank's prestige.)

No business opportunity seemed outside his aspirations. He
formed a partnership, Perez, Moisant & Co., with a Spanish
import-export firm dealing in wines, liquors, and food, with offices in Sonsonate and Barcelona. And in 1904, to the annoy-
ance and dismay of diplomatic and maritime authorities, he
beat the U.S. State Department to the scene of a shipwreck off
Acajutla and garnered a handsome salvage profit for himself by
drawing up and convincing the ship's captain to sign postdated
survey lists of his cargo.

Surviving photographs of Santa Emilia, of the main house, the
sugar mill, the smaller homes for Salvadoran workers and their
families, all project an overwhelming image of a rural aristoc-
racy strikingly similar to that of pre–Civil War plantation
dwellers in the southern United States—though perhaps a somewhat ironic image for the lively and by now trilingual Moisants,
the children of immigrants who had themselves become immigrants. This Moisant generation was working as industriously
as had their parents and grandparents, but unlike them had the
time and means to enjoy life as well. Although Josephine died in
1901 at the age of 64, Matilde, with the help of Louise and occasionally Edward's wife, Mary, immediately took charge of the

household, known throughout the area for its hospitality, good food, and good wine. Visitors and guests were a constant on the scene, either swimming in the pool or riding Alfred's horses or the "walking donkey" he had bought for the women of the family. Alfred, now commonly known as "Don Alfredo," presided at the table unless he was in Acajutla, Sonsonate, or the capital on business. Edward's family was present as well, except when Mary took the four children back to California for their schooling. George, living in the Green House, visited less frequently, having left a wife and daughter in California while eventually fathering ten more children by his mistress, Mercedes, in Sonsonate. But these children were as welcome at Santa Emilia as the constant flow of tourists, friends, and business people who stopped off on their way from Acajutla to San Salvador. Consul General and family friend John Jenkins also often stopped for dinner and an overnight stay as did other diplomatic personnel.

In 1906, by the age of 46, Alfred J. Moisant, né Charles Alfred Moisant, had achieved the goals he set for himself when his father died only two decades earlier. He was a banker, merchant, and landowner. He was rich. He was Don Alfredo.

2
THE BUCCANEER

Santa Emilia was the product and the triumph of all the Moisants, yet it was almost destroyed by one of them—John. Although he loved his brothers and sisters with a fierce clannishness, John was driven by an uncontrollable desire for adventure and wealth and an almost adolescent need to be seen as a swashbuckling hero. He was a slight, wiry, energetic man with a beautiful choirboy's face, olive-skinned, clean shaven, his black eyes sparkling beneath arched brows. He smiled frequently, his sensuous mouth curling down at the corners of full lips. He was a dandy, his clothing immaculate, expensive, and exquisitely tailored. He wore a diamond stickpin in his silk ties and a huge diamond ring on one finger. His charm alone was noted by almost everyone.

Perhaps because he was the youngest of the brothers—and because of his success and imaginativeness as Santa Emilia's chief engineer and designer—John was Alfred's favorite. But whereas Alfred drove ambitiously onward, eyes rigidly fixed on profit, John's motivation lay elsewhere. A surging restlessness left him constantly needing more than success or money. He needed the splendor as well as the success, the glamour as well as the gold.

John's friends often described him as modest and quiet. But

his babyface beauty and charm belied the spirit of a true bucca-
neer. He was, in fact, autocratic, hot-tempered, willful, stubborn, ruthless, and utterly fearless in combat. While working
and living part-time at Santa Emilia, John traveled constantly,
acquiring both property and mining rights in Central America.
By 1901 he was known throughout the region as a fearless gun-
slinging soldier of fortune. Accounts of his exploits were widely
publicized, arousing both admiration and dread. By 1910, no
less a newspaper than the *New York Times* called John's reputation "nothing short of legendary," adding, "No hero of romance ever had so many extraordinary exploits attributed to
him."

A typical incident, which was so widely reported in the world
press that it eventually became a staple of conversation within
New York City's Central American community, concerned a
tramp steamer driven ashore by a violent storm off the coast of
Honduras, where John was visiting at the time, and abandoned
with its $100,000 cargo. As the *New York Times* reported it:

That night, in the teeth of the gale, Moisant made his way alone to
the steamer and took possession of the vessel. In the morning the
storm abated, and the ship's captain, accompanied by members of
the crew, and an agent of the line, rowed out to the ship, which had
withstood the pounding of sea and wind, but which was held fast on
a sunken reef in the outer harbor. They were halted by a shot from
Moisant's revolver. There was some parleying, and the ship's skipper
rowed back to shore to inform the American Consul and the authorities that Moisant claimed the ship and her cargo as salvage, and had
threatened to "blow the head off the first man who tries to come
aboard." There was a second expedition to the ship, this time with
the American Consul and some native soldiery, but Moisant refused
to be impressed, and to show his sincerity of purpose shot a hole
through the sombrero of the native commandant.

The expedition to recapture the stranded steamer returned to
shore for reinforcements of artillery, but during the night another storm, more severe than the first, swept the harbor and
completed the wreck of the tramp. When daylight broke the

vessel was seen to have foundered. Moisant was taken off later by the American Consul, who found him lashed to the topmost rigging of the steamer, which emerged only a few feet above the water.

John's peregrinations in pursuit of adventure and wealth left his young wife, Edith, and their infant son alone at the hacienda much of the time. For the only daughter of indulgent parents, accustomed to a busy social life, life at Santa Emilia must have seemed alternately frightening—antigovernment guerrilla activity was commonplace in the countryside—and dull. Though only three miles away, the nearest town of Sonsonate, where her brother-in-law George lived and maintained the plantation's business office, offered her little of interest. There were three small hotels. One, the Blanco y Negro, housed a playhouse for itinerant theater companies, but all the productions were in Spanish, a language Edith did not speak or understand. There was a Sunday market, which Edith found equally unappealing. As one English observer of the time described it, "Every kind of article is exposed for sale, from stuffed and roasted monkeys to the cheapest kind of Manchester cotton goods and cheaper German imitations." Also on sale were "dried fish—emitting a powerful and pungent odor—live iguanas (a large species of edible lizard), squawking fowls, and repulsive-looking chunks of bleeding, freshly-killed beef."

The tropical climate brought floods in the rainy season and windstorms in the dry season that often hid the entire plantation in a swirl of dust. Added to the isolation Edith must have felt was fear of the frequent epidemics of cholera, dysentery, and yellow fever. The fear was well founded, for yellow fever had claimed the life of her mother-in-law, Josephine, barely a month after she came to Santa Emilia. With more help from John, Edith might have learned to enjoy life at Santa Emilia as much as her sisters-in-law Matilde and Louise. But John, who was often elsewhere in Central America, was either unwilling or unable to give that help, and sometime in 1899 or 1900 Edith followed her mother back to California, taking Stanlie with her.

John himself returned to Alameda in January of 1901 in the midst of fears that war was imminent between Guatemala and Mexico. Sought out by newsmen as a successful plantation owner and an authority on Central American politics, he assured them there would be no war because Guatemala was too poor and too ill-equipped to engage in a "suicidal" conflict. John was not in Alameda, however, to discuss foreign affairs but to settle his own. He told Edith she could have a divorce on any grounds she chose so long as he was granted custody of five-year-old Stanlie. Then he returned to El Salvador.

Edith retaliated in February by filing for divorce in San Francisco, calling John "a man of violent temper" who treated her cruelly from the beginning, falsely accused her of infidelity, and was so consumed by jealousy that he finally forbade her ever to speak to other men. She further charged that her husband was of such "a very cruel and inhuman disposition" that on a number of occasions and "for the sole purpose of annoying her, seized cats by the throat and choked them to death in her presence." Putting John's income at $500 a month, she asked for $200 a month in alimony and custody of their child.

John was back in El Salvador when he read about the lawsuit in the *San Francisco Call* and immediately returned to California, touching off a confusing and complicated string of events by calling on R. Dannmeyer, a liquor wholesaler and stockbroker who had been John's business associate for some dozen years as well as Edith's uncle. This triangle of seemingly conflicting alliances led to a rapid set of developments within a matter of days. According to Dannmeyer, John borrowed $1,200 worth of mining stocks to negotiate an oil deal, but when John failed to return the stock the next day Dannmeyer telephoned his niece, only to discover that Edith had allowed John to take Stanlie to a matinee at the Orpheum Theater. John and their son did not return, instead boarding a train to El Paso, en route to Mexico.

Suddenly John was a fugitive from justice. To Edith's charges of kidnapping, the San Francisco police added an arrest warrant for felony embezzlement. That night they received a telegram from a justice in Deming, New Mexico: "Man on train. Could not get him off. Have wired J.H. White, chief of police at El Paso, Texas, to hold him." A dispatch from El Paso followed: "Moisant left train at Smelter, Texas. Men are across the Rio Grande looking for him."

Both the San Francisco police and John's friends appear to have agreed that there was little legal basis for the charges against him. The reported police view was that "Dannmeyer and Moisant have had a family and business quarrel and that the charge of felony embezzlement has but little foundation." A lawyer friend of John's elaborated:

If Moisant comes back here he will do so of his own free will. . . . This story of felony embezzlement is all bosh. Moisant has not stolen any bonds of Dannmeyer and he has not kidnapped his child. His wife refused to live in the Republic of Salvador with him and Moisant has kept her well supplied with money. He sent her $200 last January, and on February 8th she filed suit for divorce. . . . Moisant read of the suit in the *Call* and came back from Salvador this month. His wife did not mention her suit when her husband called upon her, but he kept posted as to her intentions. When he found that her attorney intended to serve the divorce papers on him he made preparations to go back to Salvador and told his friends so. He took his little boy with him, as he is devotedly attached to the child.

Whatever the merits of the case, John had solved the problem of child custody in his customary style. That July Edith was granted a divorce on grounds of extreme cruelty. But she never regained custody of her son.

Young Stanlie was sent to boarding school in San Salvador but spent most of his weekends at Santa Emilia. In 1902 his devoted father wrote to American consul John Jenkins at the capital to thank him for "Stanlie's sword and air gun," stating that the boy had not been home the previous weekend but was expected that Sunday and would be pleased with both gifts.

Eventually John sent Stanlie to the United States to be cared for by his sister, Ann, following her marriage in 1903 to a former classmate at the University of California, lawyer Bertin

A. Weyl. There is no record of when Stanlie returned, but it was most likely in 1905, when he was 10. Accompanied by his Aunt Matilde, who stayed part of that year at the Weyls' house on Pine Street in San Francisco, the boy attended a nearby boarding school and spent his vacations with the Weyls and their own three children, who regarded Stanlie as their older brother.

With his son no longer there to command his attention, John Moisant began to spend most of his time in the Nicaraguan capital of Managua, where he became a close friend of, and eventually aide to, Nicaragua's President Juan Santos Zelaya. It was a relationship that would eventually threaten the livelihood of all the Moisants and indeed the very lives of his brothers. Zelaya's ambition was to restore the federation of the now five states of El Salvador, Guatemala, Honduras, Costa Rica, and Nicaragua, and to become the president of that union. The area had originally been united in 1824 as the Central American Federation, only to disintegrate into separate states again by 1839. Several attempts to reunite them had since failed.

Zelaya perceived the chief threat to his plans to be El Salvador President Ferdinand Figueroa, and his main objective was to destroy the Figueroa regime. To do this he sought to create chaos within El Salvador, leading to some incident that would provide an excuse to launch an invasion. His plan was to replace Figueroa as president with one of the Salvadoran dissidents he harbored, preferably Gen. Prudencio Alfaro, thus making El Salvador a willing participant in the recreated Federation of Central America that he intended to rule.

Why John Moisant chose to assist Zelaya in this new attempt to gain control of all five states is beyond understanding. He knew that his brothers lived under the rule and the grace of Zelaya's principal enemy, Figueroa. And he himself had prominently and publicly opposed Figueroa's election. When Figueroa learned the extent of John's alliance with his arch-enemy Zelaya, the die was cast. So far as he was concerned, if one Moisant was against him, they all were.

The first Moisant to feel Figueroa's wrath was Alfred, described by one American diplomat as "a man of little education

[but] full of energy and ambition to succeed." Unlike John, Alfred never did insert himself directly into the machinery of Salvadoran elections. But he was often publicly outspoken about Salvador's poverty, inefficiency, and government corruption. Figueroa not only resented Alfred's criticism but was further nettled by the fact that he owed Alfred's Banco Nacional $60,000, a debt he was unable to pay. In fact he owed even more than that to three Salvadoran banks whose owners were pressuring him to use his power to force Alfred's bank to close.

Seeking to solve his banking problems and harass the Moisants at the same time, Figueroa found the perfect opportunity when Alfred's friend U.S. Consul General John Jenkins nominated Alfred to be a vice consul. Figueroa, who disliked Jenkins and suspected him of favoring his political opponents, declared Alfred "not acceptable" and forced Jenkins to cancel the appointment. A day later the civil courts of the Department of Sonsonate filed suit against Alfred's brother George for "subversive language and suspicion of enmity towards the government."

After two meetings together, Jenkins suggested, and Figueroa finally agreed, that the best solution would be for George to leave the country voluntarily until the political situation settled down. Jenkins reported that he was motivated in this course of action by the near bankruptcy of the Salvadoran regime and Figueroa's own "lack of culture." He further reported to Washington that although it was evident George had committed no crime, he nevertheless "has been over free in the present state of affairs with the verbal liberty natural to Americans, as on almost every street corner secret police in plain clothes are posted to listen to and report conversations with the result jails are full of unaccused and untried victims."

Although Jenkins convinced George and Alfred they should both leave the country, their attempted departure broke down in a comedy-of-errors fiasco. Accompanied by the consul general, the brothers arrived at Acajutla the morning of April 7, 1907, to board an outbound vessel, but George was refused permission to leave because he had no passport. Jenkins raced back to San Salvador and arranged an emergency meeting with

Figueroa who assured him he would personally speak to the secretary of war, who alone could authorize George's departure. But the secretary of war at that time was none other than Figueroa himself and the promised permission never came through. George returned to his residence at the Green House in Sonsonate.

On the night of April 21, Salvadoran troops broke into Santa Emilia, cutting fence wires, destroying sugar cane, and ransacking outbuildings. Shortly after midnight, George was seized at his Green House residence, arrested, and charged with hiding arms at the plantation to be used by forces of yet another rebel leader, Gen. Potenciano Escalon, whom Figueroa had defeated in the last presidential election. But when Escalon was captured three days later in another part of the country, unarmed and without troops, the military authorities released George after holding him for four days at Sonsonate.

On April 23 the president summoned Jenkins to his office and threatened to prosecute the Moisants unless they stopped mixing in "revolutionary movements." He also requested a meeting the next day with John Moisant, who by this time had returned to Sonsonate from Managua. According to Jenkins's report, the president greeted John cordially but asked him why the Moisants were so hostile to him. Explaining that he had left in January during Figueroa's election campaign and had only just returned to look after his own business interests, Moisant told the president, "If you think that hostile, then I am guilty. Give me a hint about what you want to know. I cannot guess at it."

Angered by John's reply, the president ordered George rearrested and taken this time to the penitentiary in San Salvador. A week later Edward was arrested and jailed in Sonsonate—where he was held for the first three hours in a toilet booth—as Salvadoran troops occupied Santa Emilia and searched it for arms and other proof of revolutionary intent.

With two brothers now under arrest, the State Department in early May ordered Consul-at-Large George H. Murphy to El Salvador to investigate both "the Moisant affair" and Jenkins's handling of it. But charges and countercharges only continued to escalate and U.S.-Salvadoran relations steadily deteriorated until a third American diplomat, outranking the others, arrived on the USS *Yorktown* on May 17 to take full charge of the matter. He was William Lawrence Merry, envoy extraordinary and minister plenipotentiary, whose jurisdiction would eventually include El Salvador, Honduras, and Costa Rica.

It was clear to Merry that Figueroa was determined to drive the Moisants out of El Salvador and thus himself gain control of Alfred's Banco Nacional and the 6,000-acre estate earning $100,000 a year from sugar cane, cattle, beef, corn, and rice production. He told Washington that all the charges against them were simply a "pretence" to achieve that end. At the same time he reported that while Edward was "quiet and reserved," brothers George and Alfred consistently acted as their own worst enemies, being extravagantly indiscreet in their criticisms of the government. Alfred, he said, "has the habit of talking freely on all matters which interest him," while George "is still more outspoken having, in fact[,] no discretion or self restraint so necessary for a foreigner who would live a quiet life in Central America."

While Merry alternately pleaded and threatened Figueroa to obtain the Moisants' freedom, even hinting at a U.S. navy blockade, it was none other than John Moisant who forced matters to a head and once again put his brothers' lives in danger. He returned to El Salvador as combat commander of a Nicaraguan-backed invasion force that landed at and seized Acajutla at dawn on June 11 and advanced on Sonsonate in yet another Zelaya attempt to overturn the Figueroa government. Realizing that one of the first invasion targets would be Salvadoran jails and the release of political prisoners, Merry feared the Moisant brothers might be killed in the fighting and arranged a 10 A.M. meeting with President Figueroa and Foreign Minister Ramon Garcia Gonzales. Using "plain language," he told them El Salvador had used "illegal and inhuman" means to extort false anti-Moisant evidence from plantation workers by torture and demanded that the Moisants be freed "by sunset that day." They were released at 5 P.M.—George after 56 days in prison, Edward after 42—on Merry's promise they would no longer meddle in Salvadoran politics.

While Merry met with Figueroa that morning, the invasion landing force of 800 Nicaraguans, Hondurans, and Salvadoran revolutionaries had already steamed into Acajutla on the Nicaraguan warship *Momotombo* and under the joint command of Salvadoran generals Prudencio Alfaro (whom Zelaya planned to install as his puppet president of El Salvador) and Manuel Rivas.

Frank Wager, the American consular agent at Acajutla, was an eyewitness to the invasion.

Yesterday morning [June 11] at 4:30 we were awakened by rifle fire in front of the Agency Company buildings. I found that the "Momotombo," carrying the Nicaraguan flag, had entered the port during the night and that a party in charge of John B. Moisant, an American, had taken one of the Agency Company's lighters, and landed on the beach to the north of the pier (leaving the lighter beached), and had taken by force of arms the Commandancia [military headquarters] in this port, as nearly as I could ascertain killing one and wounding four of the guard on duty. One of these wounded died shortly afterward. . . .

A revolutionary force, in command of generals Prudencio Alfaro and Manuel Rivas, a Colonel Matta and said Moisant, was then landed, shouting *viva*s for the generals mentioned and for the revolution. They took possession of the lighters, tug, pier, etc., of the companies in the port and pressed into their service the men who could be of service to them. The party consisted of about eight hundred men with a machine gun, several pieces of artillery, and, as I heard, about a million and a half rounds of ammunition and some dynamite bombs. They also captured two small pieces of artillery when they took the Commandancia. The party was mainly composed of Nicaraguans, the rest being Salvadoreans among them some who joined them in the port.

Two trains, one passenger and one freight, fell into their hands and were used to transport the force to Sonsonate, which town they captured about noon, after a stubborn resistance in which, I am informed, the government forces lost in killed and wounded about one hundred and fifty men out of a possible two hundred and fifty.

About midnight, for I know not what reason, the trains brought the whole party back to Acajutla, and they immediately began embarking, finishing today [June 12] about 9 a.m., and the "Momotombo" left for the south shortly after 11 a.m., taking with her a lighter of the Agency Company, despatch boat and launch boats of the same company, and a despatch boat of the *Commandancia*. They also tried to take possession and carry away the tug of the Agency Company, but the men on board of her put her on full steam and escaped to the moorings, where the engineer disconnected part of the engine and brought it on shore so that the tug would be of no use to them if they took it.

A train with [Salvadoran] government forces arrived about 2:45 p.m. today and took charge of the port and everything is now quiet.

The men landed were under good control and committed no abuses after taking the port, but I am informed that they compelled one of the banks in Sonsonate to furnish them $20,000 and the "Administracion de Rentas" [government rental office] was robbed of $12,000, and when they were embarking here the men robbed some few packages on the pier and also broke into some of the houses on the beach in search of provisions and liquor, as the officers had gone on board first leaving no one in charge of the men.

The "Yorktown" arrived at 7:40 p.m. and I went on board and gave her commander the information I had.

John Moisant might well have led his men all the way to San Salvador to release his brothers as he had sworn he would but the attacking forces lost momentum when Rivas and Alfaro quarreled. By the time they settled with an agreement to split San Salvador between them, Rivas taking command in the east and Alfaro in the west, a messenger arrived with word that Figueroa himself was on his way to Sonsonate with a trainload of troops. His forces now divided by the feuding generals, John had no choice but to retreat.

Fortunately for the jailed brothers, neither Figueroa nor Merry knew John Moisant was involved when the fighting began. Had they known, it is unlikely Merry could have won their release. It is even possible Figueroa could have ordered George and Edward executed, so convinced was he by this time that all the Moisants were united against him.

Within a week, Figueroa ordered a detachment of soldiers to Santa Emilia to frighten away the workers, forty of whom were immediately impressed into the Salvador army. Merry cabled Washington that "life and property are not safe in the Moisant plantation." When jeering soldiers insulted his wife, U.S. citizen and plantation manager Andrew Leonard evacuated his family to the capital because "he feared for their lives."

On June 20 Merry witnessed the arrest at the Santa Emilia train stop of Steven Scott, the Moisants' African American engineer. After Merry protested, Scott was released. But as soon as the American diplomat left, Scott was rearrested and tortured until he signed a statement (which he later claimed was false) implicating his employers in the revolutionary movement. And when Edward Moisant asked for permission to return to the plantation from San Salvador he was told that the Salvadoran government could not guarantee his safety. Merry countered with a suggestion that if the Salvadoran government could not protect Edward and his property, then perhaps a Marine guard from the *Yorktown* could, but the ship's commander declined, saying he could not station Marines on private property.

Within one more week only Leonard and 25 to 30 of the original 150 workers were left at Santa Emilia. Production was at a standstill. The Figueroa government refused either to redeem $33,000 in bonds held by Alfred's bank or to pay an indemnity of $18,000 the Moisants were claiming for the imprisonment of George and Edward. The Moisants said, and Merry agreed, that the indemnity was vital to keeping the plantation in operation. Without it, the Moisants would lose "property worth a half million dollars" and be forced into bankruptcy and ruin. Merry proposed that Foreign Minister Gonzales "wipe the slate" clean of all charges if the Moisants dropped their indemnity claim but neither side agreed.

Apparently angered at repeated Moisant demands for indemnity, Figueroa on June 26 sent troops to seize and occupy another Moisant enterprise, the salt works jointly owned by John, Edward, and Alfred near Acajutla. Four days later Governor of Sonsonate Francisco Gomez came to Santa Emilia with 27 armed men and accused George of killing four Salvadorans and throwing their bodies into the river. Gomez threatened to "lay waste to Santa Emilia and kill all the foreigners there" even if he had to pay for it afterwards. He followed a 30-minute tirade with the promise that "things would go easier" with George if he posted a public notice promising to make no claims against El Salvador through the U.S. government.

Assistant Manager Leonard, who knew Spanish and had relatives in San Salvador, verified George's account of the incident and added that Figueroa's private secretary had personally warned him to leave Santa Emilia "for good" and as soon as possible because "it was not a safe place to be." By this time Leonard had had enough and decided to return to the United States where he could work "without being threatened with torture, for I have heard the screams of men being tortured on the *finca* [plantation]."

After a brief let-up in the government's harassment, George and Edward returned to Santa Emilia and the army troops departed. But in July Figueroa placed an embargo of $200,000 on Edward's properties, preventing him under martial law from managing any of them and placing them in the hands of a government-appointed receiver. Two days later George's property was embargoed as well and both brothers along with fourteen Salvadorans were charged with supporting the coup attempt by General Escalon.

The Moisants were not intimidated. Alfred, who had refused to close his Banco National, now added a claim for $75,000 for damage at Santa Emilia to his earlier one for $18,000 indemnity for his brothers' imprisonment. And George told his friends he might contest the upcoming mayoral race in Sonsonate.

Hearing of this, Merry wrote an undated personal letter to all three Moisant brothers informing them he was leaving San Salvador for a new post and reminding them of his official promise that they would stay out of Salvadoran politics. It ended with the wry admonishment: "Permit the people of Salvador to govern Salvador without your aid, directly or indirectly."

The warning came too late. On August 9 Merry's replacement, Consul General Samuel E. Magill, cabled the State Department that George and Edward had been charged with "treason and sedition" and would be tried before a military court. He speculated the action was prompted by Figueroa's fear that the U.S. government would officially back the Moisant demands, thus forcing his already cash-low government into payments beyond its means. The trial was eventually set to begin November 18 before the Council of War inside the penitentiary, a fortified Army garrison building. Certain they would be convicted, Magill asked Washington for permission to give the brothers asylum inside the consulate. The department denied the request but only after Figueroa received a secret cable direct from Washington. Whatever the cable contained, it obviously had the desired affect. Two hours after George and Edward arrived in Sonsonate for their trial to begin the next morning they received a notice stating, "By Superior order [only Figueroa gave Superior Orders] the council which was to meet tomorrow is suspended." The president simultaneously declared a general amnesty and the lifting of martial law.

Besides being humiliated by having obviously succumbed to Washington pressure, Figueroa was also frustrated by the fact that the person he regarded as his real enemy, John Moisant, was still at large. Conflicting rumors had him either back in Honduras plotting another overthrow attempt with President Zelaya or still hiding in El Salvador.

Figueroa wanted him in custody and Salvadoran authorities had been under standing orders since Moisant's June landing at Acajutla and foray into Sonsonate to search every American vessel docking on the Pacific coast of his country.

Reporting to Washington on an unsuccessful search of the SS *City of Sydney,* Magill said that had Moisant indeed been on board "he would have done as much damage as he could to those attempting to arrest him as he would [have felt] certain that his life would be taken once on shore." Magill said he concurred with such thinking but added he had been informed that Moisant had left El Salvador "with the permission of this government [and] on an apparently innocent mission."

Three days after the trial was canceled and his brothers released, John turned up at the Pacific Avenue home of his sister Ann and brother-in-law Bertin Weyl in San Francisco. Tanned, smiling, and dressed in an elegant suit and silk tie John gave newsmen a long interview about his experiences. Magill's information was more likely correct, but John's version was more exciting and certainly made much better copy. The diamond on his finger flashing as he gestured, he explained he had organized and led the June Acajutla landing—one newspaper said that the Moisant forces "swooped down upon the port . . . while the Salvadoran army was dreaming of bull fights and senoritas"—and continued on to Sonsonate simply to rescue his brothers from prison. John said that after Salvadoran troops chased him back to Acajutla he backtracked north by burro, over the mountains of El Salvador and through the jungles of Honduras, to the Atlantic where he boarded ship for New York, then took a train to San Francisco. John told reporters the family troubles began when the Moisants opposed Figueroa in the elections and the president retaliated by levying a "forced loan" on them, and raiding Santa Emilia where they found a few rifles and charged the Moisants with planning a revolution. Having already done so, John asked to be excused from discussing his feud with Figueroa because he had many influential friends in the United States who were close to other Central American presidents. He specifically cited Nicaragua as one country which "looked with favor on the Moisant cause" and from which he recruited most of his army.

With this single interview John once again put Moisant lives and property in danger. Back in San Salvador, his boasts and claims would not go unnoticed by President Figueroa, now his bitter but equally proud enemy. Figueroa had been forced by Washington to call a truce in his war with the Moisants. But that is all it was—a truce.

3

A TROUBLED PARADISE

The new year of 1908 heralded a fresh upsurge in the confrontation between the Moisant family and President Figueroa. Within days of his arrival, the new American envoy extraordinary and minister plenipotentiary, E. Percival Dodge, realized that of all the Americans in El Salvador, the Moisants were the most troublesome to Figueroa, and to his own legation. Dodge promptly sent off to Minister Merry, by then posted to Costa Rica, a request for copies of all correspondence relating to El Salvador since May 1907. Merry curtly refused, saying the only matter left unsettled was the Moisants' claim of indemnity for unjust imprisonment.

Concerned that his predecessors might have been misinterpreting the situation in their reports to Washington, Dodge sent the State Department an assessment of the Moisants and Figueroa given to him by the Mexican chargé d'affaires. Contrary to an earlier cable by Consul Jenkins, which described the president as "a rough soldier but good at heart," the chargé excoriated Figueroa as the illegitimate son of a rich merchant, a man who, in spite of a good education, had done nothing to end inefficiency and corruption and had left a nearly bankrupt national treasury in the hands of British loan sharks David and

Benjamin Bloom. There was no doubt, the chargé wrote, that "the American citizens Moisant were implicated in the conspiracy of General Potencia Escalon." True or not, this belief was widely shared by both Salvadorans and expatriates in the country at that time.

Seemingly oblivious to the feelings he had aroused, John brazenly wrote Figueroa from California asking for a special letter granting him permission to return. Perhaps he was counting on the fact that the president would remember gratefully that his own son and Moisant had fought side by side, comrades in arms, in an attack on Guatemala a few years before. If so, he judged the situation correctly. In San Salvador young Figueroa was confiding in Dodge that his father would indeed write the letter.

Figueroa might have been able to forgive and forget but John could forgive neither the imprisonment of his brothers in 1907 nor his own failure to rescue them. No sooner had he returned to El Salvador than he began to plot again with his old friend Alfaro. In March, Washington advised J. H. Gregory, chargé d'affaires while Dodge was on leave, that Alfaro, traveling in Mexico under the name of Smith, had received a cable from Moisant asking "when the money for the business would be ready." Suspecting that "the business" was another raid into El Salvador, the American ambassador in Mexico City reported both to the State Department and to Gregory that Alfaro planned to leave for El Salvador in a few days in disguise. With the approval of his superiors, Gregory passed all this on to President Figueroa, adding the disturbing note that Nicaraguan-backed Salvadoran rebel general Luis Alonso Barahona was also partner to the plot. Far more disapproving of Moisant than any of his American predecessors had been, Gregory assured Figueroa that he would, if necessary, request the presence of a U.S. Navy ship at Acajutla and would authorize the "immediate expulsion of any Americans seditiously involved."

John probably did not know of Gregory's assurances to the president, but they would have made little difference. The invasion plans were well under way and, with brother George's help, he was busy coaxing other Salvadoran dissidents, includ-

ing a General Pinel, to join the rebellion. He and George also offered the captain of the Salvadoran gunboat *Presidente* a
$150,000 bribe if he would steam out to sea and disappear at a
signal from shore. Their offer was accepted, but the captain was
betrayed by the ship's engineer. Gregory dutifully reported all
this to Washington, explaining that the El Salvador government
"feels very bitter against the Moisants and would resort to severe punishment but for my insistence [that] the evidence is not
conclusive."

John Moisant, whom Gregory described as "an adventurous
spirit and no doubt prepared to accept the consequences of any
seditious acts he may commit," was now under constant sur-
veillance by both Gregory and Dodge, back from leave. Dodge
reported that Moisant and Generals Alfaro, Rivas, and Sal-
vadore Toledo were all gathered in the Nicaraguan capital of
Managua on April 20, when an attempt was made on the life of
Guatemalan president Manuel Estrada Cabrera. Moisant and
the generals presumably intended the assassination to spark si-
multaneous uprisings in Guatemala, El Salvador, and Honduras.
But the attempt failed, largely because of a rare instance of co-
operative communications and intelligence-sharing among the
rulers of those countries. When the conspirators went to Tegu-
cigalpa, the capital of Honduras, ostensibly on business but actually to await the hoped-for revolution, Honduran president
Miguel Davila summoned them to his office. The angry president ordered all but General Rivas, who had legitimate business
there, to leave the country. Alfaro, in disguise, slipped back into
El Salvador while John and the others retreated to Managua.

In mid-July John risked returning to El Salvador but was refused permission to land when his ship arrived at Acajutla. For
the rest of that summer rumors circulated that he was continuing to stir up political trouble. The following month the rumors
took concrete form when the Pacific Mail steamship *San Jose*
pulled into the Nicaraguan port of Corinto. Pistol in his belt
and riding whip in hand, John stormed up the gangplank looking for Figueroa's private secretary, Vilisario Suarez, who was a
passenger. Suarez, actually more chief of staff than secretary,

had been instrumental in imprisoning Edward and George the year before. When a woman passenger tried to defend Suarez, Moisant struck her with his whip, after which several other passengers surrounded him and held him down until Suarez could escape below deck. When Moisant finally left the ship, a Nicaraguan policeman went on board and asked Suarez to come ashore and make a deposition. But Suarez refused, fearing that Moisant might kill him.

All of John Moisant's reported and aborted plots against the Figueroa regime were but a prelude to another full-scale invasion of El Salvador. To transport men and arms Moisant bought a gasoline barge in Panama and had it towed to Corinto by a Pacific Mail steamship. An alarmed Dodge in San Salvador noted that "protected as they seem to be in Nicaragua, it would be an easy matter in such a boat for a hundred or more men with rifles and ammunition to come from [Corinto on] the northern coast of Nicaragua to [the Salvadoran ports of] La Union or Triumfo in a few hours."

On December 14 Dodge's fears were confirmed when Consul H. H. Leonard reported from Managua that "the [liner] *S.S. Acapulco* arrived at Corinto December 12, towing a two-masted gasoline launch [which] I was informed . . . was purchased by John Moisant for one thousand dollars gold on his recent trip to Panama." Back in California a local newspaper headlined the story: "Moisant Buys Himself A Navy. Alameda Admiral Bravely Plans To Invade Salvador." The story warned that "a great naval fight" was imminent unless President Figueroa "first arrest[s] Moisant for disturbing the peace."

At Corinto Moisant paced on shore, staring out into the sun, waiting for his one-boat navy to arrive. His handsome, sun-browned face broke into a grin as the *Acapulco* steamed into view with his launch in tow. He remained until the launch was safely anchored where weapons could be secretly loaded at night, then returned to Managua.

Led by John and his friend Alfaro, the invasion began February 21, 1909, not with a force of 100 or more men as Dodge had expected but with almost 10 times that number. Some

1,000 men transferred from Nicaraguan navy ships to lighters, which John's launch then towed to a landing site 10 miles south of La Union on the Salvadoran coast of the Gulf of Fonseca. Largely composed of Indians and inmates released from Nicaraguan prisons, the Moisant-Alfaro-Rivas army was no match for Salvadoran army regulars who had been alerted by the U.S. minister in Managua and were massed along the coast, waiting for them. In the brief battle that followed, 200 were taken prisoner, many drowned, and many more dropped their arms and deserted. The rest were towed away in retreat by Moisant's launch.

Driven to a degree bordering on insanity, Moisant could not accept defeat and immediately set about planning yet another invasion. He and Alfaro began recruiting a new expeditionary force at Chinandega, a railway town 25 miles north of Corinto. At the same time, working at night and in secret, he transferred his one-man-navy launch by rail from Lake Managua to Corinto, ready for use again to tow troop-carrying lighters.

Back in Managua, the new American chargé d'affaires, Jose de Olivares, had heard rumors of the new expedition and decided to investigate for himself. He arrived in Chinandega on April 21 only to discover that Moisant had left there two nights earlier with 250 Nicaraguan soldiers and 50 Salvadoran political refugees for Playa Grande, a military post near the gulf, where they were to join up with Alfaro and his army and cross into El Salvador. Olivares first telephoned orders to the vice consul in Corinto to alert U.S. Navy ships there that Moisant and his men were already on the march. This done, Olivares continued toward the gulf in a search for still more proof, finally finding it in a Moisant staging area—seven large lighters each capable of carrying eighty men. After a long night's trek through the Everglade-like Nicaraguan swamps to Playa Grande, and back to Corinto, Olivares reported his findings directly to Comdr. William S. Benson, captain of the U.S. cruiser *Albany.*

Benson in turn sent Olivares to another cruiser anchored 10 miles off the coast, the *Colorado,* with instructions to organize a search for the Moisant launch. It was sighted the next day and the *Albany*, the *Colorado*, and the Mexican cruiser *Guerrero* all converged on the rebels. Benson signaled Moisant, who was manning a rapid-fire machine gun, that he would sink him and his men if they attempted to land in El Salvador. For the last time, Moisant retreated.

Himself a fugitive from the U.S. Navy, which had orders to arrest him on unspecified charges, facing possible trial in the States, his ally Zelaya discredited and soon to be forced into exile, John Moisant's buccaneering days were over. He booked passage on a ship bound for New York City and would never again return to Central America.

While John Moisant had spent the last 18 months harassing Ferdinand Figueroa with attacks from outside El Salvador, his brother Alfred had been frustrating and humiliating the president from inside his own country. But whereas John's weapons had been stealth and guns, Alfred, in a three-piece wool suit and armed with nothing more menacing than a briefcase and cigar, fought with words. Almost daily he tormented the president with a barrage of legal briefs and threats of court action to satisfy his claims for damage to Santa Emilia and the salt works, indemnity for his brothers' imprisonment, and repayment of the loan the president had taken from the Moisant bank. And when Minister Dodge claimed he was powerless to act without instructions from Washington, Alfred went to plead his own case in Washington with former minister Merry, who took leave from his post in Costa Rica to assist him in his appeals.

Figueroa was quick to note that Alfred's trip to Washington had won Moisant no help from the U.S. government and that Honduran president Davila had received no reprimand from the Americans for publicly denouncing Moisant as "a liar," "a thief," and "a revolutionary gringo," and then revoking his banking concession in Honduras. Emboldened by this lack of action from the United States on Alfred's behalf, Figueroa launched a new attack on the Banco Nacional. First, Alfred's three competitors, Banco Salvadoreno, Banco Agricola, and Banco Occidental, all refused to accept notes issued by Banco Nacional. Then, in quick succession, the government sharply restricted the amount

of currency Banco Nacional could circulate and issued an official report misstating the bank's assets, indicating it was short of
capital and questioning its stability. The result was a run on the
bank which Alfred stemmed the only way he could, by mort-
gaging his property.

For once, however, Figueroa had miscalculated in his efforts
to drive the Moisants out of the country. Contrary to his expec-
tations, Washington concurred that Alfred's bank had indeed
been singled out unfairly and instructed the Legation in San Salvador to press the Treasury to retract its statement on the bank
and make amends to Moisant for his losses. Negotiations on the
matter dragged on for more than six months, with Dodge, and
then his replacement, William Heimke, calling almost daily on
either the president or the foreign affairs minister. The Figueroa
government never did issue a retraction, but it became clear
over time that Figueroa himself was softening in his attitude toward Alfred. Perhaps John Moisant's disappearance from the
scene had something to do with it. At any rate, when Heimke
called on the president on April 2, 1910, to translate an *aide
memoire* delivered from Washington, Figueroa not only denied
ever having treated Moisant unfairly but promised Banco Nacional his full support in future because, he assured the envoy,
he and Alfred were "personal friends."

Alfred remained in El Salvador until June of that year, on excellent terms with Heimke and avoiding any action that might
offend Figueroa. With the bank now stabilized and Santa Emilia
again thriving under the management of Edward and George
(Figueroa said Alfred himself told him "he was making more
money than he could utilize") Don Alfredo was ready to invest
in a new enterprise.

4
THE AVIATOR

Before the Moisants became embroiled in their endless quarrels with Ferdinand Figueroa, before John fled to New York and Alfred followed, back when John was building the salt works at Acajutla, Matilde found him one day staring at a huge buzzard circling overhead. Pulling her hat brim forward to shade her eyes she looked up into the glaring blue sky, watching with him until the bird, so beautiful in the sky, alighted and waddled along the shore searching for carrion washed in by the tide.

"Why do you always watch the *sopalotes,* John?" she asked. "They're the ugliest things I've ever seen."

John turned and smiled at this female version of himself, small and trim of figure, her suntanned face almost as dark as his, her eyes black and sparkling.

"They're ugly on the ground, Till," he said, "but you've seen them fly, so beautiful in the air, soaring, then gliding, their wings never moving. I shot one yesterday and I've measured it—the body and wing span. And I've weighed the wings and the body, to get some kind of ratio."

John Moisant was not just an adventurer. He was a self-taught engineer with the curiosity of a scholar and the imagina-

35

tion of an inventor. He was watching birds in the skies of El Salvador when Wilbur and Orville Wright were doing the same thing in Ohio and for the same reason. All were convinced that not only birds but humans, too, could master the sky. If only they had the right machine.

John thought much about the problem in New York that summer of 1909. He undoubtedly had been thinking about it ever since December 17, 1903, when the Wright brothers—first Orville, then Wilbur—made the world's first successful flights in a heavier-than-air, mechanically propelled machine over the dunes of Kitty Hawk, North Carolina. And he was still following aviation progress from Central America in 1908 when Wilbur Wright, in France, set a new endurance record of 1 hour and 31 minutes, a marked improvement over the first Wright flights of 12 seconds (120 feet) and 59 seconds (852 feet).

The revolutions of Central America behind him, John was now ready to take part in this new revolution of the air. Undeterred by the fact he had never even flown an airplane before, he decided to build one of his own. But clearly he would have to go to France to do so. With a U.S. Congress reluctant either to investigate or invest in the future of flight, even the Wrights had gone abroad, first to Britain, then to France and Germany, seeking the funds they needed to continue their work. Besides, by 1910 France would become the center of the world's evolving aviation industry and the gathering place for air enthusiasts and aspiring manufacturers, aviators, and designers.

That summer John and Alfred met in New York where the older man frequently stopped on trips to and from Central America to further his banking and now expanding import-export interests. Matilde and Louise were with them when John said, "Fred"—which was how the family referred to their older brother—"I think I'm going to Europe. I want to see what I can do about this idea of designing a plane."

Alfred nodded. "All right. You can go. I suppose you'll need a little bit of help with that?"

John grinned. "Yes, I could stand it." No more was needed to be said. John would fly. Alfred would provide the money.

The brothers were a study in contrast. A photograph of Alfred at the time suggests the typical businessman from a Thomas Nast cartoon. His barrel chest strained at his vested suit; his neck was encased in a high, stiff collar, his derby set over a beetle-browed face; a thick moustache shaded his mouth. The only thing missing was the cigar. John, on the other hand, wore a smartly tailored jacket and slacks, his collar softer and lower, his tie a more elegant pattern. Little brother Johnny, nearing 40, looked like a rich man's young son. And, in fact, with Alfred's approval and support he lived like one, even though he had lost most of his own wealth in Central America. The bond between them was unbreakable. Alfred was proud of his intelligent, gifted, reckless, and charming brother. And John, once so independent, even defiant, of his older brother, was now willing to take not only Alfred's money but his guidance as well.

John arrived in Paris not as a typical American tourist but as an experienced expatriate who spoke French, Spanish, and English fluently and had already lived outside his own country for two decades. His timing couldn't have been more appropriate. He arrived in time to join the crowds jamming the streets to cheer their new national hero, Louis Blériot, who, on July 25, 1909, had become the first person in the world to cross the English Channel in an airplane.

Just two months later, at Issy-les-Moulineaux, an airfield 37 miles southwest of Paris, John hired workmen at the Clement-Bayard balloon hangar to help him build his airplane. Completed by February of 1910, it was pictured in a French aviation magazine that same month. He described it in a letter to his brother-in-law, Bertin Weyl, as constructed almost entirely of aluminum, braced with tubes of steel. The aluminum body was shaped like a boat and, John claimed, "would be as much at home in the water as in the air."

The Aluminoplane was powered by a 50-hp Gnôme radial rotary engine with air-cooled flanges, a seven-cylinder motor built especially for aircraft by Laurent and Louis Séguin. Weighing only 176 pounds, it was installed so as to revolve with the propeller around a fixed crankshaft. It was easy to take down and put together, to clean valves and spark plugs. Gas and castor oil passed through the hollow crankshaft to the cylinders in this motor that rarely overheated or froze because it was cooled by the spinning motion and warmed by the carburation inside the crankshaft.

Undeterred by the fact that he had never flown before or taken a single lesson, John displayed the same self-confidence, if not downright belief in his own immortality, that seems to possess many of the world's greatest adventurers. Climbing into the seat of his new plane, he signaled the mechanic to turn the propeller, waved off the six men holding the plane by its tail, opened the throttle, and took off. Ascending almost straight upwards at about 80 MPH, the would-be pilot fell back in his seat, traveling so fast he could not think of what he might do next until at 90 feet he cut the engine and descended almost as rapidly as he had arisen. By cutting the motor Moisant did what Blériot had always warned his student pilots against: If the machine climbs too fast, never cut the ignition to stop the motor because the aircraft will lose speed and fall heavily to the earth.

This is exactly what happened. The Aluminoplane crashed, its tail demolished. John was unhurt. A French pilot friend described his first flight as "like that of a man who never had been in an auto trying to drive a difficult course in [Barney] Oldfield's 200-horsepower racer."

A year later a wiser Moisant wrote, "No man should build an aeroplane and then try to fly it unless he has had experience in the air." However, he immediately started to build a second plane, this one called *Le Corbeau* ("The Crow"). Salvaging the fuselage and landing gear from the Aluminoplane, he repeated his attempt to rely on metal rather than the traditional wood and cloth used by most designers for the fuselage and wings. *Le Corbeau*'s wings were of thin aluminum, the pilot's seat and motor set on a raised surface designed to float in the event of a forced landing over water. As with the Aluminoplane, he mounted the propeller behind the Gnôme engine, again an untraditional arrangement.

Before risking a flight in his now-completed *Le Corbeau*,

Moisant went to Louis Blériot for—finally!—flight lessons. Primarily a designer and plane manufacturer, Blériot had built the world's largest airplane factory near Paris where 150 workmen had already delivered several hundred machines to eager buyers. Like Moisant, however, many of the buyers needed instructions, which Blériot gave at two schools, one at Etampes near Paris in the summer, and a second at Pau in the south during the winter.

The pursuit of this new technology was chaotic and wonderfully suited to Moisant, as evidenced by incidents related by one novitiate at Pau.

Two Blériot machines coming in opposite directions met and struck each other with full force, propeller to propeller. Result—both propellers and front carriages smashed and both engines disabled. Machines caught fire . . .

An aviator, Mr. McArdle [William McArdle, an American] stops to make a slight adjustment to his engine; another machine charges him full tilt, and smashes both machines beyond recognition.

Two pupils run into the fence dividing the ground and smash propellers and do other damage to the machine. One pupil, Lieut. Acquaviva, dismounts to restart his engine that has stopped; before he can regain his seat the machine starts off and rushes away at forty miles an hour. The rudder catches against the aviator and sets itself for turning. The machine plunges on making huge circles. Mr. Blériot is flying over the top. He descends to assist in the capture of the runaway. It is not before about a dozen mechanics come to the rescue that the runaway is caught.

John paid his tuition of 2,000 francs (US$400) for the lessons that, as per standard contract, were not to exceed a total of 30 hours within 30 days. The fee included the services of "a mechanic and aid." But the apprentice flyer—who had a maximum of 30 days and 30 hours to complete three closed-circuit flights of at least five-minutes duration—also was responsible for all accident damage and repairs and had to take out both accident and liability insurance.

In planes not yet equipped with dual controls, John and his fellow flyers first practiced "grass cutting" (taxiing up and down the field in a low-powered clipped-wing craft), then graduated to short hops and, finally, a solo flight. John did not log his first flight. But on his second and third flights, July 28 and 29, 1910, he passed the tests needed for a license issued by the Aero Club of France. That fall the license was transferred to the Aero Club of America, Certificate No. 13, making him the thirteenth American to be licensed in the United States.

Convinced that his second plane was no better than his first, the would-be designer immediately bought one of Blériot's monoplanes and received a refund of his tuition as did all student-buyers. The plane was a Blériot XI, 2 bis côte-à-côte, a shoulder-high monoplane for pilot and one passenger seated side by side in a wide fuselage. The aircraft had warped wings, a tail plane, and a rudder without a fin. There were two wheels with shock absorbers at the front and a tail skid at the back. A 50-hp Gnôme engine, which Blériot had earlier rejected as likely to destroy an aircraft by excessive vibration, fit entirely inside the fuselage, and the wings were fixed by wires to central pylons above the fuselage and below. A crossbar beneath the pilot's feet controlled the vertical rudder for turns, and a hand lever was used to ascend and descend. To Moisant the Blériot XI must have seemed the equivalent of the rapid-fire weapon he had used back in his gun-slinging days—the right equipment for a new, equally dangerous venture.

That August of 1910 the attention of all France and indeed much of Europe was riveted on the 500-mile Circuit de l'Est. Sponsored by the Paris daily Le Matin, it was the world's first long-distance air race across open country. Among the 250,000 who watched the contest takeoff from the Paris suburb of Issy-les-Moulineaux and countless others along the route in eastern France, the race stirred a level of excitement comparable to that raised by Alan Shepard's first orbit of the earth 50 years later. Viewers at the starting point could be compared to those at Cape Canaveral watching Apollo-Saturn 8 leave the launching pad, although the level of wonder at Issy may well have been higher.

As described by G. F. Campbell Wood, an Aero Club of America official who was there:

Paris, which usually stays abed Sunday morning, got up on this seventh of August in the middle of the night and set out for Issy, and at four o'clock the first signs of dawn found the streets in southwestern Paris filled with a hurrying mob of pedestrians and vehicles; the crowd at Issy was truly colossal and such a one as only aviation could at this time bring together at such an hour in France.

John Moisant had been refused entry as a contestant by officials who regarded him as a too-recently licensed amateur and "a crazy American kid." Back at Etampes, where he kept his Blériot, John invited his friend Roland Garros to fly to Issy with him anyway. The 25-year-old Garros was already a member of the Aero Club of France and one of John's flight instructors. The son of a French diplomat, he had been a law student, champion bicycle rider, and builder of automobiles before he saw his first airplane in flight. It was the Demoiselle, the world's smallest plane, designed by Alberto Santos Dumont and flown that day by a Swiss, Edmond Audemars. While the plane was still airborne Garros bought it, and 15 minutes after Audemars landed the new owner was in the pilot's seat. That same afternoon he flew it five laps. As colorful and daring as Moisant himself, Garros on his twelfth flight took the tiny aircraft up in a wind after being promised that it would be replaced if it crashed. It did. Thrown 40 feet, Garros got up and walked back to the plane and kicked it several times. Then he asked for his replacement.

With his French friend as a passenger, the "crazy American" Moisant flew for 37½ miles over the heart of Paris to Issy with only a compass as a navigational guide. As they passed over the Eiffel Tower, Garros was so delighted with the view that he stood up in the pitching, swaying machine and waved his hat, threatening to overturn the aircraft until Moisant pulled him back into his seat.

At Issy Campbell Wood observed, "Whilst the excitement was

at its height, a pigeon-tailed two-seater appeared exactly over the Eiffel Tower. Two men got down from it on landing at Issy and to those who greeted them they introduced themselves as Moisant and Garros."

Asked why he did this, John replied:

On the day that the great race started a crowd of 300,000 persons had assembled [estimates were near 250,000] and the police were keeping a great space open from which the aviators were to start. I was very anxious to see the big flyers get away on this famous journey, but I saw the only way I could do that was to fly into the enclosure. . . . [We] dropped plump down into the midst of the aviators as they were about to start. In that way we avoided the police and the crowd and accomplished our purpose and while the Frenchmen regarded me as a crazy Yankee, the fact that I flew among them with one of their own crack aviators perhaps helped my reputation a little.

If this did not help his reputation it certainly did increase his name recognition.

That day Moisant followed his unusual entry into the enclosure with an equally dramatic announcement to Alfred Leblanc, director of the Blériot aviation school, that he intended to fly from Paris to London. "Mais vous êtes fou, Monsieur!" Leblanc spluttered. Blériot agreed, throwing up his arms in dismay as he told Moisant there were easier ways to commit suicide.

Joining this chorus of disapproval was Hubert Latham, another young but more experienced pilot who insisted that Moisant would be lucky just to make it back over Paris again. Latham's admonition was probably something less than altruistic. He was about to make a second attempt to cross the English Channel, having failed in July when he became the first pilot in the world to ditch his plane in water, seven miles from the French shoreline. Now he was ready to try again, and this time he intended to beat Moisant or any other challenger.

The wealthy, dashing, 26-year-old Latham, a Frenchman of English descent, was, like Garros, a former law student. He had completed his military service in France and among his other pursuits were big-game hunting in Africa, exploring Indochina, racing boats and automobiles, and a balloon trip across the channel. Early in 1909 he bought an airplane and taught himself how to fly.

Ignoring Latham's remarks and the criticisms of Blériot and Leblanc, Moisant further stated that he planned to take his mechanic along as well. His audience blanched. Besides the fact that no one had yet flown a passenger across the channel, John's mechanic, 185-pound Frenchman Albert Fileux, had never flown before, and though his weight in the fragile aircraft would be somewhat compensated for by Moisant's scant 135 pounds, the total would still be dangerously heavy for the Blériot XI. Further noting that Moisant knew nothing of England, nothing of the English Channel, nothing of the French countryside except what he had picked up by studying maps, and that he intended to fly only by following his compass, which was unheard of, his three critics gave him up as being stark mad. Shrugging their shoulders and turning away, Blériot, Leblanc, and Latham abandoned Moisant to his fate.

Undeterred by his colleagues, Moisant took off with Fileux from Issy at 5 P.M. August 16 and landed 2½ hours later at Amien, where his rival Latham had already crashed into a tree, demolishing both his aircraft and any hopes of beating Moisant. The next morning, before Moisant took off on his 90-mile flight to Calais on the French coast, Blériot again begged him to leave Fileux behind but to no avail. The mechanic wanted to make the flight. There was nothing left for Blériot to do but offer suggestions. He told Moisant to watch for a spot at Calais that was 1,000 feet long and 20 feet wide. "If you can find that, it will make a nice landing." Moisant did find it, just 1 hour and 55 minutes later and using only a compass. Circling Calais three times he landed on exactly the same spot from which Blériot had launched the world's first cross-channel flight a year earlier.

5

WORLD RECORD

On August 17, 1910, at ten o'clock in the morning a group of reporters at the makeshift airfield near Calais huddled together in the cold wind under lowering clouds. They had originally gathered to cover Hubert Latham's second channel-crossing attempt. But the popular English flyer having crashed at Amien, they stayed on to report the arrival of John Moisant, a virtually unknown American amateur who, the other pilots said, had flown only six times, including his one lesson and two tests for his flying license. Experienced pilots at Calais advised John to wait until the weather improved. Indeed, the wind was so strong that a number of newsmen, mindful of the fierce channel winds that had foiled so many crossing attempts, wired their editors that Moisant could not possibly take off before late afternoon. But John Moisant would not, could not wait. Since Blériot's record-setting flight a year earlier two more aviators, Count Jacques de Lesseps and Englishman Charles Stewart Rolls (Rolls Royce cofounder), had both crossed the channel, Rolls actually crossing twice in a nonstop round trip back to England. Moisant intended to do something neither they nor any other man had yet done—carry a passenger all the way from Paris to London in the same plane.

The startled Calais newsmen watched in silent awe when Moisant and his mechanic, having touched down barely three hours ago and with the weather still unchanged, made it clear there would be no more waiting. With Japanese paper jammed between his business suit and coveralls as insulation, Moisant looked like a stuffed teddy bear as he climbed into his monoplane. Fileux turned the propeller until the motor sputtered to life, then clambered into his seat next to Moisant. The surprised spectators watched in silence as the wide-bodied, pigeon-tailed aircraft, buffeted by northwest winds gusting to 35 MPH, teetered and rocked but rose slowly into the grey overcast sky, then disappeared into the clouds.

Inside the pitching, tossing aircraft, Moisant fixed his eyes on his only navigational tool, an ordinary compass, its needle floating in glycerine, as Fileux read aloud from the altimeter. In the water below, the boat hired to follow them fell behind and soon disappeared, leaving them with no means of rescue if they were to ditch in the channel. Fifty minutes later as Moisant brought his plane down through freezing rain squalls, his face and goggles smeared with castor oil spewing from the Gnôme engine, he sighted several ships. Dover! Or so he thought. Flying at 1,000 feet and his hands too cramped and numb to hold the control lever much longer, Moisant headed toward a clearing when a sudden hail-like rain sucked the plane down 700 feet, forcing him to land in an oat field near Tilmanstone, six miles from Dover. He had spanned the 25 miles from Calais to England in 58 minutes, time enough for the telegraphed news to alert reporters from London and elsewhere in England and start them converging on the Dover area.

The grinning pilot leapt from the cockpit, his eyes bloodshot from wind and rain, his coveralls soaked and stained with oil. Newsmen immediately surrounded him, bombarding him with questions, then telephoning their hastily written and often inaccurate stories. The *London Daily Mirror* identified him as Juan Moissant, of Spanish origin. Several other newspapers, including the *New York Times* and the *London Daily Mirror,* spelled his name "Moissan."

"My name is John B. Moissant," the *London Daily Mail* of August 18 erroneously reported, printing the name with two "s"s despite John's almost ferocious insistence to the contrary. "That's my full name and the proper way to spell it. . . . I always put in the 'B' for Benjamin. [He had already changed Jean Baptiste to John Benjamin, but not yet changed the Benjamin to Bevins.] I'm from Chicago, Illinois and I call myself an American because I was born of American parents in America. You can say there is not a drop of Spanish blood in my veins. No, sir, not one drop."

Asked about his reputed exploits in Central America, he advised reporters to cable San Francisco, Mexico, or the secretary of state. "Yes, sir, I think Mr. Knox will tell you he knows me pretty well, but I really cannot tell you myself about my past." Moisant seemed ready to exchange his soldier-of-fortune image for that of all-American aviation pioneer.

Afraid that his plane might well be stripped by souvenir hunters, Moisant stood close by while volunteers jacked it up and moved it into the shelter of an open shed, pegging it down behind a row of hayracks to protect it from the wind and rain. In an interview later that day, Moisant exulted, "The worst part of the journey is over," and predicted he would arrive in London by evening. But when the weather failed to improve he and Fileux bedded down on rugs and a mattress next to the plane.

Moisant rose early the morning of the eighteenth, still confident of completing his record-breaking Paris-London flight that same day. (As his brother Alfred was to point out later, it would in fact be a triple record for John: not only the first Paris-London flight but also the first carrying a passenger and the first in the same plane.) With the help of ten men to drag his Blériot to a clearing, he and Fileux took off from Tilmanstone at 5 A.M., only to be forced down near Sittingbourne by a broken exhaust valve only 70 minutes later. Narrowly missing the mouth of a deep chalk pit and almost certain death, Moisant skillfully set the plane down in a turnip field. But it took 3½ hours to complete repairs and take to the air again, only to be forced down near Upchurch and Rainham in Kent just 15 minutes later. This time the plane came to rest at the bottom of an abandoned brick field "in an awkward position [and facing] so many obstacles experts wonder why" no one was injured. In addition to other extensive damage, the propeller was splintered.

Moisant immediately wired London and Paris for a new propeller for his plane, which one reporter described as stuck in the rubble of a brick pit "like a marble in a deep bowl." Within the hour 500 spectators had gathered to watch as he and Fileux, with the help of a captain and several enlisted men from a nearby contingent of Royal Engineers, went to work on extricating the aircraft. When they finished, one of the sappers gave Moisant a kitten, a blue-grey striped Maltese. He immediately named it "Paree-Londres."

Meanwhile, aviators who only a short time earlier had been deriding Moisant as a crazy kid and an amateur were now praising his exploits and hailing him as a hero. "What an airman he is," former rival Hubert Latham proclaimed, while British air notable Claude Grahame-White and his 19-year-old expatriate Philadelphia student J. Armstrong Drexel both offered to replace the broken propeller, Drexel saying he would strip the one from his own Blériot XI and send it on the first train.

The offers of assistance proved unnecessary when a replacement propeller arrived from the Blériot agent in London early Friday, the two flyers spending both nights as house guests of Sir Mark and Lady Colley at their manor house in neighboring St. LeClere. Repairing and readying the plane for flight in the face of a stiff gale that swept the area all Friday, they took off again the next morning—this time with a third passenger, Paree-Londres, whom John had placed in a paper bag held safely beside him—but managed only four miles before the winds forced them down on a patch of farmland in Gillingham. With the plane still weatherbound and the number of onlookers increasing by the hour, the farmer on whose field they sat complained that the crowds were damaging his crops. Moisant suggested he charge each of them a shilling. When the farmer observed that the people were already on his property, Moisant replied, "Then charge them sixpence each to go out!"

The following Monday, Moisant took off from Gillingham only to be blown down again some 10 miles away at Wrotham, where he walked into town to buy more gasoline, eight villagers returning with him to help him take off. Flying into strong headwinds, the Blériot covered only four miles in the next 27 minutes before it was caught by a sudden wind gust near Kemsing. This time Moisant landed safely on top of a steep hill, just missing a high hedge that bordered the road. But the wheels were damaged, the rudder buckled, and a second propeller broken. And he was still 18 miles from London.

By the time reporters reached the plane, Moisant was standing by it holding Paree-Londres, whose head emerged from the paper bag. "You ought to have seen this kitten," he said. "He enjoyed himself immensely and wasn't a bit afraid. He was still curled up in the bag, his bright eyes peeping up at me when the crash came, and even the noise of breaking wood did not disturb him." With this he handed the kitten over to a cottager who offered to care for it while he assessed the damage to his aircraft.

John turned down numerous offers to drive him the short remaining distance to London, explaining, "I'm not going to London unless I fly there," and "No other way is good enough for me." In Paris, brother Alfred, who had already spent almost $2,000 on repairs to the $10,000 Blériot, proved equally determined, hiring a second French mechanic and an additional ten workers and rushing them to England to assist Fileux.

Whether or not they realized it, the English were seeing a John Moisant quite different from the Central American adventurer of a year back. Instead of reacting in his formerly characteristic rage and impatience at the constantly occurring delays and troubles, the new Moisant seemed as unperturbed as his kitten. He had already exhibited rare traces of modesty when he told congratulatory newsmen at Tilmanstone, "I can't fly yet. Very nice of you to say I can, but I don't yet know half as much as Latham or [Louis] Paulhan or Grahame-White. I'm just learning." Now he was evincing humor as well. Acceding cheerfully to autograph requests at the repair site, he often wrote,

"John B. Moisant, the bird man, who hopes to get to London some time between now and next Christmas."

Overnight Moisant, "chivalrous to his finger-tips," had become a celebrity, attracting thousands of admirers who arrived on special trains, by autos, carriages, or bicycles. Residents of the area were calling the five-day repair period "the Moisant season" while London journalists alternately described it as "a rural rest cure" for "the intrepid aviator" and a rare chance for villagers who delighted in watching "his two merry French mechanics" in action. Perhaps merriest of all was farmer Douglas who owned the field where the Blériot was being repaired and was averaging a daily profit of 50 pounds charging admission.

Having been the Colleys' houseguest for some 10 days now, he had promised to give Lady Colley, a bedridden invalid, her first glimpse of an aircraft in flight. On the morning of the twenty-eighth, he arranged for her bed to be brought to a window and once more took off in rain and wind for London, heading first for the manor house so his hostess could watch as he flew by. But he made it only 50 feet into the air and flew barely a minute before the wind once again sent him crashing to the ground, barely missing a woman spectator, and leaving the plane, with broken wheels and a smashed propeller, "in worse condition than when it fell at . . . Kemsing a week ago." Seeing him crawl out unhurt from the wreckage, a newsman commented on this being his fourth accident and third broken propeller since leaving Calais 11 days earlier. Unruffled, Moisant replied, "Yes, sir, and you may see me smash a fourth before I get to London."

By this time, American newspapers had virtually lost interest and the *New York Times* had relegated Moisant's Paris-London story from page 1 to page 16. On the other hand, British interest and enthusiasm continued unabated, as reflected in a telegram Moisant received September 3 at the Colleys, where he and Fileux were again waiting out repairs. Signed by A. Henderson, Chief of the Great Central Railway, it read, "Dear Sir: Persevere. It took us 40 years to reach London. You have scarcely been at it a fortnight. Remember Bruce and the spider."

After a three-week flight with nine forced landings, Moisant reached London at last on September 6. Starting from Kemsing at midday, he circled wide above St. LeClere so that Lady Colley could see him and flew for two miles to a cornfield near Otford Station where he landed to adjust the wing warp and wait for the winds to die down.

He took off again at five o'clock, steering by compass until he arrived 27 minutes later over the grounds of London's Crystal Palace, which Grahame-White had used for his recent flight and where several hundred people were waiting for Moisant to arrive. But the anxious spectators were to be disappointed. Partially blinded by the engine oil that spattered his goggles and unable to pick out a landing site through the fog, Moisant flew another mile and a half before landing at the new cricket field at Beckenham in one final crash, caused by an enthusiastic spectator who ran right under the descending plane. Moisant cut his engine and came down against a fence, buckling the wheels, breaking a skid and, as he had predicted, breaking his fourth propeller.

Emerging unhurt from the debris, Moisant told the spectators rushing to his aid, "I have done what I set out to do, although I have been a long time on the way. People said I could not fly with a passenger from Paris to London, never having been over the route before and steering by compass after consulting maps. I have shown that these people are wrong!"

Besieged by admirers, John accepted two invitations to fly in air meets—the first at Folkestone in England September 19–22, and the second at Belmont Park, New York, in the international air races in October. But before going to Folkestone he returned to Paris to order a new Blériot and where Alfred was waiting to congratulate him. The proud older brother was already arranging a hero's homecoming. Louise and Matilde were on their way to New York from Alameda, where they had been visiting friends, and the family would all stay in a five-room suite Alfred had rented for the occasion at the Hotel Astor.

At Folkestone on September 19 Moisant was cheered by spectators as he flew around and around the course and as he was driven to the grandstand to meet Lord Marcus Beresford, one of the many wealthy Englishmen who regarded aviation as an exciting new sport. Moisant was amused when the band played the "Marseillaise" instead of "The Star-Spangled Banner" in his honor.

But two days later he complained to reporters that he was disgusted by "the recklessness of the crowd," especially one "cheerful idiot" who signed his name on the canvas wing of Moisant's plane, making a hole that was found only moments before flight time and could have caused a serious accident. Nevertheless he stayed on through the full four-day meet, even treating a number of people to brief flights.

Returning again to Paris, John joined Alfred for the trip back to New York on the SS *Savoie*. As the boat train to Cherbourg pulled out of Paris's St. Lazare station on October 1, John leaned out the window, waving to his friends and displaying a blanketed basket. In it was Paree-Londres, who also would be traveling first class all the way. Later he walked back to a second car of the train to chat with his former instructor, Alfred Leblanc. Leblanc, who was bringing along a 100-hp Blériot for the Belmont meet, might well have wondered how much competition he could expect from his now-famous ex-student who was suddenly a celebrity after having had only one flying lesson. Two other aviation pioneers were also sailing on the *Savoie*, French balloonist Jacques Faure and Octave Chanute, the Chicago engineer who had experimented with gliders long before the Wrights produced an engine-powered aircraft. Old and very ill, Chanute was carried aboard in a wheelchair.

When the *Savoie* arrived in New York's harbor reporters were waiting at the dock. Moisant was the perfect tabloid idol: good-looking, articulate, with an exotic reputation as a soldier of fortune, and a man who had just set a world aviation record. The self-portrayal he presented was that of a "regular fellow" who did not want his name to be pronounced "Mwa-sahnt" as the French did. The French, he said, couldn't help it, but it was "Moy-sant" and he was a Chicago man, an American.

With Fileux on one side, Alfred on the other, and Paree-

Londres wrapped in a silk comforter in his arms, Moisant held court before an enchanted and eager press. Providing photo opportunities for grateful photographers, he thanked two fellow passengers, opera singer Olive Fremstad for helping him care for the Maltese kitten and a Mrs. C. R. Miller of Baltimore for taking a picture of him with Paree-Londres.

The purpose of all this posturing was less ego gratification than a shrewd bid for national attention to espouse his views on the future of aviation. In England he had told reporters that "in five years time an aeroplane will be flying across the Atlantic in 24 hours. In less than two years time we will produce a monoplane with a 200-horsepower engine that will thrust the machine through the air at 100 miles per hour. Air stations will be great open flat places, surrounded by sheds and repair depots. Aircraft will be constantly rising from them and arriving at them after long aerial journeys." He was right about the airfields but 50 years too early.

Now back in his own country Moisant was telling his fellow countrymen that the United States was lagging behind all other nations. "America is asleep," he warned. "The American government is doing nothing for aviation, yet aviation means more to the governments of the earth than any other human organization."

John, Alfred (identified by some newsmen as a Salvadoran banker), and Paree-Londres left the docks for the Hotel Astor, where Matilde and Louise were waiting for their famous brother. There John was again interviewed, this time by Edith Day, who was writing a series on "The Personal Side of Talked-of Aviators." Describing John as an architect sharing extensive sugar interests with his brother in Central America, Day wrote that he was "very approachable. Jolly, good tempered and responsive, considered excellent company," in short, a charming 26-year-old bachelor with "no affectation." She erred on his age. He was 40.

Day was only one of many to be captivated by this modest little man with the smooth boyish face. Only a short time ago the gentle cat lover had been described as a ruthless, gun-slinging adventurer. But that image was being shoved back into the past, if not entirely forgotten. Now John Moisant was an aviator in search of approval, a zealous missionary-advocate of flight, backed by his first convert to the new faith, his brother Alfred. Together they would challenge the world of aviation, starting at Belmont.

6
FOR AMERICA!

In the green and gold suite at the Hotel Astor the four Moisants—Johnny, Fred, Till, and Lou—held a joyous reunion for the next nine days with the attention centered on the celebrity brother. On the tenth day, October 19, they drove in Alfred's chauffeured limousine to Belmont Park, Long Island, where John's new Blériot had been delivered to one of the thirty hangars erected between the back stretch of the racetrack and the Long Island Railroad tracks. It would be his first chance to test the late-model plane, especially designed by Blériot for racing, and he needed to practice before competing at the world's most prestigious air tournament, the 1910 international aviation meet scheduled to start in just three days and continue through October 30.

The novice pilot with less than four months' experience intended to challenge some of the world's best-known flyers in a speed contest for the Coupe Internationale d'Aviation, a silver cup and cash prize of $5,000, awarded by James Gordon Bennett, publisher of the *Paris Herald*. At the previous meet in Rheims, France, American Glenn H. Curtiss, the Wright brothers' chief rival in plane design, had won the trophy. Contest rules provided that the winner's nation host the next year's meet and the Aero Club of America had arranged that the race for the Gordon Bennett cup, as it was known in the United States, would climax the Belmont meet.

Eager to have Matilde and Louise see him fly, John escorted them to his hangar where several other friends were waiting to watch the test flight. Matilde, at 32, was a beautiful woman with dark eyes, regular features, fine skin, and a trim figure. Small, and appearing even smaller beneath the enormous flower-trimmed hats of the time, she often wore a pince-nez. The hat, the glasses, and the long, full-skirted dress over high-buttoned shoes combined to disguise her beauty, but she was as handsome as her brother John whom she so closely resembled.

Louise, at 27, was taller than Matilde, equally attractive but with slightly coarser features. Of the two, Louise was the more opinionated, always eager to advise others of what she perceived to be the truth. And although Matilde thoroughly approved of John's new vocation, Louise constantly voiced apprehension over its dangers.

In the car, John carried the cat in a basket on his lap. Before entering the green, barn-like hangar he handed it to Matilde. Albert Fileux and the crew of French mechanics who had accompanied John to the United States were waiting for him. They rolled the new Blériot out onto the field, watched Moisant climb into the pilot's seat, then started the revolving Gnôme motor with its fixed propeller that spewed castor oil over the pilot's goggles.

Louise looked at her watch. It was four o'clock when the plane rose off the field and headed for the inner track around which a dozen evenly spaced 30-foot-high pylons had been constructed for the meet. Leveling off at 200 feet the Blériot circled the track for five or six minutes when it suddenly turned over completely and hurtled down nose first, the noise of the impact as it struck the ground carrying across the field.

"Oh, he lost control!" Matilde cried, covering her eyes. "Don't take me over there!" she told Louise. "I don't want to see him!"

Pilots working on their planes in the track compound stopped and stared, silently watching until they saw Moisant emerge from the cloud of dust that hid the wreckage. He was un-harmed, but his new aircraft was badly damaged, the right wing crumpled, the propeller smashed, the motor shaft bent, and the fragile wooden frame turned into kindling.

"He's safe," one of the bystanders told Matilde. "I can see him walking." Both women ran to meet their brother, tears streaming down their cheeks as they embraced him. Moisant patted their backs, grinning sheepishly as he looked back at the wreck. "I simply forgot to have my oil tank turned on and when I was trying to do it, my foot slipped from the control. When you lose control, it's all off."

His competitors at Belmont all assumed that Moisant would now have to withdraw from the meet because his new plane could not possibly be repaired in time and his old one, the Blériot XI, 2-bis côte-à-côte, that had served him so well in his Paris-London flight, was too slow and bulky for the scheduled events. They were mistaken. Moisant had brought four spare parts for every portion of the plane. He sent the wreckage to Capt. T. T. Lovelace at the Lovelace-Thompson aircraft plant at Fort George with instructions that the repairs be completed by the following Tuesday. Meanwhile he registered his old plane for entry in the opening events.

Until this point, aviation news headlines in New York had been dominated by the British Aero Club's handsome socialite sportsman, Claude Grahame-White, especially since his spectac-ular landing a month earlier in Washington, D.C., on a narrow street between the White House and the Executive Building. But the Englishman made the mistake of publicly insisting that fly-ing was so difficult that "not one man in a thousand can master it," prompting one newspaper to write of him as the "King of the Air [who] comes on . . . like a conquering hero." The same paper lauded "modest, self-deprecating little Moisant" for his contrasting view that flying was "all very easy and pleasant. . . . I should blush with shame if I said anything else." The implicit difference over whether flying was an elite or a popular pastime lost Grahame-White a good deal of sympathy among newsmen while Moisant gained sympathy from his crash on the nine-teenth. But being an American flying in his own country, it was probably inevitable that Moisant's name ultimately would dominate the headlines, the New York press having bestowed on him American "favorite son" status.

The Belmont meet opened on Saturday, October 22, to near-impossible flying weather with a steady drizzle and low fog hanging over the converted race track. There seemed little need that morning for the high canvas curtains that had been hung around the perimeter to keep those without tickets from peeking. The Long Island and Pennsylvania Railroad companies had canceled their special trains and the grandstands were empty of all but meet officials, management personnel, and shivering groups of reporters. Not until later in the day when the rain let up and it became known that the meet had not been canceled after all did a few ticketholders—$1.00 for standing room only and $2.00 for unreserved seats in the two-tiered grandstand—begin to straggle in.

Although the stands were almost empty, the boxes with their reserved seats were filled with members of New York's Four Hundred, who regarded the meet as the social and sporting event of the year.

Still, until the sun came out about two o'clock, the field presented a dreary scene of wet flags—U.S., British, French, and Swiss—hanging limply from their standards while pilots huddled in their hangars debating whether or not to risk their machines in such weather. Most of the twenty-eight registered contestants, many unable to start their planes despite blankets above and heaters below their cold, wet engines, forfeited their chances at that day's portion of the $75,000 prize money. That first day, only seven flew.

Three flyers—Grahame-White in his Farman biplane and Moisant and J. Armstrong Drexel in their Blériot XI mono-planes—competed for the first event, a test for distance flown around the converted racetrack. Grahame-White won after Drexel dropped out in the ninth lap with motor trouble and

Moisant was penalized for fouling four pylons. In a repeat race the Englishman won again after Moisant fouled another pylon. He obviously needed more practice flying a marked course.

In the altitude contest that followed, the fog was so dense that the winner, Arch Hoxsey, who flew for the Wrights, reached only 742 feet, and the other two contestants got lost.

As the wind rose and the fog became even thicker, Moisant was the sole flyer who dared contest the final event, a 20-mile cross-country run to a balloon marker over Hempstead Plains and back. Flying blind through fog and rain, with only a compass and no barometer, Moisant swooped down again and again to within 100 feet of the ground to confirm his bearings, fearful only that he "might knock down a church steeple or get caught in a tangle of telegraph wires." He never did find the captive balloon marker but headed back to Belmont after spotting a clump of trees described to him as a landmark for the completed distance. As he landed in center field the band began to play and applause rose from the grandstands. In addition to winning the $850 prize money and being asked to write the story of his flight for the *Brooklyn Eagle,* Moisant clearly emerged as the day's outstanding flyer. The *New York City World* hailed the flight as "a mariner's feat in midair." A reporter from Texas said Moisant had to be "the most marvelous aviator in the world." And, calling it "one of the finest feats in the annals of aviation," G. F. Campbell Wood marveled in conclusion: "How he ever found his way back to the aerodrome after those forty minutes he was speeding through the mist over the open country, is something such men as [Emile] Aubrun—the second of the Circuit de l'Est—and [Jacques] de Lesseps—the second man to cross the Straits of Dover—are still wondering."

Moisant and Grahame-White between them had salvaged the opening day, but when they attempted to do it again on Sunday they both failed and at a heavy cost. The rain had stopped but the winds were reported at 25 MPH. The Englishman went up first, head-on into a gale, and lost control of the Farman he had borrowed from Clifford Harmon, an American friend and fellow racer. He tried to land in front of the hangar but the wind caught his right wing, tilting the Farman over, smashing the left wing into the ground and buckling its wheels. When he tried to right the aircraft he was caught by another gust of wind, smashing the other wing as well.

Moisant fared no better. Before he could even get onto the seat of his Blériot the wind wrenched the plane from the hands of his crew and flipped it over, crumpling both wings, breaking the rudder, and bending the crankshaft.

Bad weather was but one of the many problems faced by the international aviation meet management. The crowds outside the track's boundaries were larger than those within as thousands of Sunday drivers seeking to save parking and entrance fees caused traffic jams along the country roads overseeing Belmont. And when management tried to counteract this by hanging up even more canvas curtains, adjacent landowners threatened to sue unless the unsightly barriers were removed. The pilots themselves added to the committee's misery with protests about the course laid out for the Gordon Bennett cup. The 5-kilometer (3.1-mile) circuit for the 100-kilometer (62.14-mile) race was over houses, trees, telegraph wires, and train tracks, with a deadly sharp final turn and no place to land if an engine failed. Leblanc protested to the Aero Club of France, calling the plan "a death trap." Although Moisant and Grahame-White agreed that the course was too dangerous, they both offered to compete.

Moisant himself complained to the press that the meet was being poorly managed by incompetents. He said he had no plane to fly because the management lied about wind speed on Sunday when winds were actually above the meet's 25-MPH flying limit. His new Blériot was still under repair and the older one had been wrecked by the wind as had Grahame-White's borrowed Farman. In addition to this injustice employees at the gates were demanding tickets from everyone entering—even the pilots!

The next day Moisant had his old Blériot back, but James Radley, an Englishman, won the cross-country race after Moisant, Drexel, and Canadian J.A.D. McCurdy all lost their way in the fog. The other two landed elsewhere but just as the dwindling crowd began leaving in the deepening darkness, Moisant found his way back to the field by compass, a feat that captured the next day's headlines.

Since opening day the meet had been plagued by bad weather. On the fifth day, Wednesday, the wind blew at 40 MPH until three o'clock, but New York's Four Hundred continued to fill the boxes. Newcomers included John Jacob Astor and his son, Vincent; Sen. and Mrs. Chauncey Depew and Chauncey Jr.; and Mrs. Craig Biddle, who went onto the field to see the Blériot flown by young Drexel. Alfred, Matilde, and Louise spent most of the day in the hangar with John, who did not fly. He was saving his new Blériot, which the Lovelace-Thompson plant had just returned to him, for the elimination flights on Thursday to qualify for the Gordon Bennett cup.

Thursday brought gale-force winds again, forcing the committee to postpone the day's trials and reschedule them for 9 AM Friday. Since Belmont area winds were usually strongest in the morning and calmed down in the afternoon, this brought a howl of protest from all the flyers, Moisant himself becoming "so angry he sputtered in French, English and Spanish." The chastened committee backed down, permitting pilots to take off any time Friday they wanted to so long as they finished by 5:30 P.M.

On Friday Moisant qualified for the American team but only as an alternate, though he now ranked third (after Hoxsey and Grahame-White) in total prize winnings. Members of the first team were Drexel, Walter Brookins, and Charles K. Hamilton, with J. C. Mars, Moisant, and Hoxsey as substitutes in that order.

Although the winds were judged too strong that Friday to hold the race to the Statue of Liberty, news of the spectacular flying during the preceding days drew 30,000 viewers who stood and cheered each pilot as he flew by. Moisant entered only one event, the cross-country passenger-carrying race, one Grahame-White had refused to enter. He took off in his old Blériot XI with Frederick Thompson, the theatrical manager and co-owner of the Lovelace-Thompson factory, who had never ridden in an airplane. The only other contestant was Jacques de Lesseps with his cousin Count Bertrand de Lesseps as passenger.

De Lesseps was forced down by the wind at Garden City. Moisant came down in a cabbage field nearby, but Thompson was ecstatic over his first ride. "It was like hitting the pipe and dreaming," he said. "We went over a graveyard, and a White Cross encampment as well as a church spire, on which I thought we would land, all of which was cheerful—but, really, I never enjoyed myself as much before."

The next day, October 29, John Moisant was not nearly as happy as his passenger had been. As only second alternate on the American team he could hardly expect to fly in the most important contest of the entire meet—the race for the international or Gordon Bennett cup, with its recognition of the winner as speed champion of the world. Besides, the Americans seemed out of the running in their 50-hp aircraft. The daring and skillful Alfred Leblanc would be flying a Blériot monoplane with a 14-cylinder, 100-hp Gnôme engine that he had brought from France for this race. Brilliant racing pilot Grahame-Wright would also use a 100-hp Gnôme-Blériot. (The Wrights had designed a new "baby racer" for the U.S. team but it had not yet been tested under racing conditions. Glenn Curtiss built and tested his own monoplane for the race but judged it unsafe and withdrew from the contest.)

Grahame-White was the first to take off, in the early morning when the wind was more favorable than it would prove to be for the rest of the day. He finished in one hour and one minute with an average speed of 61 MPH. Leblanc followed, averaging 67 MPH and looking like a certain winner until the feedline to his gasoline tank gave way. Losing control he crashed into a telephone pole, breaking the pole into three pieces and demolishing his plane. He escaped with bruises and severe facial lacerations.

Seeing Leblanc crash, Brookins took off in the Wright "baby racer" to go to his aid. But at 100 feet a connecting rod on the little plane gave way, the motor stopped cold, and the plane fell.

Brookins ruefully commented later, "I had started over to see what happened to Leblanc. And when they brought him into the hospital tent, there I was lying on the operating table waiting for him."

The other two U.S. first-team members were quickly out of the running. Drexel withdrew after completing seven laps, saying the wind was too dangerous in the turns. And Hamilton, who had difficulty starting his engine anyway, withdrew after seeing Leblanc's speed just before he crashed, saying, "I am going to throw my machine in the scrapheap and buy a Blériot before I leave the track."

With the first team eliminated, first substitute Mars prepared to fly but was unable to start his engine. Meanwhile, sitting in his hangar eating a piece of pie, Moisant was unaware of any of this until race officials came in and told him to get ready to fly for the United States. In just 30 minutes a startled crew of mechanics readied the newly repaired 50-hp Blériot but in their haste forgot to attach one of the heavy rubber bands that controlled the elevator planes. Forced down soon after takeoff, Moisant quickly located the trouble, attached the needed band, and took off for a second time.

Moisant knew that his downtime would be included in his total and that he had no chance to beat Grahame-White and his 100-hp engine. But he realized, too, that his only rival for second place, Hubert Latham, had spent five hours grounded for repairs. Seizing the chance to win second place for the Americans, Moisant did so in 1 hour, 57 minutes, and 45 seconds, a little less than double Grahame-White's time with a motor only half as powerful. Latham was third.

Winners and losers all had comments for the press. Grahame-White said since it was the first time he had tried the course he had actually flown much more than the required 100 kilometers. Leblanc said that but for the mistake made by his mechanics he would have won for France. Latham agreed, saying France would send a strong team to England next year. John Moisant said, "The cup will not remain in England more than one year as we will get it back. I will build a metal machine before the next competition capable of flying 100 miles an hour."

The moment Moisant climbed out of his plane Allan A. Ryan, chairman of the arrangements committee, ran onto the field and dragged him into the clubhouse where he ordered champagne for the crowd of admirers. With one arm around Moisant's neck he raised his glass and shouted, "Here's to Moisant and America! Give him three cheers!" The response was so loud the window-panes rattled. Moisant lifted his glass and replied, "Here's to America—next year!"

Leaving his admirers soon after, he retreated to the hangar to discuss his Blériot's performance with Fileux and his crew. In less than 24 hours he would be challenging Grahame-White again in a race so hazardous it had been condemned by the Wright brothers as a danger not only to the aviators above but to the people of New York below.

7

"THE GREATEST RACE OF MODERN TIMES"

After a week of dreary rainy days, limited flying conditions, and disappointingly small crowds at Belmont Park, the weather cleared on Sunday. The day was cold but the skies cloudless and windless, perfect for the paramount event of the day—the race from the park around the Statue of Liberty and back.

The Thomas F. Ryan Classic was unlike previous meet events which had been held over sparsely populated areas providing flyers with vast farmlands, beaches, and manicured estate lawns on which to set down in emergencies. This race would be 35 miles over land, water, and the unforgiving rooftops of Brooklyn. Two months after the event it was denounced by *Aircraft* magazine as the most dangerous aviation contest since France's Georges Chavèz crossed the Alps a year earlier. The magazine said it should be outlawed immediately "*before* a bad accident makes it a necessity (and at the same time hurts the cause of aviation)."

Perhaps because of the dangers involved, only three of the meet's thirty-plus contestants registered for the event—Count Jacques de Lesseps, Grahame-White, and Moisant.

It was to be a day of high drama and high society. Arriving at Belmont together, the four Moisants—John, Alfred, Louise, and Matilde—walked by stands filled to capacity with 75,000 spectators, most of whom had never seen an airplane before. The box seats were occupied by members of the top social register, the Belmonts, Drexels, Vanderbilts, and Biddles, most of whom had seen airplanes before and several of whom intended to buy and fly one.

To them it was carnival time, a celebration of the impossible —men with wings. The men wore silk hats and frock coats, the women suits of satin and velvet with skirts cut in the narrow "hobble" style of the time and furs of sable, silver fox, and lamb. Their hats were of felt and fur, trimmed with feathers of yellow, blue, green, and violet in a riot of festive color. One newspaper listed by name more than 100 of these privileged spectators and described in detail the costumes of 29 of the women.

At his hangar John Moisant donned two suits, two sweaters, and a black knitted cap that covered all of his head except his face. Alfred and his two sisters stood by while Grahame-White and de Lesseps took off, then watched Fileux and his mechanics wheel John's Blériot onto the ramp. In the pilot's seat John waved to them before signaling to Fileux to spin the propeller and nodding to the mechanics holding the plane back to release it. When they did, the aircraft did not taxi out to the field but instead began to spin in a half circle, its rudder jammed. Out of control, the Blériot careened into another plane parked in front of a nearby hangar. The aircraft was Harmon's Farman, the same plane that had been wrecked by high winds the previous Sunday. Ripping off the Farman's port wing and part of the tail, Moisant's Blériot then tilted over on its side, one of its wings smashed.

As John jumped down from the crippled plane, Alfred rushed up to him. "Are you hurt, Johnny?" he shouted.

"Not a scratch, Fred, but I'm out of the statue race now."

"I'll buy you another machine," Alfred said.

A reporter at the scene wrote that Alfred could certainly afford it, being the owner of a bank in Central America and of gold mines as well. At the time Alfred was wearing "a gold nugget as big as an egg and a long string of gold nuggets as big as filberts for a watch chain."

The two brothers jumped into Alfred's car and began a hurried tour of the twenty hangars, stopping at number 7 where Alfred Leblanc's two planes were housed. Next to the 100-hp aircraft in which Leblanc had crashed the day before was a new 50-hp Blériot he had flown only a few times.

"We'll get that machine, Johnny," Alfred said. "Can you drive it all right? You've never even sat in it, but it looks to me like a good machine."

"Sure I can drive it," John replied. "Do you mean you'll get it for me, Fred?"

"I'll not only get it but you'll have it in an hour. You see that your number is painted on it, have the tanks filled, and try the motor."

Leblanc's bewildered mechanics followed John's instructions, painting "21" on the tail and underside of the wings and filling the tanks.

Meanwhile Alfred dashed across the field to the nearest telephone to call Leblanc at the Knickerbocker Hotel in Manhattan where he was recuperating from his injuries suffered the day before. Speaking in French, Alfred offered him $10,000, $3,000 more than the plane had cost in France.

Leblanc accepted the offer, arriving at the park 50 minutes later. Alfred, who had not brought a checkbook, borrowed one from a bystander, scratching out the issuing bank's name and substituting that of his own bank instead. The check finally bore the writing of three different people, the original owner who had numbered it in ink, Alfred's secretary who had hurried over to fill in all the details, and Alfred's signature.

Official spotters strategically placed along the flight route—including one in the tower of the Statue of Liberty itself—would be telephoning news of the flyers' progress to the Belmont officials who relayed it by loudspeaker to the 75,000 spectators in the grandstands and on the clubhouse lawn. Meanwhile, on this perfect-weather Sunday, thousands more jammed the streets,

Left: The house at Santa Emilia, the plantation founded by Alfred Moisant with assistance from his brothers George, Edward, and John. By 1897 their mother Josephine and sisters Matilde and Louise had left their home in Alameda, California, to join them here. (Courtesy of John A. Weyl)

Right: When not engaged in his soldier-of-fortune forays or amassing a fortune in land and mineral rights, inventor-aviator John Moisant was the charming, debonair man-about-town. (Courtesy of John A. Weyl)

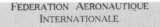

FEDERATION AERONAUTIQUE
INTERNATIONALE

AERO CLUB OF AMERICA
No. 44

The above-named Club, recognized by
the Federation Aeronautique Internationale,
as the governing authority for the United
States of America, certifies that

Matilde E. Moisant

born *13th* day of *September* *1887*,
having fulfilled all the conditions required by
the Federation Aeronautique Internationale,
is hereby licensed as Aviator.

Dated *August 17th, 1911.*

James A. Blair Jr.
President.

G. H. Campbell Wood
Secretary.

[SEAL]

Matilde E. Moisant

Signature of Licensee :

Aug 13, 1911

Above: Matilde's aviator's license, an astounding
combination of credentials and fashion. (NASM
Archives)

Left: Matilde Moisant in her smart flying suit and
helmet worn when she became a member of the
Moisant International Aviators. (Courtesy of John
A. Weyl)

Left: Matilde Moisant, the second American woman to be licensed as a pilot, with her instructor, André Houpert, chief pilot for the Moisant Aviation School at Garden City. (Courtesy of John A. Weyl)

Right: Aviator Matilde Moisant in her role as homemaker for her beloved older brother, Alfred, businessman-venturer and head of the family—Fred to his siblings but Don Alfredo at his Salvadoran plantation, Santa Emilia. (Courtesy of John A. Weyl)

The dapper John Moisant gazes fondly at his beloved cat, Paree-Londres, who missed that record-breaking flight but became his frequent flying companion. (NASM Archives)

Left: In appearance the slim, handsome aviator-inventor Johnny Moisant was the opposite of his financier brother Fred, yet they shared their firm belief in the future of aviation. (NASM Archives)

Right: Standing behind Alfred Moisant are two of his International Aviators, the French Roland Garros *(left)* and Swiss Edmond Audemars. Garros's later fame as a World War I hero was acknowledged in the naming of the national recreation center where the French Open tennis matches are currently held. With Garros, the diminutive Audemars was a master of the tiny, low-powered Demoiselle. (NASM Archives)

303

Top: Harriet Quimby, a graduate of the Moisant Aviation School and first American woman to be licensed, aboard her Blériot. (NASM Archives)

Bottom: René Simon, daring aerobatic member of the Moisant International Aviators traveling air show, listens to instructions from Alfred Moisant. (NASM Archives)

Top: John Moisant aloft at an air meet on September 11, 1910, following his record-breaking flight from Paris to London, the first airborne crossing of the English Channel with a passenger. (NASM Archives)

Bottom: John Moisant seated in the *Aluminoplane,* the aircraft he designed and built at Issy-les-Moulineaux in France before he had learned to fly. Shortly after the photograph was taken he wrecked the plane during his first flight in it. (NASM Archives)

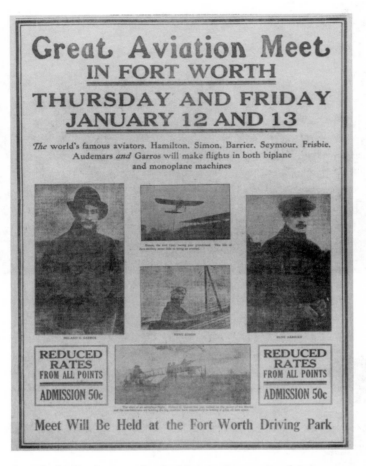

A typical advertisement for the Moisant International Aviators. This was run in the *Fort Worth Record* of January 10, 1911. (From the Texas Newspaper Collection, Center for American History, University of Texas at Austin)

bridges, rooftops, and roads of Long Island, Jamaica, Queens, Brooklyn, and Manhattan and stared up into the sky. To most of them it still seemed a miracle that humans could fly. As one reporter wrote,

The great crowd watched . . . fascinated [that] . . . man . . . was about to undertake a feat never before attempted. The history of aviation has not so far furnished an instance of a flyer crossing over a town of any size, and the danger of flying above a city like Brooklyn is regarded by aviators as almost beyond the bounds of recklessness. A fall means almost certain death.

(News of Moisant's flight over Paris had obviously not reached the writer.)

In all, an estimated one million people watched the race. Around the Statue of Liberty itself more than 10,000 stood along the Battery wall. They came in automobiles, crested carriages, by bicycle, on foot, and in streetcars, the rich standing alongside the poor. The decks of the Staten Island and Brooklyn ferries were packed.

De Lesseps and Grahame-White took off within three minutes of each other. When the Frenchman appeared over the harbor the spectators first cheered, then fell silent, watching the airplane in awe. Moments after de Lesseps began the turn around the balloon marker near the statue, Graham-White's plane was sighted from the direction of the East River.

Moisant took off an hour later because of the time required to arrange the purchase of Leblanc's plane and ready it for flight. Told just before he started that Grahame-White had just clocked in at 35 minutes and 21 seconds—slightly slower than a mile a minute—Moisant knew his only chance of winning was "to rise steadily all the way to the Statue and then, taking advantage of every bit of momentum, to coast most of the way back."

Eschewing both the Englishman's northern course and the Frenchman's southern one (which provided some safe emergency landing sites), Moisant took off on a beeline heading, barely clearing the rooftops of the most built-up and heavily populated area. Then he climbed steadily upward. Tugboat whistles sounded from the harbor as he rounded the statue at an altitude of 2,805 feet, then started home, working his engine at top speed but taking advantage of gravity by gradually descending in a series of short glides.

To spectators the plane seemed to creep until it reached Belmont then suddenly gained speed as it crossed the edge of the park. When it flashed across the finish line, Alfred, Matilde, and Louise all ran to the starter's booth. Moments later they were back, waving their arms and shouting, "He's won! He's won!"

A wave of patriotism and excitement surged through the crowd. In front of the Wright tent, Wilbur, ordinarily a man of few words and usually none at all to the press, tore off his hat and "gave a yell like a Comanche Indian," jumping at least three feet from the ground and waving his hands in the air. "That's my opinion, boys," he said.

Near the starter's box a fashionably dressed older man ran up and down, thumping total strangers on the back with his silk hat. "I don't care," he said. "It is worth a hundred silk hats to show them that Uncle Sam has a boy to hold his end up." And cheering ticketholders in the stands rose to their feet, throwing hats, coats, and even field glasses into the air in a riotous outburst of jingoism.

After Moisant climbed stiffly down from his plane, his hands and feet numb with cold, he was brought to the judges' stand in an automobile, where he was surrounded by officials trying to shake his hand. Chairman Ryan led him through the crowd to the clubhouse gate and an American flag was draped around him as he was carried to the bar on the shoulders of his admirers.

The crowd at the hangar was jubilant. In a plane similar to de Lesseps's but only half as powerful as Graham-White's, Moisant had won the meet's top prize of $10,000 by 43 seconds. His average speed of 60.6 MPH was two miles faster than was thought possible for a 50-hp Blériot. His average time for the return half of the flight was 84.5 MPH, a new world record for a 50-hp Gnôme engine.

To the throng around him at the hangar Alfred shouted, "What do you think of that! He has his machine smashed, climbs out, runs and gets another from Leblanc and the first time he drives it with its 50-hp engine he beats a man with 100!" Turning to the nearest mechanic he embraced and started dancing with him.

But as John Moisant was being hugged by his sisters and reporters were calling in their stories, Grahame-White made for the officials' stand to protest and demand a rematch. He accused the committee of changing race rules to allow Moisant's late departure. The protest was rejected.

That night Grahame-White's friend and colleague "Chip" Drexel hosted a rival dinner at Sherry's at the same time as the official banquet in the Plaza. Besides Grahame-White, meet entrants who accepted Drexel's invitation included de Lesseps, Latham, Harmon, McArdle, and U.S. team member Hamilton. In a letter distributed to his seventeen guests and the press, Drexel protested the "startling unfairness" of race authorities who, he said "juggled the Liberty prize into Moisant's hands." He then resigned from the Aero Club of America.

The American public did not agree. One reporter called Moisant's victory "a demonstration that has never been equaled anywhere in aviation." As a possible winner, he wrote, "Nobody had even thought of the game little aviator from Chicago, who since his trip from Paris to London, has held the attention of an entire world and is today the most spectacular figure that aviation in its newest, wildest and most dangerous phases has been able to produce." The *New York World* declared Moisant's victory "the greatest race of modern times."

The next morning feature writer Viola Justin of the *New York Mail* called on Matilde and Louise at their suite at the Astor. There was, she reported, "much scurrying about in kimonos. Even the cat was excited, chasing her tail while the two sisters dodged her to answer the door and the telephone."

"We knew he was going to win," Matilde said, "but for his compass he could never have done it against a 100-horsepower machine." Pointing out that her brother had flown directly over the city where there were no landing places, she exclaimed, "He doesn't fly to land! He flies to win!"

The always-proper Louise was concerned over their appearance in kimonos and asked Justin not to look at hers, but the reporter wrote that it was a lovely blue, adding a touch of color to pink cheeks and black hair.

When John entered this domestic scene, "a boyish looking man with a coat over his arm," Louise introduced him as "her wonderful brother." Asked how he liked the flight, he said, "It was bully, but just think of my goal—a lady, the Goddess of Liberty and the honor of America." With that he excused himself to return for the last day of the meet.

To another woman reporter John explained that he knew Spanish "as well as I know English" because he had been in Central America and he knew French because he studied it as a boy in Chicago. (He failed to mention it was the first language of both his parents.) He said he and his three brothers had a ranch in Mexico and they all became cowboys before going to Central America and settling near San Salvador on a big coffee and sugar plantation. (There was no ranch in Mexico and coffee was not raised at Santa Emilia.) He added that he and Alfred came to New York because they were bored with El Salvador.

On his desk in the suite was a photograph of the two children of his sister Ann (Mrs. Bertin Weyl) of San Francisco. "My niece and nephew," he said proudly. "I always carry them in my hand luggage. The trunks are so likely to get lost." (There was no picture of his son nor did he mention that he had been married.)

Asked about his role in Salvadoran revolutions, John told the reporter she would have to ask elsewhere. But she was not to be deterred. In words reflecting the nationalist fever of the hour, she wrote of the Moisants in El Salvador, "They had a real American gunboat and they made those jealous Spaniards, who just couldn't bear to see Yankee success in their little old republic, make all kinds of restitution."

In his suite, Moisant greeted Kate Carew of the *New York American* with the cat curled up on his lap. Paree-Londres had already been in the news during the meet at Belmont when the little cat attacked the French bulldog of socialite Mrs. Harry Harkness as they passed the Moisant hangar. Fileux apologized to Mrs. Harkness and John explained to reporters that his mascot was not a fireside cat but loved to fly and would go for days without purring until he took her for a plane ride. He even had to restrain her once, he said, when she tried to jump from the plane to catch a passing swallow.

Paree-Londres made headlines again when she disappeared from the Astor hotel suite. A frantic Moisant telephoned the desk saying, "My cat's gone! Find it quick! Offer a reward! Hurry up!" While the hotel staff searched, rumors circulated that Grahame-White had kidnapped his rival's mascot, but the cat was eventually found in a laundry room and returned to her owner who, "faint with relief, embraced his beloved pet and handed the laundry girl $25.00."

"My mascot," John told Carew. "I carried her from Paris to London." (By now he seemed to believe this himself although the cat had been given to him in England.) Carew wrote that Moisant had eyes "like agate set in balls of ivory" and described him as having a small, compact body, a round shapely head, a straight nose like a bird's beak, a square chin, and a full-lipped mouth. He could, she decided, be called either cute or handsome.

After introducing the cat, Moisant spoke about the impact of the new field of aviation. "It will result in worldwide communication," he said, "because aircraft will know no barrier, frontier, port or custom house. Consequently there will be no barriers to the brotherhood of man."

Newspaper editors loved the colorful copy Moisant fed them. With the press's help he created the image of a daring aviator and regular fellow, a modest man who loved his family, his cat, and airplanes. Now he felt certain he was in a position to convert the reading public to true believers—and investors—in humanity's greatest invention, the airplane.

8

THE MOISANT BIRD MEN

I n just three months of flying, John Moisant had re-
directed his brother Alfred toward a new goal—the
advancement of American aviation. If John was daring in the air
Alfred was the ultimate risk-taker on the ground. Like the
Wright brothers, these two men with very different personalities
were united in their determination to become leaders in the new
technology. John could demonstrate and, perhaps in time, design planes. But it was up to Alfred to raise the money to build
them. He was willing to risk his own money, of course. But
wealthy and successful though he was, he knew that at this
stage of the fledgling industry "none but the biggest and richest
of organizations can afford to undertake aviation from a business standpoint."

Blériot's crossing of the English Channel had begun the slow
but inexorable transformation of flying from a sport into a business. It had prompted a half million people to attend the first
great aviation meet at Rheims, France, only a month later. In
turn, meet followed meet and competition categories expanded
exponentially. As interest grew, so did the demand for planes.

In the United States, the Wright brothers and Glenn Curtiss
competed for their share of the market. But ironically—despite the

fact that the Wrights had been the first to make a flyable airplane and Curtiss had won the first Gordon Bennett cup—the center of aircraft production was not the United States, but Europe.

Flying circuses—holiday extravaganzas for the thrill-seeking, ticket-buying masses—soon became popular on both continents. But there was a difference in perception. Europeans generally worshipped their aviators—or "birdmen" as they were commonly called. Many Americans, however, regarded flyers as freaks—circus performers at best but sometimes scoundrels bent on deception. The wife of one pilot of the time wrote that the public thought her husband was trying to make them believe the impossible. "When an aviator actually got up," she said, "they thought there was something 'spooky' about it. If he could not rise because of motor trouble they would label him a 'fake.'"

Still, when hundreds of thousands of spectators lined the banks of the Hudson River to see him fly in 1909, Wilbur Wright decided that this was the way to sell airplanes. Adapting the device to his purposes he sent out exhibition teams—miniature air circuses—a year later to demonstrate and popularize his aircraft. Curtiss soon did the same. Alfred Moisant would be next to join in. Never one to think small, he set out to create the biggest and best show of all, with more planes and more pilots traveling to more cities throughout the world. He knew the risks involved. Traveling air shows and circuses were held at fairgrounds, baseball parks, and racetracks in areas too small for safe takeoffs and landings. Pilots were expected to fly their frail planes in rain, bitter cold, and dangerous winds. When motors gave out and accidents occurred, pilots returned to the air after hasty and often inadequate repairs because they knew that irate ticketholders might become violent if they didn't.

At Worcester, Massachusetts, the crowd threatened to burn one pilot's machine because he refused to fly in dangerous weather. Forced to take off, he ran into and injured a number of bystanders. In Durango, Colorado, police were barely able to hold back a crowd intent on assaulting an air circus company, and in Halifax, Nova Scotia, spectators tore bricks from a wall and pelted Grahame-White's plane with them after he refused to fly in strong winds. An editorial in the aviation magazine *Aero* suggested that the only effective means of holding back unruly crowds was the use of mounted police, although it noted that in some instances Irish-American police with revolvers and French troops with fixed bayonets had prevailed.

Ever the gambler, Don Alfredo, creator of Santa Emilia and the Banco Nacional, was planning to dazzle the American public into backing his goal to build planes, train pilots, and use them to transport passengers and freight all over the world. The airplane, he said, was already "of tremendous [military] value and importance," would soon surpass both the train and automobile in "safe and speedy" freight delivery, and had an "invaluable" future. Within two years, he predicted it "is bound to come into its own" as a carrier of special delivery letters, diplomatic correspondence, and light, perishable cargo.

On November 2, just three days after his brother John won the Statue of Liberty race, Alfred filed corporate papers for the Moisant International Aviators, Inc., with a paid-up capital of $250,000 of his own money. As president and chief stockholder he pledged another $500,000 for equipment and contracts, rented an office in the New York Times building on Times Square in Manhattan, and hired a general manager, Peter L. "Pete" Young. John Moisant would be chief pilot and in charge of recruiting aviators. Alfred would draw up and settle their contracts.

The new company had to be "international" because almost all of the well-known American pilots were already working for the Wright brothers or Curtiss. The first three flyers recruited by John were three who had competed at Belmont—Roland Garros, René Barrier, and René Simon.

Garros, 25, the friend and instructor who had accompanied John on his flight across Paris to the Circuit de l'Est at Issy, was already famous in Europe for flying the tiny, dangerous Demoiselle. Constructed of bamboo and silk it was the smallest plane in the world. Only a month before Garros had flown it to an altitude-record 1,500 feet. Dubbed the "Cloud Kisser" by Alfred, Garros was a cheerful fellow, a smile frequently lighting up his round face with its heavy brows and thick moustache. In addition to handling the Demoiselle he could also fly Blériots.

René Barrier was 26 years old and had earned a doctoral degree in law. Fascinated by machinery he sold McCormick harvesters and then automobiles before becoming an aviator. In June he had been decorated by King Alphonse of Spain for his brilliant flying during a meet in Madrid. Standing six feet and weighing 230 pounds, he was unusually tall for a pilot at a time when promoters and designers wanted small, slim lightweights to fly their fragile craft. Barrier's oval face was olive-skinned, his eyes deep brown, and a neat moustache grew below his long nose.

At 25 Barrier's friend René Simon was also a graduate of the University of Paris with a degree in law. The well-mannered son of wealthy parents, Simon was a handsome man with a clean-shaven face, heavy-lidded and sultry eyes, and a sensuous mouth frequently curved in a slight smile. He flew Blériots with a reckless abandon that earned him the title of the "Fool Flyer," but also with a skill that won him a Michelin Cup as well as several European speed and distance records.

Completing the European contingent was a Swiss, Edmond Audemars, who had inspired Garros to become a pilot by his handling of the Demoiselle. Weighing less than 100 pounds (and sporting a toothbrush moustache and bow tie), "Tiny" Audemars was admirably suited to the miniature aircraft. A former professional bicycling and motorcycling champion, he held his country's speed and altitude records. Flying Demoiselles, both he and Garros had won a special prize at Belmont for a stunning exhibition flight.

John rounded out the birdmen's roster with three Americans, the best known of whom was Charles K. Hamilton, John's team colleague at Belmont who had recently made a prize-winning New York–Philadelphia round-trip flight and was acclaimed for his daring dives in a Herring-Curtiss biplane. A former stunt parachuter and hot-air balloonist, he was scarred from head to foot, having at one time or another broken both legs and his collarbone twice, dislocated an arm, and been scalded by radiator water. Small and wiry, with red hair and protruding ears, he was also hard-drinking and prone to argument. But he was coming to the Moisant troupe with his *Hamiltonian,* the big biplane he had built from a Curtiss design with an eight-cylinder engine capable of developing 110 hp.

The second American was John J. Frisbie, an ex-balloonist and parachutist who had been ascending in man-carrying kites for almost three decades. At 46 he was the oldest in the company and had not been a licensed pilot until just before the Belmont meet. Stretching the international aspect of the company Alfred billed him as "the only really Irish aviator" although Frisbie had been born in Oswego, New York, and lived in Rochester.

The last man on the roster was Joseph Seymour, touted by Alfred as the only champion auto racer who could also fly an airplane. Seymour could fly. But in fact Alfred was hiring him to race his high-powered Fiat against the planes, a popular, crowd-pleasing act.

The salaries of the seven pilots ranged from $500 to $2,000 a month, plus expenses and a share of the profits if there were any. On top of their salaries, Alfred promised his brother and Hamilton an additional annual bonus of $10,000 and smaller bonuses to the other flyers. Moreover, the contracts Alfred drew up permitted the flyers to keep any prize money they won at company exhibitions. This was an incentive not offered by either the Wrights or Curtiss, who paid lower salaries and claimed a share of every prize from their aviators.

Alfred chartered seven yellow and green railroad cars, including two Pullmans and a diner, to carry the seven aviators, eight planes, Seymour's Fiat, some two dozen mechanics, and another thirty men who would either sell tickets or work as roustabouts, moving equipment and setting up the huge circus tent to be used as an aircraft hangar.

The company assembled and equipped, Alfred sent John to Cuba to arrange for an air show in early 1911, while he took charge of the first show in Richmond, Virginia. Press releases and feature stories flowed daily from his office in the Times Building, reminding reporters he had already spent $180,000 of his own money and signed contracts totaling half a million dollars. His daily expenses were running around $4,000, an impressive sum in 1910.

On November 20, the day before the company was to leave for its first show in Richmond, Alfred hired a truck to haul the little Demoiselle down Broadway to the Hotel Astor where curious onlookers blocked all traffic for an hour. The next day, when the yellow and green cars pulled out of Grand Central Station, one newspaper mourned the occasion by reporting, "The flyers' corner at the Hotel Astor will be deserted this morning when Alfred J. Moisant leaves for Richmond with his circus of man birds."

Louise and Matilde, holding John's cat, were seen waving from the Pullman window as the train pulled out. Alfred stood behind them, his wide smile betraying no anxiety although he had only three firm bookings so far—Richmond, Chattanooga, and New Orleans. A few minutes later he left his sisters chatting with the company's secretary-treasurer, A. E. Wupperman, and Mrs. Wupperman. He may well have been looking for the telegraph operator in his continuous search for more engagements. The train had become his office, the operator his secretary. Alfred Moisant was in the aviation business to stay.

9
BEGINNERS' LUCK

Roland Garros made the first flight of the first show ever given by the newly created Moisant International Aviators, Inc. Soaring over Richmond on a cold, clear day, he crowned his performance by halting a speech being made by the president of the United States. William Howard Taft, no friend of aviation, was speaking from the steps of the governor's mansion when the Frenchman zoomed down, the roar of his Gnôme engine silencing the president and capturing his audience.

Hotels were filled that day with delegates to a convention of educators, cause for Alfred to anticipate a successful opening. During one of the seven later events at the fairgrounds, Hamilton, Simon, Barrier, and Garros were all in the air at the same time, bringing a clapping, whistling, cheering audience to their feet. Alfred soon realized, however, that although many were watching, few had paid. The fairgrounds were so open that anyone could watch from outside without a ticket. There were other problems as well. Frisbie's biplane needed repairs and Joe Seymour's Fiat had been damaged in transit.

The next day was Thanksgiving, when competition from the annual football game between the Universities of Virginia and

North Carolina—always a sellout—forced Alfred to reschedule flights from the afternoon to the morning. Never one to admit setbacks, he explained that he did so because Virginia's team captain feared fans would abandon the game in favor of his show. Alfred also distributed complimentary tickets to children attending public schools and living in orphanages, as well as to the residents of the Soldiers' Home. But again paid attendance was low.

On Friday gale winds grounded much of the show. Frisbie was still having mechanical troubles. An accidental gasoline fire burned away the fabric of Hamilton's plane. And Barrier flew over Richmond, which meant little to the fairground audience who couldn't see much more than his takeoff and landing.

As the several thousand spectators waited restlessly for flights that were either delayed or canceled, Alfred sent Joe Seymour racing his Fiat around the track at a mile a minute to keep them entertained. When Seymour raced around the track a second time, Matilde was seated beside him. A disapproving Louise shuddered each time the Fiat zoomed by in a cloud of dust. "I don't like it," she muttered. "She shouldn't have gone." But Matilde loved it, grinning at the cheering crowd when she left the track and telling a reporter that her brother John, who would arrive from Cuba early next morning, had promised to take her up in his new plane as soon as it was finished. In fact, she confided, she intended to learn how to fly it herself.

Matilde's ride with Seymour was hardly enough to mollify the fidgety spectators, nor could the police prevent many of them from running across the course while the Fiat continued to speed around. Once again there were more people outside the fairgrounds than in, many watching from parked cars. And again Alfred tried to salvage the day, this time by inviting ticketholders to see the planes inside their tent hangar and by giving out wind checks for the next day and promising that the aviators would fly no matter what the weather.

On the fourth and final day the weather did improve and the show was further revitalized by John's arrival from Cuba. After persuading his brother to lift a ban on flights over the city John made one past the city limits, across the James River and back again, diving low to cut a figure eight for the 1,200 prisoners watching from the yard of the state penitentiary. Over Capital Square he flew so low that spectators crowding the rooftops could read the numbers on his plane. Soon after that Garros, Barrier, and Simon all flew together, racing to City Hall and back while the rooftop spectators waved and cheered.

That night the planes were packed up for departure to Chattanooga for a three-day engagement starting on Monday, November 28. In spite of the miserable weather, the canceled flights, and the meager ticket sales, both Moisants thought Richmond had been a credible start for their new air circus. Although attendance was poor, they said, they had never expected to make money at first.

If Richmond had been a limited success, their next stop was a disaster. Chattanooga's Olympia Park was too small, the stands dilapidated, and chill winds from the nearby mountains buffeted the crowds and endangered the flyers.

Ten thousand people came the first day but, faced with a choice of standing on wet ground or huddling in the broken-down stands, one-third of them left before the long-delayed first flight was made. Later delays were so long and numerous that during them, one reporter wrote,

a gang of husky negroes hiked over the big lot, and as if hired by a junk dealer, gathered unto themselves some old tin cans, other trash and carefully stored it in holes and low spots, like dogs hiding bones. The crowd waited, wandered, gossiped and stamped its feet to keep the blood in motion.

Finally, a "clarion voice" over the loudspeaker announced that even though the aviators were rushing to instant death, the crowd should not be disappointed, and Col. John J. Frisbie of Ireland would make the sacrifice. Col. Frisbie, after several false starts, got his Curtiss biplane started toward the north end of the park. It was a hop and a hobble, rather like a boyish game of hop-scotch. At one end it was probably 25 feet off the ground. Then it ducked toward the ground, rose again and down it came, a few feet from the north fence.

During another long wait the crowd surged across the field to the hangar tent where Alfred announced he would send up two more men "even if it busted the show." Garros went first in the Demoiselle but had to circle the small field repeatedly to avoid landing on one or more of the remaining spectators still milling around. Simon followed in a Blériot and, like Garros, flew around and around searching for a clearing on the tiny field.

"They came, they saw, they conquered, maybe," the *Chattanooga Times* editorialized. "They took $600 of Chattanooga's money, having spent some $12,000 of their own, or so the management says."

An additional sour note was sounded by a summons served on Hamilton by John P. Daly, a local promoter who accused Hamilton of having defaulted on a contract to fly there the previous spring.

Alfred decided he had had enough of Chattanooga. Despite the fact he had booked the stadium for three days, he told the flyers to pack immediately for their next stop at Memphis—one he had arranged from the train. While the flyers closed up shop in Chattanooga, he, Matilde, Louise, and Paree-Londres took the night train to Memphis to prepare the ground.

Increasingly aware of mounting irritation over delayed and canceled performances, Alfred assured the press that Memphis was about to see real flying, not a repetition of an earlier "fiasco" by another air group that had been jeered for its cheap stunts and barely-off-the-ground flying. "Our men are not grass-cutters," he said, promising they would treat Memphis to honest, complete flights which he described as three circuits of the field at an altitude of at least 400 feet.

Alfred had good reason to expect a repeat of the Chattanooga disaster. December 1, opening day of the Memphis show, was miserable for flying. It was stormy and the temperature was below freezing. To make matters worse, the Tri-State Fair Grounds were six miles outside the city, a one-hour haul by streetcar. But despite the cold, raw weather a surprisingly enthusiastic crowd turned up and "forgot the chilly blasts that swept through the grand stand" as they concentrated on the spectacle above them.

Displaying his customary disregard for even minimal prudence, John opened the show with an 18-minute flight, during which he climbed to 1,500 feet in a 35-MPH wind, standing his Blériot nearly on end. Simon followed with "a daring exhibition . . . [of] air tricks . . . that until recently had been considered impossible except in biplanes." Garros then set an American record (8 minutes, 44⅕ seconds) for sustained flight in his Demoiselle, and John closed out the day with a second flight of almost 19 minutes, skimming the house tops of the eastern part of the city. The Moisant International Fliers sent home an audience happily surfeited after a day of risky maneuvers that Curtiss aviator Beckwith Havens called "the kind of crowd pleasing that killed pilots."

Describing a typical air show of the time, Havens recalled, "The program said you were going to fly at two-thirty. Well, maybe the wind was blowing pretty hard. You were always watching the wind, you know—watching smoke, watching flags, laundry on the line. I think the crowd's yelling at them and everything, some pilots would take off when they shouldn't." Many did, and many were killed.

On the second day Moisant, Simon, and Barrier all took to the air simultaneously, Hamilton set a speed record of 79.2 MPH, and Garros reached an altitude of more than a mile. The third day, a Saturday, the flyers drew their largest crowd ever for a show highlighted by Garros climbing to 5,500 feet and Hamilton bettering his previous day's record at 81.6 MPH.

The Moisant flyers were indeed giving "crowd-pleasing performances" but at a fearful cost. Two planes were damaged. Frisbie rose to 25 feet, then crashed when his motor stopped. Garros demolished a Blériot after the warping wire on his left wing broke at an altitude of 100 feet. Just before hitting the ground he lifted his feet from the rudder to avoid breaking his legs and emerged from the wreckage moments later with legs intact but with a broken nose and a badly cut eye.

For the next three days of rain, sleet, and then snow, Garros recuperated in a hotel bed while his colleagues stood around the lobby waiting for a break in the weather. It came on Wednesday, initiating a series of stunning flights during the next 11 days in which the Moisant International Fliers proved they were not only great but possibly the greatest of all circus flyers. Barrier set a speed record of 87.93 MPH over a 16-mile closed-circuit course, winning the $5,000 prize offered by the *Memphis Commercial Appeal*. The stands were packed day after day and local businessmen launched a campaign to raise $10,000 to prolong the aviators' stay.

Garros and Barrier flew brilliantly, but Moisant was the star of the show. In attempting to break an altitude record he reached 9,264 feet before the cold and approaching darkness forced his descent in an aircraft whose metal parts were covered with ice. He was gone so long Alfred and his sisters grew worried, Frisbie built a bonfire to light up the field in the growing dusk, and Simon flew for two miles around the area looking for him. Matilde was the first to spot him coming out of the darkening sky. Grasping Louise's arm, she shouted, "I believe—yes, there he is!" When he landed the half-frozen flyer was almost mobbed by cheering fans.

One of Moisant's stunts was to *vol plane,* cutting off his motor at 3,000 feet and heading down, at a 45-degree angle or in corkscrew turns, until just a few feet above the field, then coasting in for a perfect landing. On one occasion he kept coasting across the field toward the hangar tent and scattered the startled mechanics before suddenly restarting his engine and taking off again, barely clearing the canvas top.

One Moisant maneuver that caused alarm among knowledgeable observers was a reckless turn one newsman described as "banking the machine even closer to the perpendicular than the ill-fated Johnstone" who had been killed in a crash just a week before. "It was excessive banking in thin air that caused Johnstone's death, yet Moisant repeatedly stands his Blériot nearly on end and turns it so quickly that it seems to an observer on the ground as if the inside wing is nailed to a board."

Not only did Moisant achieve a near-perpendicular position. He then turned to the right (in opposition to the propeller and the Gnôme motor, which were rotating together to the left), thus creating a stress that could have torn his plane apart in midair.

Moisant's feats in the air were no less colorful than his forays with the press on the ground. He once bragged to newsmen how simple it would have been for him to sink the U.S. Navy ship *Amphitrite* as it lay anchored in the Mississippi River. "How easy it would have been," he told them,

to drop a detonating explosive on that big expanse of deck! And all the while I should have been perfectly safe far out of reach of either turret or fighting top guns. And if I had wanted to drop an explosive on the city of Memphis itself, what forces could have stopped me?

Never did a flight of mine prove so clearly to my own satisfaction the remarkable part that aeroplanes are certain to play in the very next war. I could have taken a passenger aboard just as readily as not and he could easily have photographed and mapped the country below him. The inside defenses and gun emplacements of a fort would have been permanently recorded by the camera. All kinds of huge sums could be extorted as tribute from big cities by an enemy who sent one or two bomb-dropping aeroplanes over the community with a warning that the number of these flying machines would be multiplied by hundreds of thousands unless the sums demanded were immediately forthcoming.

Despite John's vision anticipating by two or three decades how air power would be used in bombing, reconnaissance, and even terrorism, he was a firm advocate of peace. Calling war "licensed wholesale murder," John said it would continue until people learned to settle difficulties by other means or "until warfare is made so horrible, so deadly, that no nation will dare enter upon it."

The daily shows continued in Memphis even in wind, rain, and sleet. There were accidents and near accidents. In a second crash Frisbie dropped 200 feet after his engine stalled, smashing his steering gear and both ends of his plane. While taxiing at high speed, Barrier almost hit the post of an old water trough protruding six feet above the center of the landing field, clearing it by inches. Held over by popular demand, the Moisant show remained in Memphis for 16 days, the longest continuing flight exhibition ever held in the United States.

From Memphis the flyers went to another of Alfred's last-minute road bookings—a two-day engagement in Tupelo, Mississippi, before a scheduled appearance in New Orleans. In the town of 4,000 news of the show had filled every hotel and lodging house with visitors, most of whom had never seen an airplane. On the afternoon of December 19, 8,000 shivering spectators watched John Moisant take off into a storm-darkened sky and gale winds reaching 70 MPH. Climbing to 3,500 feet he *vol planed* down in a glide that sent the crowd into paroxysms of applause, followed by demands that he be brought before the grandstand where women were standing, shouting and applauding, and men were tossing their hats into the air. That night an ebullient Moisant promised Tupelo promoter W. H. Armstrong he would fly again the next day regardless of the weather.

During the night the temperature dropped and snow was falling by morning. Gale-force winds kept the audience low, but John kept his word and made several flights. On his last landing a blast of wind struck his Blériot just as it touched down and tilted it dangerously. Joe Seymour rushed out on the field, grabbed the tail of the plane, and held it until spectators racing from the stands could help him pull it to safety. They lifted Moisant from the aircraft and carried him on their shoulders to the grandstand where he was given a glass of warm milk and $1,000 collected from an admiring crowd.

By the time the Tupelo show was over, Moisant International Fliers, Inc., had established its reputation as a bona-fide air circus featuring head pilot and star performer John Moisant supported by three other skilled and daring aviators, Garros, Simon, and Barrier. Joe Seymour and his Fiat added to the excitement. Frisbie and Hamilton drew less notice because their touted biplanes, the *Rochester* and the *Black Demon* (formerly the *Hamiltonian*) were under repair during most of the tour. But all had learned that the only way to please the crowds was to fly, no matter how bad the weather, how great the risks. They took off for New Orleans with applause ringing in their ears and determined to win the considerable amount of prize money that had been offered for their eight-day stay.

10
WHEN IT'S WINTERTIME
DOWN SOUTH

O n the night of December 21 all eyes were on John Moisant as he strode across the lobby of the St. Charles Hotel to meet his unofficial welcoming committee. Aside from his well-cut suit and expensive jewelry he arrived in New Orleans clad in a legend of fact and fancy based on sometimes inaccurate newspaper reports and spiced up with material from brother Alfred's often imaginative press releases. One could almost hear the contradictory stories whispered around the room about the soldier of fortune . . . Central American millionaire . . . daring pilot . . . loyal friend . . . ruthless enemy . . . as John, followed by Alfred, headed toward the group of reporters, old friends, and leading citizens awaiting his arrival. Some in the group would indeed have given credence to the whispers. One was Crawford H. Ellis, manager of the United Fruit Company's New Orleans office and chairman of the committee of twenty-five businessmen sponsoring the Moisant air shows. Another was Nicaraguan Consul General Francisco Altschul, who had fought beside John when they were both armed supporters of President Juan Santos Zelaya.

John told the gathering he would fly over the city the next day and that within the week he would be taking possession of a new aviation wonder—a three-seater aircraft. Neither event came to pass. The circus planes and equipment were on railroad cars blocked by a train wreck somewhere between Tupelo and New Orleans. They did arrive and were assembled a day later but by then rain and bitter cold made flying impossible.

Yet the expected wonder plane never did materialize. Actually Alfred had referred to it earlier in a telegram to Ellis, promising it would be available for the New Orleans show. He described it as an all-metal aluminum-steel "limousine monoplane capable of carrying three passengers [and] the pilot in a glass cabin to protect them from the wind and capable of reaching 175 miles an hour." He referred to it again in a long press release as having wings of rubber-impregnated silk and a body shaped "like birds or fishes" with none of the conventional wires or straps except for three of each to secure the wings, adding that it had been tested three times in "private flights." John did Alfred one better by telling the *Picayune* it would be able to carry four passengers and had been shipped from France with both 50- and 100-hp engines.

When it finally did make its appearance, the much-vaunted wonder plane turned out to be too small to carry anyone except the pilot, came with only a single 50-hp engine, and was simply a new version of the Aluminoplane John had built—and crashed—in France. And there was no record of it having been tested, privately or otherwise. (It was flown later by plane designer Harold D. Kantner, who said it was "wicked" to handle and wrote it off as "John Moisant's funny little plane that he built before he learned to fly.")

The wonder plane the Moisants were ballyhooing did not exist. Built partly from John's overenthusiasm and partly on Alfred's anxiety to sell planes, it was a product of the Moisant imagination. It was also evidence of the brothers' faith in the future of aviation and their determination to become aviation leaders. They were convinced, as John said in an article written especially for one of the city's newspapers, that "where today there is one aeroplane there will be 100 in a year and in three years, no fewer than 10,000. In another five years hundreds of planes will be flying over American cities."

The opening of the Moisant New Orleans air show was scheduled for the afternoon of December 24. But John hadn't forgotten his promise to fly over the city. Early that morning he sneaked out of the hotel while his brother and sisters were still asleep and took a car to the City Park racetrack. His mechanics assumed he was taking his plane up for a test spin but when he took off into the cold, windy skies he headed southeast for the center of New Orleans.

The drone of the Blériot's motor above the rooftops was soon followed by the ringing of telephones throughout the city as the news spread that an airplane was actually in the skies over New Orleans. The hotel operators awakened Alfred and the Moisant pilots, who rushed to the park.

Louise and Matilde, left behind, watched from the sidewalk outside their hotel entrance. Looking upward, they saw their brother doing seemingly every aerobatic stunt he knew, twisting and turning, dipping and spiraling, climbing, then plunging toward earth. Both women understood the risks John was taking. And after a few minutes they could no longer bear to look, returning to their rooms to wait and worry.

Meanwhile John had brought the city's phone and street traffic to a virtual halt. The Cumberland Telephone Company reported later that 20,000 calls were made during 10 of the minutes John was in the air, causing a temporary delay in service. Pedestrians, necks craned, peered skyward while streetcar conductors stopped their cars to join passengers who had alighted to watch the "birdman."

For the 25 minutes that John flew over downtown New Orleans, Canal, St. Charles, Carondelet, and Camp Streets were impassible, jammed with an estimated 100,000 spectators. Another 100,000 saw him as he flew over Lake Pontchartrain and the Mississippi River as far as the town of Gretna in a wide circle of more than 30 miles until he descended 46 minutes later with just three pints of gasoline left in his tank.

John's morning flight over the city was probably more successful than brother Albert would have wished. With more than
half of New Orleans having witnessed Moisant's stunning aerobatics in what for many was surely a first-in-a-lifetime experience there couldn't have been too many left wanting to pay for
a repeat performance. The opening show that day included long
exhibitions by six of the seven birdmen, including Barrier's as-
cent to 6,133 feet and another 57-minute flight by John, all feats
remarkable for the times. But only 2,000 tickets were sold.

The weather in the South that winter was decidedly miserable
and dangerous for flying, so much so that back when the
Moisants' men were still in Memphis, four Glenn Curtiss pi-
lots—Eugene Ely, August Post, J. A. D. McCurdy, and James
West—were grounded for eight of their ten scheduled days in
New Orleans. But the next day, Christmas, the International
Fliers again flew in strong winds and near-freezing temperatures.

Five thousand New Orleans residents bought tickets for the
holiday show and thousands more watched from outside the
park, bobbing up and down, stomping their feet and clapping
their hands to keep warm. They were treated to ten flights, each
averaging 24 minutes, by Moisant, Barrier, Simon, Hamilton,
and Garros. Each time three flyers were aloft at the same time
the bleachers rocked with deafening cheers. The cold was so in-
tense that Barrier, who had forgotten his earmuffs, was brought
down by the pain of frostbite. Hamilton's engine worked loose
when two bolts shattered and he barely managed to clear the
spectators' stand before landing. Garros made it to 7,200 feet in
an altitude contest before his carburetor froze and shut down
his engine. Without power he hurtled down to what seemed certain death when his engine caught again only a few feet above
ground. When the Frenchman alighted his goggles were frosted
over, his plane covered with snow, and icicles hung from his
gasoline and oil tanks. The only warmth of the day came from
a fire that broke out in the hangar tent, prompting one reporter
to declare that the Moisant flyers had again set a world record
—for the first aviation fire to be extinguished by a fire engine.

That night a jubilant John hosted a Christmas dinner at the

St. Charles. His guest list included all of his fellow pilots; Crawford Ellis and William Allen, another old friend, and their wives; Alfred, Louise, and Matilde; Mrs. Joe Seymour, general manager Peter Young, and Albert LeVino, the new public relations man Alfred had brought with him from New York.

After dinner Garros, Simon, and Barrier returned to the De Soto Hotel where Alfred had rented a suite for them. The three Parisians were delighted to be in a city were many of the 340,000 residents spoke French and where Garros, who spoke some English, no longer had to serve as their translator. In the evenings they were free to go to restaurants like Fabacher's at Royal and Iberville Streets where a 75-cent *table d'hôte* was served from 6 to 8 P.M., a trifle early for them but at least white and claret wines were offered with dinner. On the nights they took in a show at one of the city's nine theaters, it was often followed by a visit to the St. Charles' Italian Garden which featured a Neapolitan quartet. All three pilots were avid music lovers, so much so that the De Soto manager provided a piano for their suite "so that we may enjoy life," Garros said. Simon was the pianist and all three sang. They were also befriended by the performers at the French Opera House which they attended often, mingling comfortably in the audience with men in evening dress and silk top hats and women garbed in the latest fashions, frocks trimmed in gold, silver, jet, and crystal, and narrow skirts tapering from hip to ankle.

When air-show attendance fell off the day after Christmas, John tried to stimulate it by attempting an altitude record despite the high winds and freezing temperature. He made it to 9,000 feet before his carburetor froze, just as Garros's had on Sunday. Attempting to return to the park by using a spiral glide, he was driven westward by the wind over swampland where he was seen heading straight for a huge oak tree. Like Garros he was saved at the last minute when his motor kicked in and he pulled up to clear the tree by six feet, then landed safely inside the park.

Still, despite his heroics, more onlookers were cheering Moisant from outside the park than were paying for seats inside. So two days later Moisant repeated his effort to draw crowds with another hazardous performance, only to be caught at 4,000 feet by the sudden approach of a gulf hurricane. Flying into a gale that tore at his plane's cloth-covered wings, his Blériot was brought to a dead halt, at one time for three full minutes, then blown backward for another three. He battled the gale for 26 minutes before he was able to take advantage of a lull in the battering gusts and land, exhausted.

While the fifteen-piece band played "Dixie" and the crowd howled its approval, Simon, Garros, and Barrier all rushed to the plane and lifted Moisant out bodily. In something of an overstatement, Chairman Ellis congratulated Moisant on "the most wonderful flight ever made in the history of aviation." However, Moisant's colleagues and officials all agreed that no one before had ever dared challenge such a gale in a 50-hp Blériot. And Moisant was the only International Airman to fly that day.

By December 30 John's spectacular flying had finally pulled thousands of ticket-buyers back into the stands. Garros, Barrier, and Simon all flew that day, but it was Moisant, waving from the cockpit in his red sweater and knitted cap, whom they had come to see. He clearly loved it. Basking in the attention, he walked from his plane to the grandstand after each flight and bowed before the cheering crowd. That day he could do no wrong. Even when he lost his race with Seymour's Fiat, the crowd was "delirious."

Much as he enjoyed the crowd's adulation, Moisant had not risked his neck all week simply to hear applause. He had put the Blériot to every conceivable endurance test he could devise in preparation for an attempt to win the Michelin Cup with its prize of $4,000 for the longest nonstop distance flight of 1910. By waiting until the last possible moment he knew exactly what mark he would have to beat. It was 362.7 miles flown by Frenchman Maurice Tabuteau in 7 hours, 48 minutes, 31 seconds just the day before.

That night, after all four Moisants had dined with the Ellises, John told his host, "I want to win that cup tomorrow because I want America to have it. If I am fortunate I intend to leave it in

New Orleans with the Aero Club here where everyone has been so cordial to me."

On his way back to the St. Charles, John stopped off at the De Soto where the three French flyers were giving a party, one of many they had held in their suite since acquiring the piano. When he arrived, four members of the French Opera Company were leading the singing, interspersed with frequent toasts. Moisant sat but drank no wine, soon returning to his hotel for a proper night's sleep.

He wanted to be ready for tomorrow.

11
MORE THAN ANY MAN

For a man considered impetuous and foolhardy by many of his colleagues, John Moisant awoke to the last day of 1910 having taken infinite care and being exceptionally well prepared for his try at the Michelin Cup. Waiting out all other aspirants had not only been good theater but also assured him of being the only challenger to know beforehand precisely what he would have to accomplish to win. Only two days earlier he had staked out the course to be flown with the help of Alfred, General Altschul, and G. F. Campbell Wood, the Aero Club of America official who had come from New York to verify the time and distance. White flags already marked the elliptical four-mile flight path at the Illinois Central's Harahan Station, 12 miles west of downtown New Orleans. And railroad officials had already prepared a makeshift field for him within the swampland between the Mississippi River and Lake Pontchartrain.

That Saturday morning those going to Harahan assembled at the offices of the United Fruit Company where they were herded by Crawford Ellis into two cars and driven to the St. Charles Hotel. John was waiting for them in the lobby reading a newspaper while Alfred paced up and down, repeatedly looking at his watch. The two brothers, accompanied by two mechanics and several newspapermen, rode in one of the cars and Pete Young and other friends in the second for the ride to City Park.

At the park John dressed in the costume he himself had devised: flannel underwear, two sweaters, and two suits of coveralls, each item insulated by a layer of newspaper. His feet were covered by three pairs of socks and canvas shoes, each again insulated with paper. Finally, each leg was wrapped in woolen cloth and more paper, all bound by strips of wool. Friends had to help him walk to the plane. When one of them remarked that the outfit looked like a suit of armor, John laughed and replied, "I do believe if someone shot at me, it wouldn't touch me."

Someone gave him a cup of hot bouillon before he climbed into the plane. He would be flying in freezing temperatures with a 14-MPH wind augmented by gusts sweeping westward along Lake Pontchartrain and down the Mississippi and he would have to sit in one position for almost eight hours, his hands and feet never leaving the controls.

The 50-hp Blériot, the same plane that had carried him to second place in the Gordon Bennett race, was now equipped with an extra gas tank, a 35-gallon reserve almost directly below and slightly forward of the engine. But Moisant did not take on a full load of gasoline at the park, preferring to do so after reaching the course at Harahan. Alfred was to deliver the tins of extra fuel in his car decorated with white streamers and carrying the necessary tools.

As the plane neared the field that had been prepared, Campbell Wood waved a white flag to guide Moisant toward a second official, Edward J. McCormark, who was stationed on a riverbank levee. Passing by the levee Moisant circled the field twice at 300 feet, descended to 200 feet, then made a right-hand turn to land with the wind behind him, a procedure Moisant himself had repeatedly called "one of the most dangerous experiments" an aviator could try. While still in the turn, a gust of wind lifted the Blériot's tail, forcing its nose down into a sudden dive. Watching on the ground, T. E. Hill, Louisiana superintendent of the Illinois Central who had directed the field's preparation, said, "When the thing was a few yards above the earth the full horror dawned on me. The machine struck the earth, rebounded and plunged forward five or ten feet." Hill said Moisant's body seemed to ascend "as though shot from a cannon into the air, describing a circle before falling on a mud heap about 30 feet from the wreck." Others said that as soon as the plane reached a vertical position Moisant was propelled into the air "as if he had been shot from a gun."

Running across the muddy swampland, General Altschul was the first to reach Moisant, closely followed by two other friends, William Allen and M. B. Trezevant. The aviator lay on his back. Someone muttered, "He's dead!" Altschul replied, "Dead! Bah! That dear boy Moisant has more lives than a flock of kittens! Lift up his head and I'll bet you he'll smile." But his smile was a grimace, his eyes glassy, and his pulse racing rapidly. No bruises or cuts were visible except for a small mark on his nose made by his goggles.

Allen and Trezevant carried him to a nearby flat car where two railroad men laid him down, putting a pillow under his head and covering him with overcoats. Hill ordered a locomotive attached to the flat car, then called down the line to clear the tracks. Boarding with Moisant were Trezevant, Altschul, Allen, and five railroad workers.

Back in the middle of the makeshift field Garros and a mechanic were waiting for Moisant to arrive. "He must have come down somewhere," Garros said. "He was due here at least two or three minutes ago." Looking over to the grandstand, he saw a man waving a white flag and yelling, "You're wanted on the telephone." When Garros picked up the receiver he heard the caller say, "He's down but we haven't got to the machine yet." Ten minutes later the phone rang again. This time the caller said, "Well, he's killed." The Frenchman raced to his plane and took off for the marked race site, only to return and report, "No use flying up there—you can't land!"

Alfred was the last to learn of the crash. On his way from City Park to the field in the car loaded with gasoline tins, the driver was delayed by a detour and then lost his way. When they finally reached the river road Alfred shouted to people as he passed, "Where's John?" and was told that the plane had passed overhead 15 minutes before. Seeing a handcar on the tracks, he commandeered it, loaded the fuel tins, and jumped aboard. About 300 feet along the track leading to the field he met a switch engine with a half-dozen men going in the opposite direction. One of them pointed to the gasoline tins and shouted, "They don't need that!"

"Why?" Alfred asked.

The man replied, "The machine is wrecked and the aviator killed."

When Alfred motioned that he couldn't hear, the man repeated the news. This time Alfred reeled back into the arms of one of the railway men. Embarrassed when told that Alfred was the pilot's brother, the speaker changed his message, claiming the pilot was alive. A second man added that John was already on a train headed back to the city. Returning to the car, Alfred murmured to the driver, "I must tell them."

He was thinking of Louise and Matilde.

By the time Alfred's car reached the railroad station John was no longer there. The engine carrying John and his friends had taken just 13 minutes to travel 12 miles to the station where an ambulance was waiting and police had been assigned to keep back the crowds. An intern in the ambulance performed artificial respiration but on arrival at the hospital John was declared dead. A hearse took his body to the McMahon Funeral Home.

At the funeral home a coroner had already pronounced the cause of death a broken spinal column when the weeping Alfred arrived. A hush fell over the place as he walked slowly to the bier, gazed mutely at the body, wringing his hands before walking to the back of the room and sitting on a folding chair. At intervals he rose, returned to look at his brother again, then sat as Ellis and Trezevant kept offering to take him back to the hotel to break the news to his sisters.

Within an hour the news of John Moisant's death was telegraphed to the West Coast where his 16-year-old son, Stanlie, was visiting relatives in Los Angeles. A student at the Hitchcock Military Academy in San Rafael, he had lived in San Francisco for the last decade with John's sister Ann Marguerite and her husband, Bertin Weyl. At the time of his father's death Stanlie, who was in Los Angeles with his uncle, was staying at a hotel in order to view the summit of Mount Lowe. When Weyl was informed of John's death he asked the journalists to keep the news from his nephew, explaining that "the boy has been enjoying himself so much that I want him to have one more day before he learns of the tragedy."

This request was subverted five hours later when a United Press reporter found Stanlie roaming near the crater of Mount Lowe and told him his father had been killed in New Orleans. For a moment the boy did not speak. Then he said, "I have not seen my father for five years and now he is dead."

Also in Los Angeles at the time was Wright flyer Arch Hoxsey, who had come to take part in an air show and learned of Moisant's death from a newsboy shouting outside his hangar. "There's another good man gone," he said, adding, however, that he wasn't surprised because Moisant "was awfully reckless . . . and a reckless man and a Blériot machine do not go together. He took more chances than any man I know."

Ironically, Hoxsey himself died only minutes after hearing of Moisant's death, losing control of his plane while attempting to beat his own world altitude record of 11,474 feet which he had set only five days before.

Back in New Orleans, Alfred was finally persuaded to return to his suite at the St. Charles after selecting a casket and making tentative funeral arrangements. Louise and Matilde embraced him at the door while Paree-Londres circled them, rubbing against their ankles and mewing pitifully.

During the evening Alfred returned to the funeral home where John's body lay in a copper casket, his head resting on a pillow of flowers sent by his fellow flyers. A long line of mourners shuffled past while women knelt in prayer and men stood in small groups at the back of the room, speaking in hushed voices.

As floral arrangements and telegrams of condolence poured in from around the country and Europe, Campbell Wood was eulogizing Moisant as "not merely an aeroplane driver" but "a great believer in the future of aviation and a designer and builder of machines himself." With his death, the Aero Club official added, "Not only his country but the whole world lost a man destined to pre-eminence in the development of the art" of flight.

But it was John's colleague, Edmond Audemars, the quiet Swiss master of the Demoiselle who had just joined the troupe in New Orleans, who best expressed the loss felt by his fellow flyers. "He was really king of the air," Audemars said, "as much ahead of all of us as the great soaring birds are ahead of the aeroplane."

Alfred left it to Ellis to announce the names of the pallbearers for the funeral service the next day. They would be Alfred; LeVino and Young, to represent the Moisant Fliers; Ellis, Palmer Abbot, and William Allen of the Citizens' Committee; and General Altschul and Charles Weinberger, friends of John since the early days in Central America.

Later Alfred told reporters outside the funeral parlor, "You may say for me that my sisters and myself are deeply grateful because of the sentiments expressed to us in the death of our dear brother. I am broken-hearted and it is impossible for me to say much now, but I do want to thank the people and especially Messrs. Ellis, Weinberger and the other gentlemen of the committee." Saying he was deeply touched by the number of people who had come to the funeral home, Alfred added, "My mother was a Catholic and we were all christened in that faith. I want to be an active pallbearer because I wish to take my brother to his temporary resting place in a city where the people have shown him so much courtesy."

On New Year's morning, after thousands had viewed John's body during the night, more mourners stood in the rain on the sidewalk outside the McMahon Funeral Home. A senior police captain and eight uniformed men stood guard while almost fifty cars, taxis, and carriages arrived with those attending the funeral—a private service for family and close friends. At ten o'clock, under low, darkening clouds, his robes flapping in the wind, the Reverend Father James Malone, preceded by two acolytes bearing a cross, walked across the street from St. John the Baptist Church to the funeral home. John Moisant, who had been baptized Joseph Jean Baptiste, was not to have a funeral mass in the church he had ceased to attend. But Alfred had done what he could to honor their mother's faith by asking a priest to officiate.

During the service Alfred kept glancing at the black ribbon on his coat sleeve and back at the casket. Tears glistened on his cheeks and in his thick moustache as he entered the carriage with his sisters to follow the hearse to Metairie Cemetery where the casket was sealed in receiving vault No. 24.

The rain continued to fall as the three Moisants rode back from the cemetery on that dark winter afternoon. At the hotel Alfred told Louise and Matilde he could no longer bear to remain in New Orleans. He asked them to pack immediately and be ready to leave with him and LeVino on the nine o'clock train for Jacksonville, Florida. From there they would board ship for Havana so that he might complete whatever arrangements John had made for the air meet in Cuba.

Alfred said he had arranged for Trezevant to care for John's personal effects. These included $12,000 in cash and a collection of jewelry. His diamond ring would go to Pete Young; his estate, estimated at between $100,000 and $150,000, to his son, Stanlie. There would be no more flights in New Orleans. General manager Young and the seven remaining International Fliers would go to Dallas, Texas, for another air show beginning on January 4. That night the flyers saw Alfred, his sisters, and LeVino off on the train for Jacksonville, then ate their last dinner in New Orleans, a dismal gathering followed by an 11 P.M. departure on their special train for Dallas.

When the three Moisants arrived in Jacksonville, the January issue of the *Air-Scout* magazine had already appeared with a lead article written by John B. Moisant and titled "The Gentle Art of Aviation." Printed too early to include any mention of his death, the article was an impassioned argument that aviation was "no longer a mere toy and plaything" but an art. His conviction of this was embedded in the final paragraph, which read:

Two centuries ago, yes, even as late as the middle of the Nineteenth Century, the people prayed as they had long prayed, "Oh God, annihilate but time and distance and make two lovers happy." I do not know much about the "lovers" part of it, but the aeroplane has come to annihilate both time and distance, thereby advancing the material prosperity and the moral progress of the world and bringing that much nearer the universal brotherhood of man.

In time for news of their deaths the new issue of *Aero* magazine opened with a combined article-editorial story on the Moisant and Hoxsey crashes, attributing both to "the overdaring of the aviators." Optimistically titled "Fatalities Will Make Flying Safer," it managed to mix mourning with criticism, saying the two deaths would make future air meet flyers "abandon all idea of trying to give the spectators . . . more than they deserve in performances of doubtful safety."

In New York, meanwhile, the same Blériot that Moisant had flown from Paris to London was one of fourteen planes on display at Grand Central Palace. Only now it was draped in black crêpe.

The cause of Moisant's crash was never determined. He himself had written that crashes involving experienced aviators were the result of their own failure to check their plane's condition or from negligence aloft.

There was no evidence of either when Ross Browne, an American who had known Moisant in France, went with Garros and the mechanic, Maurice, to view the wreckage. They all agreed with Campbell Wood that Moisant had descended too rapidly, forcing the remaining fuel to the front of the auxiliary tank and shifting the plane's center of gravity too far forward to pull up in time. But they guessed that only some unexpected problem such as ignition trouble would have caused him to come down and attempt to land so swiftly.

Alfred denied that the forward flow of gasoline in the tank could have caused the accident. John had won second place in the Gordon Bennett cup race with the same plane and the same tank, he said, adding that excess weight could not have been a problem since the tank still held 20 gallons when he landed at

Belmont but only six gallons when he crashed. Something must have gone seriously wrong with the plane, Alfred insisted, forcing John to come down regardless of the danger inherent in landing with the wind.

Others differed as to what caused Moisant's death. *Aero* attributed it to "his endeavor to land with a stiff wind while his Blériot was unusually heavy forward. Undoubtedly the wind and the extra weight combined pointed the monoplane too sharply downwards, which threw Moisant from the machine."

English flyer James Radley implied concurrence with Hoxsey that Moisant had been a reckless flyer. He recalled seeing him dive at Belmont in the same plane with engines at full speed and ram the aircraft's nose into the ground before rebounding 100 feet. "No air machine," he commented, "can stand that sort of thing."

Joe Seymour spoke for the more fatalistic of John's colleagues, saying, "He was due. Poor old John had hundreds of hairbreadth escapes but his time had come."

Careless, overly daring, impetuous—John Moisant was all of these. But it was left to his dear friend Roland Garros, himself destined to be idolized by the French for his bravery during the world war to come, to deliver the accolade John would have wanted. "He did more than any man," Garros said, "to arouse the enthusiasm in aviation which will bring this science into its own. . . . Moisant was ahead of his time. He saw farther than any of us and realized better than all of us how aviation would benefit and improve mankind."

Garros could have added, "And he did it all in only five months."

12
CIRCUS SOLDIERS

Within hours of the interment of his brother, Alfred Moisant's grief metamorphosed into action. Alfred would preserve his brother's memory by making John's vision of aviation a reality. He would accomplish this through the Moisant International Aviators' air circus, supported by a barrage of press releases to government and military officials and newspapers throughout the country. His releases made up in inventiveness for what they often lacked in fact, giving his birthplace as Chicago, not L'Erable, and his age as 46 instead of 49.

But the news-hungry press devoured them eagerly. Even before the air-show flyers left New Orleans, Dallas newspapers were reporting they would arrive with "a limousine monoplane capable of carrying three passengers besides the aviator . . . and . . . developing a speed of 175 miles per hour." Advance man H. F. McGarvie was boasting that Texans coming to the state's first-ever air show could expect to see a number of record-breaking flights because Dallas offered mild weather, flat countryside, and the best airfield in the States.

McGarvie was wrong about the weather. For 48 hours starting on opening day rain and freezing temperatures forced the flyers to delay or cancel most of the flights before a meager audience of 3,000 while another 6,000 watched for free from outside the fence. When they did fly, Frisbie and Hamilton both crashed, Frisbie's biplane losing a wing and Hamilton's a wheel. On the third day, another 30,000 people watched gratis from downtown streets and rooftops as Barrier made four flights over the city, but at least 20,000 ticketholders in the stands saw Simon crash and disappear from sight under the mangled plane. Seymour ran to the wreckage shouting, "Are you hurt? Are you all right?" From under the plane came the answer, "No. Ver' good."

"Here I was," Simon said later, "alive, whole, not a bone in my body broken and my friends afraid to lift the machine for fear they would not find enough of me left to make a decent funeral."

That same day a monkeywrench left on top of Frisbie's plane fell into the moving propeller, destroying it, and Hamilton's motor exploded when he tried for a speed record. Yet the thousands who saw them led to more thousands until 25,000 packed the stands on January 8, forming what one newspaper called one of the largest-ever crowds in Dallas "except for the state fair, presidential visits and the Confederate Reunion." They cheered for Simon when he flew six feet off the ground along a racetrack lined with spectators, touching his wheels to the earth briefly, then skimming up again. Another 300 waited until after dark to make certain that Garros was all right after a forced landing miles from the enclosure.

The next day Texas governor-elect O. B. Colquit gave the spectators an unexpected thrill when, posing for photographers in the seat of Frisbie's plane, he accidentally stepped on the foot throttle, starting the craft leaping and bounding down the field while Frisbie ran frantically alongside and mechanics were alternately tossed into the air or dragged in the dust as they clung desperately to the tail. The plane traveled erratically for some 100 feet before Frisbie managed to reach in and release the throttle, allowing Colquit to emerge, somewhat ashen but otherwise unharmed.

Shortly after midnight January 12, the flyers reached their next stop at Fort Worth to face more gale-force winds for two days of performances before thousands of spectators who had come from as far north as Amarillo and as far west as Big Spring. They arrived in automobiles, on horseback, on trains, in buggies and rigs, and on foot. Children were let out of school at noon while stores and factories released half their workforces on alternate days to allow them all to attend the two-day engagement.

On the first day a good-natured crowd of 17,000 watched the planes being assembled and ground-tested, Seymour raced his Fiat and Audemars dared a few short hops in his Demoiselle. When after three hours of this the wind still hadn't died down, Garros risked taking off in a 35-MPH gale, rose to 60 feet and almost crashed when a wind gust caught him, but righted the plane and flew over north Forth Worth. When he returned a mob of men, women, and children broke through the police lines and ran across the field to meet him. On the second day Simon and Audemars flew in even stronger winds but this time the star was Seymour who flew his man-lifting kites, once rising to 100 feet. After the diminutive Audemars also rode one, a number of women left the grandstand and begged for their chance as well.

The Fort Worth shows were followed by five successful days in Oklahoma City before returning to Texas for a show in Waco. But like Chattanooga, Waco was a disaster. On the first day all flights had to be canceled. On the second, gale winds continued and a delivery of substandard gasoline had to be drained from all the tanks while 16,000 chilled spectators waited for hours. On the last day 15,000 outraged ticketholders endangered the aircraft by rushing from the stands and demanding at least one flight for their money. This time it was "the nervy young aviator" Simon who saved the day by a perilous flight which ended with the unruly throng carrying him from the plane on their shoulders.

If the crowd was satisfied, the *Waco Times-Herald* was not. It excoriated the Moisant group for having "fleeced" the people by luring them to a "so-called aviation meeting" which was long on promises and short on performance. The flyers left Waco with only $5,000 in gate money, just a fraction of their expenses. And they left convinced that they would have to fly in Texas regardless of the weather or face violence to their aircraft and themselves.

As winds continued to lash the state the flyers went on for two days in Temple and five in Houston, with Garros and Simon emerging as just as daring, colorful, and reckless as the late John Moisant.

Simon won the adulation of Texas ranchers in Temple when he flew from the enclosure to the open prairie, circled a herd of cattle, and stampeded them back to the fairgrounds while startled cowboys looked on in astonishment and the crowd shouted itself hoarse. "Then . . . to demonstrate he could really drive cattle with an aeroplane, he cut across the herd and started them back to their original grazing grounds." The stunt was reported in newspapers throughout the country, leading one of them to suggest that farmers would soon have "tame, tractable aeroplanes" for common use.

The next day it was Garros's turn to become the idol of 8,000 in Houston. Shutting off his motor at 3,000 feet and still a mile from the grandstand, he began "a sensational glide to the field" and cleared the heads of spectators at the top of the stand by only six feet. As he came to a perfect landing in the center of the field, "automobile horns, sirens and claxons mingled with the cheers" and "spectators in the grandstand stood up and applauded [in] the greatest ovation . . . [of] the present meet."

Still, as the flyers had feared, the Texas fans were as quick to riot as they were to applaud. Twenty-four hours later many from the audience of 15,000, angered by long delays caused by high winds, charged out of the stands onto the field, breaking through the lines of mounted police. When the mob surrounded two of the Blériots and a Demoiselle parked on the field, frightened mechanics tried to push the planes out of danger but were followed by the crowd as the police stood by helplessly. To save his Blériot Simon spun the propeller, climbed in, and taxied ahead, scattering the mob just enough to take off but barely missing the heads of the people in front of him. Garros followed. But no sooner were they airborne than the crowd surged back onto the field, leaving no clearing for a landing. Simon gave up and landed outside the enclosure. Garros tried to clear the area by diving on the crowd but the demonstrators stood their ground, forcing him away from the field. He finally landed on prairie land several miles away as a Mr. and Mrs. T. C. Dunn were driving by, followed by their son, T. C. Jr., in a second car. Unable to restart the motor, Garros left his plane in the field and rode back to town with T. C. Jr. On the way they were joined by Mr. and Mrs. W. R. Nash and five other friends and they all had tea at the Nashes' before returning Garros to the Rice Hotel where the flyers were staying.

Altogether there were more good days than bad in Houston. On one Garros again thrilled spectators with a repeat of his dive to the top of the grandstand, this time clearing the heads by just two feet. He also dived on parked cars, sending their occupants running for cover, then chased a cow up and down the field. On January 31, the last day of the Houston meet, Garros and Simon competed for a $1,000 prize put up by local businessmen for the fastest flight over Houston. Garros went first, finishing the 16 miles in 16 minutes and 22 seconds. Flying into a blinding sunlight, Simon lost his way and landed in a field seven miles away 20 minutes later. Drivers rushing to his rescue found him sitting in his plane, wiping oil from his goggles. When he tried to take off again the rudder of his plane hit one of the cars. Garros won the prize but the businessmen also gave Simon a sizable sum, declaring the Houston meet highly successful.

On the evening his International Aviators were giving their first show in Texas, Alfred boarded the SS *Governor Cobb* for Cuba with Louise, Matilde, publicity man Albert LeVino, and Paree-Londres to complete arrangements John had made for the air show in February. At Havana's Ingleterre Hotel Alfred told Cuban officials he had come to complete arrangements for the February air meet begun by his late brother, "the greatest aviator in the world." John had told Alfred he wanted to make the tournament rival the great French air meets and to demonstrate the practical uses of airplanes. As for both Moisants, LeVino explained, the tournament was planned not merely to make money or as a personal "road to fame" but to further the brothers' hopes of manufacturing airplanes and establishing aviation schools in the United States—and also in Cuba if there was sufficient interest. Besides, he added, the Moisants were already widely known from their activities in Central America, France, and Mexico.

When told the Cubans had not even set a definite date for the tournament Alfred said his aviators would come to Cuba only after contests dates and programs were firmly established and only if guaranteed at least $40,000 in prize money. Within days the Cubans founded the Aero Club of Cuba to gain FAI approval, set the opening date for the second half of March, and began raising money and issuing invitations.

Once assured of the engagement Alfred returned to New York where he heard conflicting reports from Washington on the state of military aviation. Official interest was so low that in its weekly "News and Gossip" column from Washington, an aviation magazine characterized a talk by Chief of Staff Gen. Leonard Wood as "a fair sample of what the government is not doing in aeronautics." Discussing the possibilities of the airplane in scouting, the general said "the present aerial equipment of the army consisted of one out-of-date aeroplane" which would cost $70 or $80 to be put in flying condition although he had been assured the money could be "raised . . . by private subscription." Only a few days later, however, despite the opposition of two representatives, "neither of whom knew a flying machine from a threshing machine," the House military committee approved a surprise amendment appropriating $125,000 for Army aeronautics.

Alfred had been positioning himself for exactly such an opportunity. Just before John's death he had filed corporate papers in New York for the Hempstead Aviation Company (soon reincorporated as Hempstead Plains Aviation Company) with capital stock of $50,000 and 1,600 acres of land for an airfield just east of Garden City, Long Island. He said hangars would be built for a flight school to be opened in the spring and exhibitions and contests would be held at the field. Alfred was self-appointed chairman of the board that included Allen W. Evarts, Charles Steward Butler, and George E. Tarbell.

Shortly after John's death Alfred bought at auction the planes and motors of the bankrupted Lovelace-Thompson Aeroplane and Motor Works at 197th Street and Amsterdam Avenue and hired Lovelace to build Moisant planes for him in the factory he had relocated to nearer downtown New York on Ninth Avenue in Manhattan.

Now, seeing the chance to sell planes to the Army, he informed officials in Washington of his activities in an increased flow of press releases. Where these failed to interest the Army his pilots in Texas succeeded. Arriving in San Antonio from Houston on February 2, Garros, Simon, and Barrier called on Lt. Benjamin D. Foulois, an Army pilot attached to the Signal Corps at nearby Fort Sam Houston, and volunteered to act as air scouts. Foulois accepted and set up a three-staged military maneuver as part of a February 4 show. Knowing only that there was an "enemy" camp somewhere within a 10-mile radius, the flyers were to locate it and report back on the number of men and guns, undergo an artillery attack, and "bomb" the "enemy" position.

Garros went first, flying at 2,500 feet. Simon was next, but at 1,500 feet and with the wind at his back was first to return, telling Foulois he had found three guns and 50 to 60 men, some on horseback. Garros's report generally duplicated Simon's but lacked the latter's details because of his having flown at a much higher altitude. Consequently Barrier was sent out to confirm the two reports. He was airborne for just four minutes when gunfire was heard at the field, from which the Army officers decided he had obviously flown within range of the guns and that in actual warfare he would have been shot down. Flying at 500 feet Barrier thought so, too. He told Foulois, "I was not ver' high when they shot at me. The explosion was ver' bad, shaking me all over and doing the machine this way," with one hand demonstrating his airplane rocking and tilting.

To entertain the crowd of 10,000 Garros and Simon then took off on exhibition flights when an artillery battery, caissons rumbling, harnesses and equipment clanking, and bugles sounding dashed into the enclosure. Minutes later a deafening artillery salvo startled the onlookers out of their seats and frightened Simon, too. Less than 500 feet from the gun muzzles, he came down in a hurry, while Garros flew out of range. Barrier closed the exercises by attempting to drop flour bombs on the guns but the wind was so strong he was unable to hit the targets while trying to control his aircraft.

The next day Garros, by now a favorite of the San Antonio fans, was caught in flight by gale-force winds and hurled toward the stands. Pulling up over the heads of the screaming spectators, he was forced to land at 50 MPH, his plane twice bouncing 20 or 30 feet into the air before mechanics managed to grab the fuselage and drag the plane to a halt a few feet from the grandstand.

As Garros tore off his goggles and cap and ran toward his fellow pilots, who were racing across the field to congratulate him, some of the crowd broke through the line of soldiers and surrounded him, one woman saying, "Mr. Garros, I thought that you were going to kill yourself."

"Madam," he replied, bowing, "I could not do that for you today; maybe tomorrow."

As the airmen were closing out their show in San Antonio, *Aero* magazine was preparing a cover story that would laud them for enabling the Army to reach some important conclusions about the effectiveness of aircraft in wartime. They had demonstrated that an air scout could locate and identify the enemy but would need an observer-passenger at high altitudes, that the concussion of ground artillery could upset a plane at 800 feet, and that two men would be needed for a bombing run, one to fly and one to drop the explosives.

Encouraged by their accomplishment, the airmen volunteered to attempt another reconnaissance mission, but this time in a real war. They proposed to Lieutenant Foulois that during their next show in El Paso they scout the fighting between Mexican Federal troops and insurgent forces just across the border. When their proposal was accepted—after both sides in Mexico agreed to withhold fire provided the airmen observed strict neutrality and reported their observations only to U.S. Army officers— Garros cabled Alfred in New York.

Delighted, Alfred issued a press release stating that since this was "the first time since the development of the aeroplane that we have had war anywhere," he was not going to miss the "opportunity . . . to demonstrate the practical military uses to which the aeroplane may be put." Therefore, he continued, "my men will try to make just such reconnaissance flights over the Juarez battlefield and its vicinity as they would make were they actually enlisted in the signal corps of an army facing its enemy."

Within 48 hours Alfred, his chief engineer, and the head draftsman of his new airplane factory were on the train to El Paso. From the train he sent a formal notice to the War Department in Washington that he was offering it seven planes and aviators. (In addition to the three Frenchmen, he was including Audemars, Hamilton, Frisbie, and Seymour, even though neither of the last two had an airworthy plane.) General Wood replied that the offer "would be taken into consideration."

Two days later Alfred's balloon was deflated when the chief of staff announced that he planned to mobilize members of the Aerial Reserves, six of whom were among "the best known aviators in America" and would probably be assigned to air-scout duty on the Mexican border. Not only were none of the chosen flyers (all now reserve lieutenants) Moisant's, but at least five of them represented his chief rival, Curtiss. Making matters even worse, press reports of the announcement directly echoed Alfred's claim that this would be the first time in history that flying machines were used in warfare.

Alfred no doubt worried during the trip that he probably also faced opposition from President Taft, who disapproved of all military flights, saying planes were still too primitive and the risk of death to Army officers too great. The president was further convinced that aviators flying above 400 feet were incapable of making accurate observations. Perhaps Taft thought that when Garros halted his speech at Richmond the Frenchman was unable to see that he was interrupting the president of the United States.

When he arrived in El Paso, Alfred's concerns about official disapproval proved unwarranted, although he now faced difficulty from an unexpected quarter. As an alien in the United States on a visitor's visa, Garros was having second thoughts about crossing the border, a legal deterrent that applied equally to Simon, Barrier, and Audemars. This left Charles K. Hamilton with his *Black Demon* as the only available volunteer.

In the final event, Alfred was not to be denied seeing a Moisant pilot become the first in the world to fly reconnaissance in battle. Within hours of Alfred's arrival and watched by thousands in the streets, on rooftops, and along the banks of the Rio Grande, Hamilton took off for a flight into Mexico, covering the 22 miles to Juarez in 19 minutes. "As I crossed the river," he wrote in a bylined dispatch for a New York newspaper, "I could see the glitter of the sun on bayonets of the American soldiers patrolling the border to preserve neutrality. . . . On top of the Mexicans custom house floated the colors of [Mexican President Porfirio] Diaz. . . . Juarez is under martial law, troops are garrisoned in nearly every house and guards are kept night and day on top of the churches, the bull-fight ring and the theatres."

The first time he circled Juarez the troops on guard ran for cover, but the second time they came out and waved. On his return he again passed over the U.S. customs house and a guard post, shutting off his motor and diving at the soldier on duty. Terrified, the man jumped into the river, feet first, his hat floating on the water as he stood up in the mud, "cussing and shaking his fist at me."

Although Hamilton saw no rebel troops his feat was featured

in hundreds of American newspapers by editors who jingoistically headlined the fact that it was an American who made the historic flight.

No doubt they were as pleased as their readers by Hamilton's boast that "one more flight over Juarez and I think the Mexican soldiers will be ready and willing to capitulate to Pascuel Orozco, the insurgent leader, that is if he can give them anything like the scare I gave them yesterday."

The newspapers were impressed by Hamilton but General Wood was not. Less than two weeks later the chief of staff ordered Lieutenant Foulois and Wright aviator Philip Parmalee to report to Laredo for air-scout duty. With Laredo as a base they were to cover the Texas border between that city and El Paso, observing the Mexican fighters with powerful binoculars and reporting their findings by wireless radio—a two-man team, just as *Aero* had suggested. Wood also spared the Army expense by borrowing a new Wright model airplane for the job. After the initial test flight *Aero* reported, "It is rather a feather in the Wrights' cap that while there were many offers of assistance on the border patrol from different aviators, the Dayton men were the first to detail a man to devote his whole time to the work."

When the article went on to paraphrase Parmalee's praise of the Wright biplane as superior to the Moisant monoplane— because it could carry two men and more gasoline, was steadier in the air, and could fly slowly allowing the observers more time —it was simply adding insult to Alfred's injury.

Alfred's bid to become a supplier of planes to the U.S. military was clearly unrealistic. At this point he owned only a handful of planes purchased from Lovelace-Thompson and had yet to build any of his own. But the entrepreneur gambler who had already made a fortune in high-risk Central America was not to be discouraged. If the Americans weren't interested in his monoplanes he would just find buyers elsewhere.

13

SHOW AND SELL

W ith his flyers and planes already on the border and Mexico engaged in a revolution Alfred, not illogically, chose that country as his first sales target. Several days before his airmen finished their engagement in El Paso, he boarded a train for Mexico City to negotiate two air meets—a two-day warmup in Monterrey followed by ten days in the capital. They would be the first ever in Mexico and, as Albert saw it, a great opportunity to merchandise his aircraft.

Air-show entrepreneurs of the time customarily negotiated subsidies from promoters and/or ticket sales and prize-money guarantees to protect themselves from financial disaster. Only a few weeks earlier, for example, the Aero Club of Connecticut left Mexico City in disappointment after failing to get such assurances from the Mexican government. But for some reason Alfred's normally shrewd business instincts seem to have temporarily abandoned him. Whether starstruck, unaccustomed to his new role as an air-show impresario, or simply overcome by the prospect of mass sales to a country at war, he agreed to stage the Mexico air shows with neither subsidy nor guarantee, or as one newspaper put it, "willing to take all financial risks" on himself.

His initial business completed in Mexico City, Alfred joined his airmen in Monterrey, where Simon was credited with being the first pilot to take off in and make an extended flight over Mexico. For the next two days the city went "aviation mad," as one newspaper headline put it, while everyone at Zambralano Park "from the dignitaries in their autos to the small boys in the treetops" watched the International Aviators. The paper rated the first day "a howling success." The second day was equally successful, as the packed stands cheered Garros and Simon as they played "follow the leader" over the skies of Monterrey, making right-hand turns "against the turning of the mighty propeller wheel, a feat which has resulted in mishaps to more than a third of the men who have been martyrs to the sport of aviation." The enthusiasm turned into near-chaos as cheering fans broke through police lines until a Mexican general in the audience ordered a lieutenant and his infantry company onto the field to restore order.

Despite his show's success, Alfred himself was somewhat less than ecstatic, having arrived in Monterrey only to learn that Charles Hamilton had broken his contract and ordered his mechanics to dismantle his biplane and pack it up for shipment to the United States.

Alfred countermanded Hamilton's instructions and ordered the plane loaded on the company train for Mexico City. When Hamilton, whose wife had joined him in Monterrey, appeared to accede to the reprimand and asked for permission for both of them to take the Moisant train to Mexico City, Alfred took it as acquiescence on the flyer's part and assumed the matter was settled. But when they reached the capital Hamilton hired a lawyer and charged Alfred with illegal possession of his airplane.

If Alfred was surprised by Hamilton's actions, he probably shouldn't have been. Even when Moisant hired him, the flyer was embroiled in legal action with the Curtiss group—Curtiss suing the flyer for $6,200 owed him as a percentage of the flyer's show winnings and Hamilton countersuing for $14,000 in contract and other obligations. Later Hamilton also led a pilots' revolt against the Wright brothers for engaging in unfair employment practices. As Moisant and Hamilton were both vain, pompous, contentious, and obstinately single-minded, the surprising thing is not so much that Hamilton quit but that he and Alfred hadn't clashed sooner.

A Mexican judge ruled Alfred had a right to hold the plane, along with another, a Blériot that Hamilton had sold to Garros, until Hamilton completed the contract with Alfred on which he had already received a $10,000 advance. In defiance of the court Hamilton persuaded his two mechanics and several helpers to break into the railroad car and remove the planes but the men were caught by manager Pete Young and another member of the staff. Later that same day the Mexican police arrested Hamilton at his hotel.

Imprisoned for three days, Hamilton bribed his way out by paying the judge 200 pesos, or so he said on his return to the United States, accusing Moisant of still owing him more than $1,000 in back pay. He claimed he had been held incommunicado in a cell without food, water, and, worse yet, cigarettes—this for a man seldom seen without a cigarette dangling from his lips.

Hamilton's experience in jail left him a champion of the revolution and a bitter critic of the Mexican government. He praised the rebels, who he said "do not waste lead and ball on the Mexican soldiers but drag them over the ground with their horses galloping at top speed till they are ground to pieces. Some artistic death, what?"

Alfred answered Hamilton's charges with a claim that from November 23 in Richmond until February 20 in Monterrey the defecting pilot had flown for a total of just 1 hour, 51 minutes, and 50 seconds. For this Hamilton was paid $16,302.42, this at a time when the annual wage of the average U.S. worker was less than $1,500. Alfred further claimed that this did not include the wages, travel, and living expenses for Hamilton and his two personal mechanics, all of which was also paid by the Moisant company.

Moisant and Hamilton filed charges and countercharges in both Mexico and the United States and the case dragged on in both countries until Hamilton's death from pneumonia in January 1914.

In deference to his host country, Alfred saw to it that the first flyer to take off on the first day of his Mexico City air show was not one of his own men but Mexico's first and only pilot, Alberto Braniff, demonstrating his new Farman biplane. Garros followed and was in the air 48 minutes, flying four times around Chapultepec Castle, the presidential palace. Barrier flew for a half hour across the capital. The second day provincial governor Guillermo de Landa y Escandon, his staff, and "the elite society . . . of the Republic" attended while a cordon of police and soldiers surrounded Valbuena Plains and more than 100 automobiles flanked carriages along both sides of the grandstand. Although the airmen set no records, the National Railway did by putting fourteen cars in operation and carrying more than 3,000 passengers safely and without delay from the field to San Lazaro station.

The third day in the capital was actually the formal opening of the Moisant air show and Alfred staged it like a Broadway extravaganza. Dramatically positioned around Valbuena Plains, Mexico's red, white, and green flags and those of the pilots' countries fluttered in the wind as a flare of trumpets announced the arrival of President and Mrs. Porfirio Diaz, who along with cabinet ministers, war department officials, and select members of the foreign diplomatic corps, had all received special invitations. Five hundred cavalry and foot soldiers presented arms as the president and Mrs. Diaz passed through the long line of soldiers stationed below the grandstand and entered the royal box in the middle. When the crowd of 30,000 stood for the national anthem Alfred noted with satisfaction the large number of army officers in the stands.

Invited to fly first, Mexico's Braniff opened the show by flying his 50-hp Farman five times around the field at 30 to 40 feet while the president watched him with binoculars. Then Simon and Barrier took turns in an array of stunts that brought ovations from the crowd. Afterwards both men were brought to the dias to be presented to the president and Garros took off in a demonstration of high-altitude flying. At this point the situation suddenly turned precarious as delirious spectators overwhelmed the troops and police on the field, rushing from the $1-enclosure to join standees in midfield, all clamoring for an up-close look at the pilots and their planes. Garros barely managed to land right in front of the presidential box.

The more unruly among the crowd surrounded the aircraft, attempting to clutch the aviators and to cut off pieces of their clothing and even fabric from their planes. The desperate pilots and staff first used persuasion, then force to fend off the attackers. Tiny Audemars in his white shirt and bow tie climbed aboard the Demoiselle and tried to take off but was unable to find a clearing. At the peak of the disorder the band began to play and the presidential party departed. Simon was left standing on the seat of his plane, trying to wave away the crush of spectators jammed against the sides and wings of his Blériot. Not until night fell did the crowd drift away from the battered aircraft and weary pilots.

During the week that followed, in continuing bad weather, at least one and sometimes more of the aviators flew in the thin air of Mexico City's high altitude, drawing daily crowds of up to 20,000. A new vehicle entrance did little to relieve congestion at the gate, causing one observer to complain, "The road was inches deep in dust and the air from heavy traffic stifling. At four o'clock carriages were lined up three abreast for more than two blocks waiting their turn for the narrow passage." This was but one of the problems that prompted a further observation that "the International Aviators truly live up to their name, for they have flown now under practically every condition they are likely to meet anywhere on the globe."

For Alfred the red-letter days of the meet came on the two days before it closed. On March 2 Garros won a special prize for soaring to 12,740 feet above sea level, a record height for the meet and possibly for the world as well. On March 3, Army Day, Mexican flags outlined an imaginary man-of-war on the field. Following Simon's stunning demonstration of the Blériot's aerobatic capacity, Garros and Simon capped the show by with an exhibition of bombing. Zooming across the field at some 150 feet, they bombarded the "ship" with oranges, hitting it four times in four passes.

Congratulated by army officers, a smiling Alfred was convinced that some of them would be future students at his aviation school and that their government would buy planes from the Moisant factory. He had every reason to consider his Mexico City production a resounding success. Three of his men—Garros, Simon, and Barrier—had all flown without trouble at more than 12,000 feet above sea level, shattering the prevailing belief that such high-altitude flights were beyond the capabilities of existing aircraft. President Diaz had personally assured him not only that he would soon establish an army aviation corps but that its future members had "greatly benefitted" from watching the Moisant flyers. And similar interest had been hinted at by the diplomatic corps of China and Chile.

Cheered by the escalating gate receipts, Alfred seemed oblivious to the fact that his expenses were steadily rising. On top of his original investment in the International Aviators, Alfred had now reached the point where he was supporting an entourage of sixty-five people, twelve planes, and a special train of Pullmans, sleepers, dining car, and baggage cars at a minimum daily cost he estimated at $4,000 excluding salaries and living expenses, besides which he had chartered a ship to take the entire company to Havana.

At the outset of the International Aviators' Mexico visit an aviation correspondent reported it would probably "not be a financial success because of the large expense of carrying their organization about."

It is not known whether Alfred saw the story or not. But while the show continued to Vera Cruz for two final performances in Mexico, Alfred returned to New York to spend more money on a replacement for Hamilton and more planes for Cuba. Though still to sell a single plane of his own, he considered the additional aircraft essential for another prospective customer.

In New York Alfred sent six more planes to the Ward Line docks to be shipped next day to Cuba along with twelve pairs of extra wings, tail planes, and other parts. The *New York Times* called it the "largest shipment of planes ever made" from the United States. He also hired a new International Aviator, St. Croix Johnstone, and sent him and his pretty young wife to Cuba on the same ship with the planes. The blond, blue-eyed, 26-year-old Johnstone had been licensed in England less than three months before.

The Havana meet almost ended before it began. The day before it was to start, Alfred's pilots learned that two members of the Aero Club of America appointed to represent the FAI at the meet had disagreed about the prize money. After one refused to sanction the meet because he considered the original Cuban offer of $30,000 too high it was reduced to $10,000, a saving readily accepted by the sponsors. Their potential earnings suddenly slashed by two-thirds, the flyers were ready to quit. But as there were no ships leaving for the United States for another week they had no choice but to fly for the diminished rewards.

Equally troublesome to Alfred was the earlier appearance in Cuba of several Curtiss representatives. He had wanted his own men to be the first to fly in Havana, but a four-man Curtiss exhibition team beat him by a matter of days. One of them, Beckwith Havens, recalled how they "had to chase cows off the field before we could take off . . . [and] flew across the town, around Morro Castle—me thinking all the time about all those sharks."

Alfred was even more irritated to learn that J.A.D. McCurdy, yet another Curtiss man, had already competed for the Havana City Council's Morro Prize of $3,000 for the fastest round-trip flight in an established route directly over the city to and around the Morro Castle. Alfred persuaded the council to extend the original contest deadline from February 28 to March 31. If his men could not be the first to fly over Havana they could at least beat McCurdy while putting on a better show than Curtiss with better flyers and better planes.

On March 23, the second day of the Havana meet. René Barrier did better McCurdy's time—by 1½ minutes. McCurdy protested on grounds that the contest deadline had been illegally extended and that the Frenchman had flown a shorter route by taking off from a point closer to Morro Castle than he had, but the protest was rejected and Barrier came away with the $3,000.

Before the meet even opened, however, another International Aviator set another record. Just after 7 A.M. on March 22 sleeping Havanans were awakened by a strange buzzing from overhead. Those few startled citizens who were outdoors at first ducked their heads as the "dragon fly" zigzagged overhead. It was newcomer St. Croix Johnstone, who had just taken off in his Gnôme-Blériot in an unannounced flight from suburban Le Coronela. As they gradually realized what was happening, the rest of Havana streamed into the streets and parks along the Malcon seawalk, lining the waterfront to watch what for many was the first plane they had ever seen. Flying over the Morro Castle, Johnstone dropped two oranges on it, one hitting the target but the other falling into the water. An enthusiastic onlooker jumped in and retrieved it for a souvenir. Johnstone crashed and demolished his plane irreparably on returning to Le Coronela. But he had just won $2,500 for becoming the first person to fly over the whole city of Havana.

Young Johnstone was not the only flyer to be caught in the city's confusing vertical air currents. Garros crashed, too, damaging the undercarriage of his new $6,000 Blériot XI, Audemars wrecked his precious Demoiselle, and Frisbie fell in his Rochester biplane while attempting a flight to the castle. One reporter described the air currents as similar to those over Sahara and wrote that the Moisant flyers' experience "illustrates what should become a maxim, that a drooping flag [wind sock] is no sign of the air at rest."

In scheduled competitions for speed, duration, altitude, and other designated flights, Garros led with $3,700 in prize money, Barrier was second with $3,400, Johnstone third with $2,500, and Simon last with $900.

At the close of the meet Garros set a kind of record of his own by keeping his vow to provide the first passenger ride in Cuba. Though intending to take off with his mechanic, he deferred to Dr. Orestes Ferrara, president of the Cuban House of Representatives, who was enchanted with the idea of becoming the first

Cuban to fly. Seconds after takeoff the plane listed to starboard, stalled, and fell 60 feet to the ground. After a moment of silence while both men sat amidst the wreckage, Garros turned to his guest and asked, "Pardon me, are you hurt?"

"No, thank you," Ferrara replied. "Are you?"

"Thanks, no," said Garros, reaching over to shake hands with his passenger. Then they both crawled out from under the wreckage.

Aero magazine praised the Havana meet for its "good exhibition flying," but otherwise wrote it off as "rather a disappointment to the officials because of the small interest shown." There was more than enough disappointment to go around. Though fascinated by the "birdmen" the general populace was effectively barred from the show by the shortage of public transportation. The airmens' prize money was paltry compared to what was being offered in Europe. And the low attendance meant a huge loss to Alfred, who no doubt found Havana a chastening experience. Still, he had suffered huge losses before in El Salvador and bounced back with a fortune. Returning to New York with his two most mature and skilled pilots, Garros and Audemars, he sent the rest of the air show on to New Orleans to continue the schedule of appearances he had already set up for them in the American Middle West.

14
A NEW ST. EMILIA

During the first three months of 1911 Alfred
Moisant was assailed by renewed reminders of
the terrible loss of his brother. Shortly before he left for Havana
he learned that the FAI had ruled that John had not won the
Statue of Liberty race after all. The committee disqualified him
for failing to meet the entry requirements by first completing
a continuous flight of one hour's duration. It also disqualified
Grahame-White for fouling a pylon on landing and declared de
Lessups the official winner. Alfred vowed to challenge the ruling.

Returning from Havana he walked into his Times Square office to find on his desk the watch John had been wearing on his
last flight. J. T. Dopp, the railway official who had marked the
Harahan field circuit for John to fly in his pursuit of the Michelin Cup, was walking at the crash site almost four months later
when he stumbled over the expensive timepiece, undamaged in
its gunmetal case, the carved gold hands on its three-colored
dial stopped at the moment John crashed.

A few days afterward in San Francisco, Alfred's brother-in-
law, Bertin Weyl, applied to the probate court for control of
John's estate on behalf of his ward, John's son, Stanlie. That

same day in New Orleans John's friends began a collection for a monument to be erected at the scene of his death.

Alfred was relieved to learn that young Stanlie would continue to be cared for by the Weyls and touched by the news that John's friends were setting up a memorial, but he remained convinced that only he could assure his brother's lasting reputation as a champion of American aviation by persisting in the pursuit of their original plans to establish an airfield, a factory, and a school. This is why he had reorganized his principal asset, the Moisant International Aviators, Inc., and established the Hempstead Plains Aviation Company.

Alfred acted quickly when reports reached him from New Orleans that Simon, Barrier, Frisbie, and Seymour, now back from Havana, planned to break with him and go to Hutchinson, Kansas, with an air show of their own. He reminded the four flyers that although they were originally under contract to him personally he had assigned the contracts to the company and that he and secretary A. E. Wupperman had every intention of enforcing them. He then sent them their schedule for the next two months. In April they were to appear at Hutchinson and Pueblo, Kansas. In May they would go to St. Joseph, Missouri; Omaha, Nebraska; and Atlantic, Sioux City, and Des Moines, Iowa, where he planned to join them in early June and give them their schedule for the next two months. The rebellion, if that's what it had been, was over.

For his two best pilots, Garros and Audemars, Alfred had other plans. They would take two aircraft built at his Ninth Avenue factory in Manhattan to Europe. The planes were of a new design Alfred called the Moisant Junior, halfway in size between John's original Aluminoplane and the Demoiselle. He described them as all metal "except for the surface of the two main wings, the vertical rudder and the tail plane."

Though he offered no pictures, they were probably a smaller version of the basic Blériot whose standard model had a 50-hp engine. But the Moisant Juniors he was sending abroad were powered with 70-hp motors capable of speeds from 90 to 100 MPH.

Alfred ordered Garros and Audemars to demonstrate the

planes in Europe, flying them in cross-country races and in the elimination trials for the French team for the next Gordon Bennett cup race in England. The two pilots must have looked forward to the substantial prize money being offered on the Continent, especially after the comparatively paltry pickings in the United States and especially Mexico and Cuba.

Scheduled to sail with the Moisant Juniors on April 13 aboard the French liner *Provence,* Garros and Audemars missed the boat. They arrived 20 minutes before sailing time, assuming their luggage and the aircraft were already on board, only to be met by customs officials who accused them of violating the bond under which they had previously brought airplanes into the country. Audemars established that the plane he had been using was imported by the Moisant company on a bond which had not yet expired. But Garros was told that the two Demoiselles and the Blériot XI he had brought from France lacked the necessary papers for their export to Mexico and return to the United States. Garros saw the vindictive hand of Charles Hamilton behind the delay at the docks since he had filed suit against the American for selling him a plane he had no right to sell and repair parts that turned out to be nonexistent. Mailing a request to the Aero Club of America to take official recognition of Hamilton's conduct, Garros sailed with Audemars on another ship a day later, saying he would try to have Hamilton's license revoked.

With all his aviators now deployed, Alfred announced that his Hempstead Plains Aviation Company was about to begin work on the 1,600 acres of land recently purchased for the flying, training, and production aviation complex. Part of the land, the Mineola aerodrome, was already in use by more than thirty pilots and the office staff of the Aeronautical Society, a private club, and Alfred gave them six months to evacuate. The site, on Hempstead Plains between the Mineola and Garden City stations of the Long Island Railroad, was ideal for the purpose with no trees or houses to obstruct flying and room for five-mile and two-mile runways and racing circuits. Glenn Curtiss had been the first to use the area, in 1909, just east of the Mineola fairground on what became known as the Washington Avenue field. Alfred's land was to the east of Curtiss's within the present-day boundaries of Old Country Road, and the Long Island Motor and Meadowbrook Parkways.

Alfred said construction would start immediately on the first 25 of what would eventually be 100 aircraft hangars. Near the southwest corner he planned a long, roofless grandstand seating 25,000 and a clubhouse with showers, sleeping rooms, a restaurant, and a café. Already, he added, forty-two school applications had been received from prominent businessmen, sports stars, and military officers. With a 25-foot fence enclosing the field, his own men would hold an aviation meet every month. And at some later date his company planned to open other flying schools in Havana, Santiago, Mexico City, New Orleans, Chicago, St. Louis, Los Angeles, and Seattle.

In a press release sent to all Brooklyn newspapers and the Associated Press, Alfred further disclosed he would build an aircraft factory outside the north end of the field and just east of the hangars for manufacture, assembly, and repair. The 1½-story plant would have 59,000 square feet in the shape of a hollow square inside of which would be the company's two-story office building.

At the factory Alfred planned to produce three types of aircraft—the Moisant Junior, like the two he had just sent to Europe with Garros and Audemars; a Moisant all-metal monoplane; and a passenger-carrying monoplane for the military. In the all-metal model, the pilot would be enclosed in a "limousine" with three mica- or glass-covered slits through which he could see up, down, and straight ahead. The military plane would provide a clear view for an observer to make aerial maps, photographs, or sketches.

All that spring Alfred sent out lengthy press releases on his progress. Many detailed false or clearly unattainable accomplishments. And as time went on more and more of them indicated that Alfred's reach was beginning to exceed his grasp. One release, for example, said Garros and Audemars would visit "the Moisant factory in France" where "limousine-bodied tourabouts" were being made and tested before shipment to the United States. There was no Moisant factory in France. And there were no "tourabouts." When one did arrive it was the same old Aluminoplane his brother had built and Harold Kantner had dubbed "John's funny little plane."

On April 23 the first monoplane built for use at the school was delivered from the Ninth Avenue factory to the field. Like most aircraft of the time—concoctions of wood, cloth, metal braces, and piano wire—it was frail but flyable. It was, in fact, a modified Blériot with a fuselage of ash and hickory, stanchions and struts of Oregon spruce, and landing cradle of bamboo. The wings were rubber-treated silk and the propeller wood.

The next day Alfred announced in the *New York Herald* that his new school would open May 1 with seven planes and forty-two students. One delay followed another, however, and opening day was constantly postponed. But even while promise continued to outpace performance, Alfred kept up his flow of press releases whetting the public appetite for the many good things to come: The 50 hangars—down from the original 100—would have electric lights, running water, and underground fuel tanks. The students would be taught by a corps of six experienced instructors, among them some of the best flyers in Europe. Students who finished the course could get immediate delivery of a Moisant monoplane at generous discount—a 50-hp single-seater for $6,200; a 30-hp model for $3,800; or a higher-powered two-seater for $6,500.

A promotional pamphlet advertising the school said students would have to take a week of instruction in basic aircraft operation and maintenance before actually getting in a plane. They would be taught in 30-hp Blériots with Anzoni engines. Tuition would be $750 plus any charges for aircraft damage that was considered to be the student's fault.

The Moisant Aviation School, operating as a subdivision of Alfred's Hempstead Plains Aviation Company, finally opened in late May but not at the factory-school-airport complex. Because the complex was still under construction, Alfred had to lease hangars and a three-year-old workshop adjacent to his property at the old Mineola airport to get the school started.

The school started with six students, not forty-two. With one plane, not seven. And with one instructor instead of six. Garros and Audemars were in Europe, Simon and Barrier were with the air circus in the Midwest, and Johnstone's contract was for exhibition flying only, not teaching. The sole teacher would be Frenchman André Houpert, whom John and Alfred had met in Paris. Trained and licensed at Blériot's school in Pau, Houpert spoke some English and had an older brother, Henri, who lived in Manhattan where he operated a foreign-car garage.

Alfred was three months behind schedule. His aviation complex was still mostly on the drawing board and barely under construction. But finally his Hempstead Aviation Company was up and running and Alfred could be forgiven for envisioning a new Santa Emilia—a Santa Emilia of the air.

15
ANGELS IN THE AIR

I n the spring of 1911 Long Island newsmen were quick to notice the unusual flurry of early morning activity at the Moisant School of Aviation. A story by *New York American* aviation reporter Arnold Kruckman typified the attitude of wry amusement that colored much of their reporting.

Rain and fog usually take the starch out of even airwise flyers, but it does not dampen the ardor of that joyous bunch of aerial collegians who shout the yell of Don Alfredo's heavenly institution of learning at Mineola. Male and female, hobble trousered or hobble skirted, they were "all there" in the classic language of Times Square, on the aviation field yesterday. They rise early. With the first streak of dawn you'll find them shivering around the sheds where their instruments of learning are housed.

The first to enroll was a woman, Harriet Quimby, well-known drama critic and feature writer for the popular New York magazine *Leslie's Illustrated Weekly,* who had made up her mind to fly the day she saw John Moisant's Statue of Liberty flight at Belmont.

"When Moisant landed that Sunday, I told him my ambition and he agreed to teach me," Quimby said. John died before he could keep his promise but Quimby, who was introduced to the Moisants at the Belmont meet, continued to see Alfred and his sisters in New York. Soon after John's death she placed an article Alfred had written on the safety of flight in *Leslie's*. Then she persuaded the magazine to pay her $750 tuition at the Moisant school in exchange for a series of articles.

Quimby's enrollment was to bring Alfred's flight school more free publicity than all of his hyperbolic press releases. She was "tall and willowy," Matilde said, "and the prettiest girl I've ever seen." A veteran feature writer, she well knew how best to attract the attention of other reporters, many of whom took the bait, writing about the mysterious woman who arrived at the school at dawn, heavily veiled, took her five-minute lesson, then sped away in a car before anyone could question her.

On May 10 her identity was revealed by the *New York Times* as "a magazine editor of Manhattan who lives with her parents at the Hotel Victoria, a slender, youthful figure in an aviator's jacket and trousers of satin, leather puttees, heavy goggles and an aviator's cap." A few days later she began wearing a more flattering costume designed for her by the president of the American Tailors' Association, a one-piece, fitted and hooded suit of wool-backed purple satin with a skirt that could be converted into trousers.

Once Quimby's identity became public knowledge, Alfred seized the opportunity to exploit her position with the magazine by sending her a memo suggesting that she tout the monoplane as faster and safer than the biplane. The United States was saddled, he wrote, with old-fashioned, unsafe biplanes and phony schools with unqualified instructors, whereas he, Moisant, had monoplanes and employed only expert French teachers. Alfred could not resist adding that in the past three years only nine men had died in monoplanes, whereas forty were killed in biplanes, twenty-one of which belonged to his rivals Wright and Curtiss.

Quimby chose to do her own writing instead. In "How a Woman Learns to Fly" she advised would-be woman aviators to buy a one-piece suit like hers, which had no flapping ends to catch on wires, struts, and ailerons, and freed her hands and feet to manipulate the controls. And she advocated washable over-alls to wear over the flying suit to protect it from the castor oil constantly spewing from the motor. Once properly garbed, she wrote, they could begin their lessons, which would be in a Moisant monoplane with a 25- or 30-hp Anzoni engine. While four mechanics gripped the tail of the plane to hold it in place a fifth would spin the propeller until the engine started, at which the student pilot would attempt to steer it across the field for a mile or more in as straight a line as possible in an exercise called "grass-cutting." Quimby was quoted elsewhere as calling this exercise (also referred to as "trimming the daisies")

deceptively easy—'til you discover that an airship possesses a large share of the perversity supposed to be common to all inanimate objects. . . . If no mishap occurs your first dash across the field will take about two minutes, and after two dashes . . . the wise teacher will dismiss you for the day for you have had all that your nerves ought to be asked to stand at the outset.

Houpert imposed a strict five-minute limit on all Quimby's lessons.

After grass-cutting came "kangarooing" during which, in a slightly larger plane dubbed "The Grasshopper," students rose five or ten feet in the air, touched down and rose again, leaping and bounding across the field. When Houpert decided his students were ready to fly he assigned them an even more powerful Blériot in which they circled the field, learned to make turns and, finally, perform figure eights, all maneuvers required by the FAI to qualify for a license.

Quimby told reporters at the field she caught the 3:45 train from New York to Hempstead Plains every morning and started flying "about 4:30 after a thermos bottle breakfast," then returned to New York for her regular day's work schedule for *Leslie's.*

The 36-year-old Quimby, who admitted to 27 but looked even younger, was not the only woman pilot at Hempstead Plains. Another, Blanche Stuart Scott, was taking lessons from

Capt. Thomas Baldwin, who had sublet a hangar from Alfred. Scott made her first public flight in the fall of 1910 in Indiana, where she had been a pupil of Glenn Curtiss, but left him when Curtiss refused to accept her as a member of his exhibition team for fear of bad publicity if she were ever injured. She came to New York after being similarly spurned by the Wright brothers, who "absolutely refuse to sell their planes to a woman or any-one who intends it to be used by a woman."

A second woman, Bessica Raîche, soloed in September 1910, but abandoned aviation soon after to become a doctor. Neither Scott nor Raîche was ever licensed.

The first woman in the world to get a flying license was Baroness Raymonde de Laroche, who won her award March 8, 1910. Two other record-setting French woman flyers of the period were Hélène Dutrieu and Marie Marvingt, but neither was licensed. Marvingt that November set the women's speed record of 28 MPH. And in a nine-month period between 1910 and 1911 Dutrieu became the first woman to fly with a passenger and set women's records for both distance and altitude.

Four men joined Quimby's class—Ferdinand de Murias, Mortimer F. Bates, Shakir S. Jerwan, and Harold D. Kantner. De Murias, son of a wealthy Cuban businessman, proved an apt pupil. "Buddy" Bates was best known as the bumbler, a man who one observer said "up and hit a flagpole for the umpty-umpth time." Also prone to accidents was Jerwan, called "Dude" because of his fashionable suits.

The fourth man, Kantner, was a self-taught plane builder, the only student with a considerable knowledge of aircraft. He walked into Moisant's Times Square office at 42nd Street with $500—all the money he had—and offered it to company secretary A. E. Wupperman with a promise to pay the remaining $250 later. Wupperman accepted Kantner's offer and the young man moved into Anderson's boardinghouse in Mineola with a number of other students. Rising early at dawn, they would raise the window and check for rain or strong winds that might cause cancellation of the lesson that day. Houpert never allowed beginning students to fly in winds stronger than five miles an hour.

Kantner walked to the school to take his lessons in the short-winged plane designed not to leave the ground, which Quimby named "Saint Genevieve" after France's patron saint for flyers. The first time Kantner went grass-cutting down the field he ground-looped, making a rapid turn that caused the plane to tilt and swerve around in a circle, one wing scraping the ground. "They came and got me," he said. "I promptly ground-looped again."

Students were not the only plane wreckers. Testing a new Blériot one day before allowing Quimby to try it, Houpert landed to adjust the tailpiece, turned down the throttle and set back the ignition, then got out to make the adjustment, after which he made the mistake of trying to start the plane by himself. At the first turn of the propeller, the engine caught and the pilotless plane started down the field with Houpert racing after it. The rough terrain and the jar of his body as he tried to climb back in shook the throttle wide open and the craft suddenly roared down the field at 30 MPH, Houpert clinging to the fuselage until he fell and the plane ran over him. Rising, he grabbed the tail and hung on, shouting for help as he bounced along. Three mechanics who attempted to rescue him were themselves thrown to the ground, one after the other, while Houpert, still clinging to the tail, accidentally turned the rudder, forcing the plane into circles until it crashed into a hill, its propeller shattered. Harriet watched in safety from behind a tree.

Late in June Harriet asked Matilde, "Till, why don't you come and learn to fly? You've got just as much sense as I have." Matilde confessed she had thought about it ever since first seeing her brother in the air, but Alfred had been like a father to her and she was reluctant to ask his permission so soon after John's death.

Harriet continued her urging until one day Matilde walked into Alfred's office and said, "Fred, I want to fly." She recalled years later: "He looked at me very seriously. If he had said, 'You can't,' that would have ended it, but he looked at me and said, 'What do you want to fly for?'

"'Just for fun,' I said.

"He said, 'Well, if you promise me you will not fly commercially, I'll let you go.'"

Alfred rented rooms for her at the Atlantic City Hotel near the field where she recalled having to wait 12 days for her first lesson because of the weather. On July 13, with the wind down to four miles an hour, Houpert helped her into the plane and instructed her to head for a clump of bushes at the end of the field, warning that while running on the ground the machine would veer to the left and begin to turn in circles. The instructor's final words were to assure her that "we're going to hang onto the tail, and then you'll give us a sign and we'll let the tail go, and we'll go on over there. But don't forget to cut off your motor as soon as you start to turn."

Matilde recalled saying to herself, "If I make a turn this first time I'll never sit in the machine again. That was going to end flying for me." As soon as Houpert walked away she told the man assigned to help her when she cut her motor to go instead to the bushes at the end of the field. "I won't even cut off my motor, I'll just play with it, and you just spin the tail, and hang onto it if you want, but turn me around on my track." Completing her run as planned, Matilde taxied back to her starting point and asked, "Did you like my circle?"

Houpert growled. "Well, you'll cut [your motor] the next time." Then he said to Alfred, "You know, your sister is what I call a natural born flyer."

Matilde's appearance was as misleading as her public demeanor. At 33 she looked a good 10 years younger, and she unassumingly passed herself off to the press as Alfred's housekeeper, never noting that this was not in a self-sufficient New York apartment but in El Salvador, an undeveloped land plagued by bad weather, tropical disease, and political turmoil. On the surface she appeared to follow the code of delicate femininity called for by the tenets of her time. But she had already defied one of those tenets deliberately, remaining an "old maid" by choice. And beneath the surface was a woman who did whatever she wanted to, limited only by her deep regard for the views of her siblings.

In the last week of July Harriet told Matilde she wanted to take her licensing tests. Matilde, who was also ready, recalled, "I could have had my license first . . . but to me, I only took it up for fun. [Harriet] took it up for commercial reasons. She was taking care of her mother and father, and it [being first] meant a good deal to her, because she intended to make aviation her livelihood." This suggests Matilde deliberately passed up the honor to help her friend. At any rate there can be no question as to the qualifications of either woman. Houpert himself, who originally objected to allowing women in the school, was so impressed by both of them that he ended up believing "a flying machine was safer in the hands of a woman than it is with a man."

Other men felt differently. Arnold Kruckman, who had written so sardonically about the "hobble skirted" aviators and also that women were too emotional to fly, further questioned if a woman would be granted a license even if she passed the test since "no woman is accepted as a member of the Aero Club [of America]." Even stronger disapproval came from British air star Claude Grahame-White, who said flatly that women "are temperamentally unfitted for the sport."

In the late afternoon of July 31, Quimby took the first test given by the Aero Club of America in the presence of two officials, G. F. Campbell Wood and Baron Louis D'Orcy. Under recently revised rules she was required to make two flights of approximately three miles each, turning right and left in figure eights five times around two pylons, one at each end of the field. In addition she had to climb to at least 164 feet, then land within 150 feet of her starting point. She failed the landing, cutting her engine too late and coasting past the mark.

The two judges offered to stay overnight at Garden City so she could try again in the morning. When they met again at five the next morning a dense fog blanketed the field for another hour and a half. But neither her previous failure nor the long wait seemed to rattle the student who had taken just two hours of lessons over two months. This time she cut her engine properly and pulled to a stop only seven feet, nine inches from her takeoff point, something of a record for a beginning flyer. After her third flight that day when she saw her barograph reading of 220 feet she turned to D'Orcy and said, "Well, I guess I get that license."

"I guess you do," he answered. Holding flying license no. 37, Quimby was not only the first licensed woman flyer in the States but the second in the whole world. Flying the same plane that same day, classmate Ferdinand de Murias won license no. 38.

Like Matilde's brother John, Quimby was a feature writer's delight. The "first suffragette of the air" was as eloquent as she was beautiful and practically wrote the story for her interviewers. She promised that other women could do what she had done provided they could "control their nerves." Quimby could certainly control hers. Again like John, she was not averse to embellishing her background, telling people she was born in California in 1884 when she was really born near Coldwater, Michigan, nine years earlier. Nor did she discuss the fact that between high school and writing for San Francisco's *Examiner, Dramatic Weekly,* and *Call-Bulletin* she helped her parents make and sell herbal medicines.

Twelve days after Quimby and de Murias, Matilde, with only 32 minutes of instruction, earned license no. 44. "Why shouldn't a woman fly if she wants to?" she asked at a Chicago air meet two days later. "Now I'm not a suffragette and I'm not of the opinion that just because a man does this and that a woman has a right to also, but I do believe a woman is entitled to enjoy good sport as well as her brother."

Matilde went on to say, "I'm not, in the strict sense of the word, a society woman. I have my household duties to perform as I live with my brother, Alfred, in New York, and in New York keeping house makes no few demands on a woman's time." And she expounded on her love of flying, saying "there is a tremendous exhilaration in an early morning flight. The grass is cool and wet with dew. The air is clean and sharp and the speed at which one flies gives one an appetite for breakfast that must be experienced rather than described. I have never felt so well in my life as since I have been taking my early morning flights."

That August the next student to pass the test was Shakir S. Jerwan for license no. 54, and in September latecomer but fast learner Jesse Seligman became no. 64. Kantner and Bates followed in October as nos. 65 and 66.

By the end of the year six more students had enrolled and passed their tests. Alfred's money, Houpert's skill, and the publicity-drawing talent, charm, and attraction of Matilde and Harriet had made the Moisant School of Aviation a recognized major center for pilot training.

16

MIXED REVIEWS FOR A BOX OFFICE FLOP

As fast as Alfred was spending money building his aviation complex in Long Island, his International Aviators were losing it in one of the most difficult and trying engagements of their brief existence. Hempstead Plains Aviation Company manager Pete Young led a Moisant crew of fifty pilots, mechanics, and other personnel on an ambitious and arduous three-month town-hopping tour through eight states of the American Middle West—Kansas, Colorado, Missouri, Nebraska, Iowa, Illinois, Indiana, and Michigan. Though not a company officer (there were only two, Moisant and Wupperman), the 26-year-old Young, born in Anita, Iowa, had three years of aviation experience and all the confidence of a successful young married man returning home. But his foray into the Midwest turned out to be a never-ending battle against freak erratic winds, accidents, unexpected expenses, and dwindling audiences. As the returns of each day were tallied, the occasional small success stood out depressingly in a sea of substantial losses.

Starting with the first show in Hutchinson, Kansas, René Simon became the acknowledged star, ably supported by René Barrier, while Seymour and Frisbie alternately wrecked and fretted over their already beat-up biplanes. Fierce winds totally wiped out the second day of their initial three-day show in the Sunshine State. But "Fool Flyer" Simon lived up to his name by taking off in a gale on opening day and chasing a spectator down the field while fans from Hutchinson, Salina, Wichita, Mcpherson, Great Bend, and Larned screamed their approval and Simon himself chortled, in his exuberantly personal style, "Ze man, I make heem run!"

At their next stop, in Pueblo, Colorado, the winds continued so savagely that the Pueblo Commerce Club refused to hand over any of the $21,000 guarantee money unless the troupe flew on at least two of their three scheduled days. Barrier, Frisbie, and Seymour flatly refused to take off on the last day and again it was the "Fool Flyer" who came to the rescue. On opening day Easter Sunday the fearless Simon flew into a gale while hundreds of churchgoers plus some 6,500 at the field watched in a mixture of fascination and horror as he almost overturned and bounced "like a cork on a millpond" at 1,600 feet. Terrified for his friend's safety and "on the verge of tears," Barrier raced to the plane when Simon landed and in a very French show of concern embraced him and "planted a kiss on his forehead." Three hours later Simon insisted on flying again in conditions an aviation reporter said made a cyclone look like a mild breeze. This time he landed so heavily his plane bounced 20 feet into the air, breaking the struts of the landing gear. Simon called it "ver' good fun" but Barrier said nothing but luck had saved his friend's life.

On the third day, many of the close to 12,000 spectators, certain he had been injured, left their seats and raced outside to where Simon had been forced down. But before they could reach him he took off again, flying over their heads and circling the enclosure before landing safely just outside the fairground.

Although Barrier, the "Cloud Kisser," tended to be more cautious than Simon, he too flew in dangerous weather, often simultaneously with his friend, the two stunting and competing together. Considered by some to be the "more skillful and graceful" of the two, Barrier astonished a crowd in Omaha, Nebraska, by taking off in a near hurricane that only moments earlier had almost blown away the tent hangar. As one newsman reported, after watching him "careening from side to side" like "a feather in the blast of an electric fan," the crowd heaved a "sigh of relief" when the Frenchman "wobbled to the ground directly in front of the appalled multitude with a perfect landing."

During the first six weeks of the tour rain and gale winds blasted across the Midwestern plain. Crowds were small and invariably far more people watched from outside the gates than in, thus saving themselves the usual fifty cents admission. At Topeka, Kansas, some 5,000 customers went home disgusted two days in a row, their money refunded, as storms wiped out the entire scheduled program. In St. Joseph, Missouri, manager Young, counting 500 people in the grandstand but 30 times that number just outside, again repaid the ticketholders and canceled the day's show, saying, "I will not risk the lives of any of my men when the attendance is so small."

There was the occasional respite, such as in Sioux City, when Simon landed after flying at 3,500 feet over the Iowa–Nebraska–Colorado tristate area to be greeted by an embrace, a kiss, and a rose from the famed French actress Sarah Bernhardt, who then took Simon and Barrier as her guests to her performance that evening as "Camille."

Such moments were few, however, and more often the general tone of the tour was one of futility, failure, and frustration. Flying in dangerous weather simply to pacify audiences growing ornery from hours of waiting, Simon demolished a Blériot at St. Joseph and Barrier crashed his biplane in Newton, smashing its wing. Also at St. Joseph the sheriff's son punched Frisbie in the nose as the flyer was trying to help police stop crowds from the new Metropolitan Golf Club from crossing the flying field to the grandstand. That night the fighting "Irishman" from Rochester, probably far from sober, and company transport manager Charles Davis were arrested when they refused to leave a Chinese restaurant after a brawl with the waiter.

Neither Frisbie nor Seymour had been of much help to their two French colleagues. The planes each had brought with them to the International Aviators were now unserviceable. Seymour's was not much to begin with since he had signed on primarily to race his Fiat automobile against the other flyers. And Frisbie gave up totally on his Rochester biplane after it dropped into a hole in Newton. He finally settled for a replacement aircraft built by Omaha brothers Charles and Gus Baysdorfer. In a deal worked out by Young, Frisbie could use their plane, for which Young would provide a 50-hp Gnôme engine, and hire the two Omaha men as mechanics with a possibility of taking them on eventually as Moisant pilots.

Scheduled to join his flyers in Des Moines, Alfred instead spent six days in Chicago, where he entered Simon, Barrier, Frisbie, Seymour, and Johnstone in an air meet scheduled for August. Then he went to Detroit to book another show there before the one in Chicago. While Alfred continued on the road negotiating booking after booking, his International Aviators plodded on to six more cities, struggling as best they could to fulfill their earlier commitments.

But it was becoming increasingly apparent that they all needed a rest and their planes needed a complete overhaul. During a three-day show in Ottumwa, Iowa, Frisbie made a forced landing when the rudder controls broke in his new Baysdorfer. The next day winds forced Simon down into a cornfield, for which he was hauled into court and forced to pay farmer John Manuel $25 for tearing up his crop.

The next shows were equally punishing. In Davenport, Barrier was badly shaken up and smashed his propeller by crashing into the gravestone of Maud A., a famous racehorse who died at the same track. Then company chauffeur René Porsch was fined $10 plus costs for speeding, frightening a horse, and causing a woman to be thrown from her carriage. In a three-day show at Galesburg, Illinois, Frisbie was still unable to get his biplane off the ground (this time it was motor trouble). Flying in his place, Barrier went up in his monoplane and was quickly forced down into another cornfield.

As the tour continued, press coverage became increasingly critical. After the aviators opened at Terre Haute, Indiana, a local newspaper came out with one of the most unflattering articles to date. It said the Moisant flyers spent most of their time "fuss[ing] around with [their] planes until spectators began to wonder if the first aviation meet in Terre Haute was a joke," and "not until then did the 'World's Greatest Aviators' aviate." Conceding that "even a daredevil cannot be expected to fly in the face of a gale that means certain death," the paper said it still appeared to the crowd, who demanded its money back, that there was "an unnecessary amount of stalling." When, in one of only a few brief flights of the entire day, Frisbie made a short flight into town and back, the paper quoted "one disgruntled viewer as commenting: 'Huh! If I'd known he's goin' t' fly downtown, I wouldn't have come out!'"

Troubles only escalated during the last two stops of the tour. At Logansport, Indiana, a rainstorm forced cancellation of all flights and badly damaged the wings of the planes. With a show scheduled for the next day in Marion, Indiana, Young ordered new wings to be sent from Detroit to Marion by express that morning. The wings arrived too late in the afternoon for any flights that day, and on the next day more wind and rain made flying impossible. Outraged ticketholders called in the law. The sheriff arrested Young, Simon, Barrier, and Frisbie and attached the company's planes until Young deposited $528.90 in the local bank to repay all ticketholders.

One newspaper editorial accused the airmen of simply not bothering to attach the wings the first day and needlessly canceling flights the next. It concluded, "The Moisant International Aviators have been branded as a company of men out to obtain money through fraud." Another Indiana paper echoed the complaint, reporting that "a number of cities in the northern part of the state have contracted with the aviators and have experienced considerable trouble with the men. In a number of cases they disappointed large crowds by not giving exhibitions as advertised."

The weary pilots were glad to see the end of Ohio when they entrained for Detroit for the Collegiate Aviation meet at the Michigan State fairgrounds from June 29 through July 4. As always, Alfred's advance publicity and press releases were larded with promises, and attendance was expected to be high. Press reports said at least eight institutions had reserved tickets—including 5,000 from the Aero Club of the University of Michigan and 3,500 from the Michigan Agricultural College—while delegations were also expected from "every college within 500 miles of Detroit." Many no doubt would be responding to Alfred's promise that at least two of his men would give flying instructions to any student interested, for which reason he had ordered Johnstone to leave the flying school on Long Island and join the troupe in Michigan. Alfred's contract flatly guaranteed appearances by Johnstone, as well as Simon, Barrier, Seymour, and Frisbie. Alfred further spurred interest by suggesting he might move his factory and school from New York to Michigan because land on Long Island was so expensive. And he said that for $10,000 two of his planes would fly to Grand Rapids to pick up a furniture order there and fly it back to Detroit as the first commercial air freight into that city.

The second night of the meet Detroit businessman E. Leroy Pelletier hosted Moisant and his aviators to a dinner at the Hotel Pontchartrain. Places were laid for sixteen but there were only fifteen chairs and at the empty seat a bouquet of blood red carnations. "It's just six months ago today," Johnstone murmured to Barrier as Alfred glanced at the empty setting and bowed his head in silence. After an awkward pause, the dinner resumed with Alfred entering a long discussion of the wonders of aviation and predicting that in another six months he himself would be a passenger on a plane that would cross the Atlantic. But for the guests of honor it was in fact a sad reunion, marking the first time they had all dined together since their leader, Alfred's brother John, plunged to his death in New Orleans.

During the entire meet Alfred never stopped talking about the future of aviation, his brother, his school, and his factory. While he talked, his pilots flew, all of them eager to impress officials of the Chicago Aero Club who would be sponsoring another international air show in Detroit on August 12–20.

Despite, and perhaps even because of the customary accidents and crashes (Simon broke the wheel of his Blériot and Johnstone fell 30 feet, slamming down right in front of the grand-stand), Detroit showed its approval of the Moisant International Aviators with frequent bursts of enthusiastic applause. And the Chicago Aero Club was more than satisfied with what they regarded as a preview of their own show in August.

But, as one newspaper reported, while "from the standpoint of flying," the Moisant air show was a success, "from the financial end it was a tremendous loss."

Despite their pretense of affluence the Detroit promoters were actually heavily in debt and operating on a shoestring. On the third day of the meet two armed men burst into the cashier's office beneath the grandstand and seized concession and gate receipts of $1,713. Only after they struggled with the men and called the police for help did the staff realize that the intruders were not robbers but deputy sheriffs serving a writ of attachment for an unpaid advertising bill of $785.

Despite its comic overtones the incident had unfortunate repercussions for Moisant. When the deputies insisted on holding the money to cover expected legal fees and payment of possible debt claims to come, Alfred sued them for $2,500 on the grounds that the writ of attachment was sworn against the promoters but the money that was seized belonged to him.

A Detroit newspaper reported that, although his contract entitled him to the first $12,000 of gate receipts, Moisant eventually received only $3,000, thus losing the greater part of his investment plus another $5,000 the paper said he had advanced the promoters as start-up money. Alfred denied having made any such advance but did admit that the Detroit meet had been a financial failure, costing him "upwards of $20,000."

When the meet ended, Simon, Barrier, and Frisbie went on to New York to finish shows Alfred had booked for them in Rochester, Elmira, and Troy. But the results there were simply more of the same. Thousands watched from outside the enclosures. Only a few hundred paid for tickets.

After seven months on the road, the Moisant International Aviators were hailed by a national aviation weekly on the cover of a special Moisant edition as "The World's Greatest Aggregation of Airmen." But the cost of that claim was now reaching into thousands and thousands of dollars, more than even Don Alfredo himself could afford to lose.

17

BIG PLANS AND BAD LUCK

By the summer of 1911 Alfred Moisant claimed the 10-month venture into the financial wilderness of aviation had cost him $200,000. The air circus had brought the Moisant name widespread recognition but the shows lost money. The aviation school had five hangars, not the fifty he had promised. So far only five students had graduated with another six currently enrolled, their combined tuition fees totaling $8,250, less than the amount he lost at the Detroit air meet. A businessman less zealous about aviation would have cut his losses and run. But Alfred had become as reckless with capital as his late brother had been with airplanes, so he decided to expand his company by raising even more money.

In July he increased the capitalization of the Moisant International Aviators, Inc., from $250,000 to $1,000,000, bringing the air circus, the school, and the factory under one corporate umbrella. To raise the money the company went public, issuing $500,000 in preferred 7 percent cumulative stock at $10 a share. (With each share of preferred subscribers received a half-share of common.) The company directorate was increased from three to seven with Alfred as president and treasurer and Wupperman as secretary and general manager.

In August Alfred placed an entire page of advertising in *Aero* magazine boasting that his recordbreaking aviators used planes built in his own factory and inviting fair managers and aviation meet promoters to engage any or all of them "to appear ANY- WHERE in the WHOLE WIDE WORLD." He listed them all: veterans Garros, "2d Prize Winner in European Circuit Racers"; Simon, "The 'Fool Flyer'"; Barrier, "A Wonder"; Johnstone, "The Record Breaker"; Audemars, "The Marvelous"; Frisbie, "of United States"; de Murias, "of Cuba"; Houpert, "instructor by arrange- ment with Moisant Aviation School"; newcomer Abram Raygor- odsky "of Russia"; and "Miss Harriet Quimby of U.S.A. (A Rec- ord Breaker). The ONLY WOMAN LICENSED PILOT IN AMERICA."

The advertisements also offered students exclusive use of a 1,200-acre field "level as a billiard table. . . . Ten Square Miles of Hempstead Plains for Flying" unimpeded by trees, hills, or electric wires. Another advertisement detailed the new stock of- fering, explaining that although the Moisant factory at 276- 278-280 Ninth Avenue, Manhattan, had built sixteen planes in three months, it was currently behind in orders, so more funds were now needed to obtain a larger factory capable of produc- ing 500 airplanes a year. Only the first of many such notices purchased over the next few months, Alfred's ad said expansion was necessary because "we mean to keep our position as THE FOREMOST AEROPLANE MANUFACTURERS IN AMERICA." (He did expand a month later, buying an abandoned Queens Boulevard building on two acres of land in Winfield, Long Island, origi- nally built in 1849 as the first Singer sewing machine factory.)

Pending a response to his advertisements, Alfred was forced to rely on his existing assets, namely his aviators. He knew they were fed up with flying for impatient audiences and paltry prizes in the United States when tantalizing purses totaling $1 million in 1911 alone were ripe for the plucking in Europe. The largest U.S. prize—$50,000 from William Randolph Hearst for a flight across the continent—held little incentive when set against the available European trophies of $80,000 for Paris to Rome, $85,000 for Paris-Brussels-London and back, and $100,000 for a cross-country race over Russia.

To placate his restive crew he announced a new Moisant policy of competition for prize money rather than exhibition flights for box office guarantees. As a first step he had already sent Garros and Audemars to Europe to compete in races from Paris to Rome, to Madrid, and to London, he said, adding that if no cross-country prizes were posted for the United States by the close of the Chicago international air meet on August 20 he would send Barrier and Simon to Europe also to vie for the $500,000 prize money still to be won.

Alfred brought Audemars back from Europe and sent him to Chicago for the international air meet along with Raygorodsky, Simon, Barrier, Frisbie, and Johnstone, posting a bond of $1,000 for each pilot. Their equipment included eight monoplanes, insured for $49,000, two biplanes insured for $10,000, and parts worth $9,200.

Chicago clearly was "aviation mad," the *Chicago Daily Tribune* said when thousands of persons lined Michigan Avenue and the Van Buren Street viaduct before noon and traffic made Grant Park almost impassable on opening day. Seventy thousand people filled the Aviation Field grandstand while tens of thousands lined the entire lake front or stood on rooftops overlooking the mile-and-a-half course along the shore of Lake Michigan. Pennants flew from 70-foot-high pylons while below them wealthy Chicago women left their expensive box seats to stroll along the promenade clad in colorful frocks and wearing their "aviation hats." These were the standard inverted spittoons of the era covered with flowers, feathers, and ribbons but with veils over the entire hat and face to protect against sun and rain.

Little happened that first day to advance Alfred's hope of raising the Moisant name right up there alongside those of Wright and Curtiss. Simon's plane was wrecked before it left the ground when Wright pilot Frank Coffyn aborted a takeoff and smashed into it. After Coffyn failed to apologize, Simon protested to the committee, accusing him of illegally turning right, a violation of meet flying rules, when by turning left he could have avoided the collision. That same afternoon Johnstone, against Alfred's orders, insisted on flying because his parents, Dr. and Mrs. A. R. Johnstone of Chicago, had never seen him fly and were in the grandstand. Johnstone himself had arrived only that morning from Long Island where, two weeks earlier, he had broken distance and sustained-speed records with a flight of 216 miles in four hours and two minutes in a Moisant monoplane. This time, with his parents watching, Johnstone barely left the ground before his engine stopped and he crashed into a tree. He escaped injury but the plane was demolished.

The next day Simon performed a spectacular flyover of the audience but was fined $25 by the judge for "risking his own neck and the lives of spectators flying too low over the grandstand." Then Frisbie, by now dubbed "the world's champion aeroplane wrecker," narrowly missed hitting a bronze statue of the goddess Diana atop the tower of a lakefront building and was caught by a gust of wind that overturned his plane in midair. Attempting to adjust the steering control for a glide down, his hands became entangled in the wires and he suffered severe cuts to both hands and arms before he made a successful landing.

The plane Frisbie was flying was the one built by Charles and Gus Baysdorfer of Omaha although the brothers had yet to be paid for their mechanics' services. While Charles and Gus were in Chicago Gus received a letter from their older brother Otto in Omaha saying he was "sorry to see your company don't pay as your agreement." Otto advised Gus to "call it square" by taking possession of the Gnôme motor Young had installed.

On the third day of the meet Simon, who had been having trouble with his engine all day, was flying over the water about a mile from shore when his motor shut down. He glided down to the lake surface and was sitting cross-legged on the wing, flicking drops of water from his natty tan shoes, when Curtiss flyer Hugh Robinson taxied up in his hydroplane. "Can I give you any help, old sport?" Robinson asked. "Bonjour, Monsieur," Simon replied, pointing to a launch at the lakeside, "I'm all right, thank you kindly. They'll catch me." But Simon eventually accepted Robinson's offer to help him start his motor, then took off briefly, only to fall again. Guards in the launch rushed to the overturned plane and towed it to shore with Simon perched nonchalantly on the fuselage smoking a cigarette.

On the fourth day of the meet Matilde, who had just arrived from Long Island after passing her licensing tests two days earlier, went with Alfred to the Moisant hangar. There, with Simon, Frisbie, and the wives of Frisbie and Johnstone, they watched Johnstone who had been aloft for almost four hours in an effort to log time for an endurance prize. As Johnstone flew over Lake Michigan about a mile from shore Alfred saw his plane halt in midair, then tip and plunge down, its wings crumpled back against the fuselage. Alfred looked at Mrs. Johnstone, who stood speechless for a moment, her face a mirror of fear. When the crowd began to run toward shore, Johnstone's wife, her voice quivering as she fought down hysteria, said, "Let's go. I'll bet he's good and wet."

Hydroplane pilot Robinson, who had helped Simon just the day before, was flying nearby and witnessed the accident. He saw Johnstone flying at about 1,000 feet when the engine of his Moisant monoplane exploded and dropped through the fuselage, followed by plane and pilot all hurtling down into the water. He rushed to the spot where a number of small boats were headed but Johnstone was trapped in the wreckage for 10 minutes before a boat reached him and was so entangled in the debris that rescuers were unable to free him until the Harbor Police arrived after another 10 minutes. A doctor on board tried to revive him on the way back to shore but Johnstone was dead.

Robinson hurried ashore and ran to Mrs. Johnstone. Afraid to tell her the truth, he mumbled, "He's all right. They have a boat out there to get him." The others stood silent as Johnstone's wife looked from face to face until someone suggested she go back to the hotel to get dry clothing for her husband. Then the young woman cried out, "Oh, he isn't all right! He isn't and you won't tell me!" Hysterical with grief she was taken to the hotel.

Taking exception to Robinson's report that Johnstone's engine exploded, Alfred later claimed the pilot had simply misjudged his fuel supply and run out of gas. He also said he had tried to ground him that day because Johnstone had been losing his nerve for some time. Moisant may have been trying to divert attention from the frequent failure of his company's Gnôme engines during the meet. His allegation about Johnstone's loss of nerve does not jibe with the pilot's insistence on flying for his parents the day before even though Alfred had forbidden it.

The Chicago meet was declared a success with more than 2 million witnessing part or all of it, never less than 300,000 on any one day. But most of them watched from outside the enclosure, making the meet a financial failure that cost its organizers "some fifty or sixty thousands of dollars" which one aviation expert said "they cheerfully paid, satisfied they had furthered the education of their fellow-citizens and helped to maintain the speed of mechanical flight's uninterrupted progress."

How cheerful the organizers, who included 250 of the city's most prominent residents, were is open to question. But clearly Alfred Moisant had nothing to be cheerful about. The Chicago meet had failed to enhance his prestige as a rival of Curtiss and the Wrights. Seven of his eight aircraft had crashed one or more times, each one costing from $500 to $3,000 for repairs. Only three of his men—Simon, Frisbie, and Johnstone—had won any prize money. And one of his best men, Barrier, never flew at all. Ailing ever since the Detroit meet in July, he was confined to his hotel room almost the entire time with a severe bronchial infection.

Not only ill, but homesick and tired of air-circus flying as well, Barrier told Alfred he was taking his plane and going back to France. But Alfred refused to turn over the plane, claiming it had been given to Barrier in lieu of a $4,000 payment for the last three months of his contract. Pointing out that Barrier's contract didn't expire until September 20, Alfred told Barrier to either stay with the circus until then or go back to France without the plane. The Frenchman chose to go home, leaving the plane and the Moisant International Aviators.

Alfred's best flyer, René Simon, was another homesick Frenchman whose contract also expired September 20. Although agreeing to complete his contract, Simon left no doubt that he, too, would be glad to leave both Moisant and the United States. He said he was offended by an American public that granted the same status to aviators as they did to circus clowns. In France, he said, 90 percent of all pilots were college graduates and members of the best society. But, he complained, "in ten months here I can remember just six times I have been invited to the homes of nice people. We were invited to hotels and banquets where we were stared at."

Of the remaining Europeans, Garros was still in France and Audemars went back to Europe as soon as the Chicago meet ended. Alfred's advertising and publicity continued to claim that both men would be rejoining his troupe, but it was clear neither one had any intention of doing so.

The Moisant International Aviators, handpicked by John Moisant and only recently hailed by *Aero* magazine as "The World's Greatest Aggregation of Airmen," was breaking up. So, too, was the original basic structure of the brothers' foray into aviation with Alfred in charge of finances and John supervising the aviators and design. Something would obviously have to be done.

18
RESIGNING, REGROUPING, REPLACING

From the first day of the first air show by his pilots at Richmond Alfred Moisant remained a devotee of the flying exhibition tour. Refusing to call it an air circus, he would not abandon what he considered his chief means of marketing his aircraft. Neither the accidents suffered by his flyers at the Chicago meet nor their subsequent disbandment changed his mind.

When the Detroit show ended he took his last two pilots, Simon and Frisbie, on the road again in another exhibition tour. Although Simon's contract would expire in less than a month and Frisbie was rumored to be seeking other employment, Alfred had already booked them for six stops, the first three in the Illinois towns of Joliet, Freeport, and Kankakee.

Alfred planned to accompany them as far as Kankakee, where a warm welcome had been promised him by his cousin, city alderman S. E. Moisant, who had come to Chicago to see him. With only two planes and a small support group the hitherto-free-spending Alfred attempted to economize by stripping down to two railroad cars, one freight and one Pullman, in place of his former seven. Riding in the Pullman were Alfred, Matilde, Young, Simon, Frisbie with his wife and two children, Charles

Baysdorfer and his wife, and chief mechanic Charles Davis and the maintenance crew.

In Joliet the first show immediately experienced traditional air-circus difficulties. The park was too small for safe flying and the crowd either overran the field or stood outside it to avoid paying for tickets. Simon tried to herd the people off the field by flying directly at them and skimming over their heads. But not until Young told meet officials they would have to assume all responsibility for deaths or injuries was the field cleared.

After the second of their two days in Joliet, John Frisbie boarded the night train for Norton, Kansas, with his wife and two children. His only notice to Alfred was a telegram telling him to look for a substitute because Frisbie was ill with typhoid fever. Frisbie was not ill. He had arranged a series of one-man flights at the Norton County Fair without Alfred's knowledge.

Left without a man to fly the Baysdorfer plane at their next stop in Freeport, Alfred sent to Chicago for a local flyer, Fred Heegel, to replace the defecting Frisbie. The first time Heegel took off he lost control and demolished the aircraft, escaping serious injury himself but injuring six others as his plane fell into the crowd. The next day Baysdorfer sold the broken bits of his plane for 10 cents a piece, the eager buyers described by one observer as gathering "like vultures over a dead animal." The sale netted $15.00 for the plane that Baysdorfer and his brother Gus had worked on for two years.

While Baysdorfer was selling the wreckage of one aircraft in Freeport, Frisbie was demolishing another, a Curtiss biplane, at Norton. After falling 40 feet in it, bruised but not seriously injured, Frisbie decided the machine could not be sufficiently repaired to withstand another flight. But when he announced this the following day angry demonstrators accused him of cowardice and taunted him with cries of "fakir" until he finally agreed to fly. After ascending to 100 feet the aircraft tipped and Frisbie appeared to lose control. Spectators saw him fight to right the machine before one of its wings smashed into the side of a barn at the edge of the field. The plane plowed into the ground, crushing Frisbie to death in the heavy wreckage. That night Mrs. Frisbie, who with her daughter and son witnessed the crash, bitterly denounced the spectators for "forcing her husband to make the flight with a disabled machine." In Indiana, meanwhile, Alfred's Chicago representative, Lt. J. P. Anderson, told newsmen that Frisbie "was not flying the Baysdorfer machine in which he was to give an exhibition here but . . . a Curtiss machine. Nor was he flying under the auspices of the Moisant aviators."

To publicize the shows at the Kankakee fair on September 4 and 5 Alfred sent Albert LeVino ahead from Chicago. Within two weeks LeVino placed eight long front-page stories in the leading local daily stressing two themes. The first was the return of Alfred, the hometown boy who had become a millionaire aviation backer, and his pilot-sister, Matilde. The second was the participation of two brilliant pilots, Simon and Frisbie. Now, without either Frisbie or the Baysdorfer plane, Alfred promised to provide an internationally known replacement for Frisbie but none ever showed.

Left to carry on alone, René Simon entranced audiences of between 20,000 and 30,000 each day, capping his aerobatics with the very same spectator-skimming dives that cost him a fine of $25 at Chicago for "endangering lives." As compensation for Frisbie's absence the show was extended from two to four days of what the press generally described as the most successful performances ever given by any or all of the Moisant flyers.

Before returning to New York with Matilde, Alfred sent Simon and Charles Baysdorfer and their wives along with Davis and his crew to the next stop in South Bend, Indiana. This time Simon's Moisant Blériot was the sole winged occupant of the freight car. Alfred had also promised to send Quimby to fly with Simon as a second pilot but she declined. Although she said she could not leave her magazine work, she may have refused after hearing what financial failures most of the Moisant shows had been. The phenomenal attendance at Kankakee could be accounted for by the fact that Alfred's parents had lived there and Alfred himself had worked there for his uncle. But at South Bend gate returns plunged again. Admissions for the three days did not reach $1,000 and everyone lost money. The promoters and city merchants had to dig in their own pockets to make up the box-office deficit and pay Simon the $1,500 they had guaranteed, and even that did not cover the flyer's expenses.

From South Bend Simon with the Moisant crew went 500 miles to Menominee, Wisconsin, then back to the Illinois towns of Danville and Watseka, giving shows on his own. At the end of September Alfred sent a biplane pilot, Abram Raygorodsky, to fly a new plane Baysdorfer had put together, bit by bit, along the way. It was finished and operable when the group reached Danville on September 26. But by that time the weather was so bad that neither Raygorodsky nor Baysdorfer dared fly, leaving "Fool Flyer" Simon once again to perform on his own.

Simon stayed with the group until September 28, eight days after his contract with Alfred expired. Rumors that he might be persuaded to join a new assembly of Moisant pilots at $1,000 a week ended on October 12 when he boarded the French liner *La Lorraine* for France. He would never return, he said, to be classed with circus clowns.

Alfred soon learned that Simon was irreplaceable after he sent Jesse Seligman to give a three-day show in Canton, Ohio, in late September. The 22-year-old New York banker's son, who had been licensed just five days earlier after completing his training at the Moisant school, made a miserable showing on all three days. On the first he was forced to land after his motor stopped during his one and only flight. On the second day he didn't fly at all after several bolts that had fallen out of his aircraft could not be replaced in time. And on the third day his motor gave out once again. Dropping suddenly from an elevation of 100 feet, Seligman's plane slammed into a fence. Unhurt but humiliated, the dazed rookie said, "That's the worst luck I ever had in my life. That was my second fall. The machine worked terribly. It's a wonder I didn't kill somebody!" He left for New York the same night, his shattered aircraft following him on a freight car the next morning.

With no one to fly for him Alfred was forced to abandon the exhibition circuit and return to New York to concentrate on selling stock in his reorganized company, increasing his aircraft production, and expanding his school. He had gained his first military student in late summer, Capt. George Mackay of Company A, Signal Corps, Michigan National Guard. That fall Mackay and his thirteen fellow students continued their lessons at the old Mineola field, adjacent to the land Alfred had leased at Hempstead Plains. While they used rented hangars and Albert Triaca's shop for repairs at Mineola, Alfred went right on telling the press they would soon move to the new field with its five concrete hangars (still unfinished). Either ignoring or forgetting his earlier announcement that he would build a new production plant at the field, he said that the Hempstead Plains Aviation Company, now a subsidiary of the Moisant International Aviators, would soon move to a new factory in Long Island City. In a later announcement he changed this to Bridgeport, Connecticut, but no move was made.

All this talk without action may have been the real reason Christopher J. Lake resigned from the board of directors. "I thought I had better be out than in it," Lake said, adding he was unwilling to make any statement that would reflect on the company. But it is likely that Lake, himself the vice-president of a successful boat-building firm, had lost faith in the future of Alfred's new company.

In his pursuit of aircraft buyers, Alfred even changed his former stance that monoplanes were superior to biplanes and commissioned Albert Triaca and designer Philip Wilcox to build a passenger-carrying biplane for him in Triaca's workshop. An illustrated magazine article described the plane as similar in size and dimensions to the Henry Farman Michelin Cup type, its wooden frame covered with Goodyear fabric "tacked to the ribs and bottom." The article noted that the center of the lower wing "looks a little odd, having a hole cut . . . just ahead of the rear spar." The hole was made to fit the Blériot Gnôme engine Alfred favored because Gnôme engines for biplanes were not yet in production. Lest the pilot worry about safety, the magazine further noted that the plane's center section was trussed with double wire, and wires near the propeller and engine were "wrapped with string to keep them from flying into the propeller" if they happened to break!

In spite of these enticements buyers did not rush to purchase the new plane nor did they seem eager for shares in Alfred's reorganized company. Unable to move to Hempstead Plains until the flying field was prepared and the hangars completed, Alfred found himself stymied, unable to expand either his school or his aircraft production, until help suddenly arrived from an unexpected source—his sister Matilde and her friend Harriet Quimby—and in the form he loved best, exhibition flying.

The previously retiring Matilde had taken to flying with the same fervor as her brother John, making flights almost daily. On one occasion when she was flying for some visiting friends from El Salvador her aerobatics were so impressive that five visiting Arabs sent an emissary to the hangar to ask her about lessons and the availability of planes. Frequently interviewed by feature writers, Matilde was becoming a feminist in matters of aviation, criticizing men flyers who doubted that women could set records. Like Quimby, she claimed to disapprove of aerobatic stunting for women but within weeks of receiving her license she was flying with the same daring as her brother John.

Harriet backed Matilde's claims, maintaining that women were "born to the sport" because of their innate sanity and instinct, which she called basic principles of flight. Ascribing most air fatalities to recklessness, overconfidence, or neglect, she held that a woman's sanity led to a careful examination of one's plane before leaving the ground, while once in the air her instinct would protect her.

Quimby's views were soon seconded by the possibly fictitious Professor Rudolf Hensingmuller of the University of Vienna. In a feature newspaper article titled "WHY A WOMAN CAN RUN AN AIRSHIP BETTER THAN A MAN," the professor listed eight reasons for female superiority. First, the professor wrote, comes the fact that a woman sees through "her full retina." Presumably this skill, derived from "enforced modesty and flirting," gave her wider peripheral vision than men. Second, a woman "has scattered attention more than concentration," which is "invaluable to the aviator who must notice many things at once." The professor further wrote that because women were less affected by altitude than men, reacted more quickly to atmospheric changes, and required less oxygen to breathe, they were therefore "the natural aviators, the cautious, the conservative, the primitive [who] will step in and rule" the air.

It is difficult to determine who was the more demeaning, the verbose Professor Hensingmuller or the British air star Claude Grahame-White who wrote in rebuttal, "I have taught many women to fly and I regret it. The air is no place for women."

Of the two women, Harriet was the first to make an exhibition flight, on September 2 at the Richmond County agricultural fair on Staten Island. She arrived in Alfred's big yellow limousine accompanied by Alfred, Matilde, and aviators Capt. Tom Baldwin and Lee Hammond. Clad in her purple-satin flying suit with the hood up to protect her face from the sun and the sharp winds outside, she sat quietly in the car. The wind died down just as she left the car, removed her long coat, and climbed into the seat of her Moisant monoplane.

Once airborne she flew a circuit over the island's meadowland and the Narrows, pushing the satin hood back from her face and smiling and waving at some 15,000 people below as she passed over them. The crowd "went wild," swarming onto the field until traffic police had to clear a place on the grass for her landing, which was a poor one. First diving from 200 feet she pulled up sharply, only to drop again to the ground where she bumped along to a stop. Just as the noise of Garros's engine had once interrupted a speech by President Taft, the roar of Quimby's motor now quelled one being given by governor of New York Woodrow Wilson, who was launching his presidential campaign at the fair. Wilson "could not possibly hold the attention of his audience until [the sound of Miss Quimby's motor] . . . had faded in the distance."

Two days later Quimby made a night flight, ascending with the rising moon to circle the racetrack four times while 10,000 grandstand spectators—not to mention her parents in Alfred's car—watched anxiously. Again people ran onto the field and

Quimby dived at them, feinting right and left to clear a space before making another rough landing that bounced her 10 feet into the air before her plane rolled to a stop just a few feet short of a tall fence. As Quimby jumped from the plane she was mobbed by people trying to shake her hand and, "wriggling and squirming and twisting," was passed from one group to another before Alfred's chauffeur drove through to rescue her. In just seven minutes in the air on two different days, Quimby had completed her first contract as a professional pilot, earning $1,500, twice the annual salary of an unskilled laborer.

A few days later Harriet and Matilde took off together from the Moisant field in a heavy ground fog while a nervous Louise watched them head north toward the Meadowbrook Hunt Club. During that flight Matilde cruised for much of the time at 1,200 feet. She was practicing to break the women's altitude record, which she did on September 15 when she ascended to 2,500 feet. Her only rival, Hélène Dutrieu of France, had achieved 2,000 feet but no more.

That fall both Matilde and Harriet were getting nationwide newspaper coverage, more effective publicity than Alfred had ever achieved with his countless press releases. Hastening to exploit their fame, Alfred enrolled them in the first major air meet offering contests for women, to be held September 23 through October 1 at Long Island's Nassau Boulevard airfield. In his sister and her friend, Alfred once more glimpsed promise of the success that so far had eluded him.

19
RISING STARS

The Nassau meet was the first in America to include competitions for women, an innovation that attracted nationwide interest from the press. The fact that four women were on hand when the meet began, Americans Matilde Moisant, Harriet Quimby, and Blanche Stuart Scott, and famous French flyer Hélène Dutrieu, raised interest in the air show to a level beyond even Alfred Moisant's aspirations. The publicity was also welcomed by the meet's organizers, the Aero Clubs of New York and America, who hoped to make Nassau Boulevard the major flying field for that part of the country, serving both as the eastern terminus of all cross-country flights and the official center for official tests and record-setting.

The committee of arrangements was headed by wealthy aviation enthusiast Timothy L. Woodruff, one of the aviation aficionados just beginning to crop up around the country and, like Chicago's Harold McCormick, willing to back aviation with "real money" as well as enthusiasm. Woodruff, a one-time New York State lieutenant-governor, put up most of the money for the Nassau meet, which provided a seating capacity for 8,000 (excluding 160 special boxes) and parking space for 10,000 automobiles.

161

On opening day, Saturday, September 23, 15,000 people paid from fifty cents to two dollars to see some fifty planes and thirty-five pilots from England, France, Russia, and the United States. At first, however, a good number of the audience seemed to be more interested in one of their fellow spectators than in the planes. The presence of Gaby Deslys, beautiful French dancer and mistress of the former king of Portugal, was so disturbing she had to be "removed from the grandstand and hurried off" after parading the length of the field in a skin-tight purple sheath and a skirt slit to the knees.

That same day five aviators flying as air scouts spent an hour searching for twenty U.S. infantrymen who had been sent into hiding. The search, one of a number of such specially staged demonstrations catering to and indicative of the growing interest of the military, was fruitless.

The day also marked the first air mail delivery in the United States when Earle L. Ovington flew five miles from Nassau Boulevard field to Garden City, New York, clutching a 75-pound bag of letters and postcards between his knees and dropping it to a post office official on the ground. Another 100 pounds of mail traveled the same route less dramatically by car although it also bore the postmark, "Aerial Station No. 1, Aerial Special Service," in honor of the occasion.

Watching these air-show events from the Moisant hangar were Ferdinand de Murias, the Cuban who had been licensed from the Moisant school, René Simon, Matilde, and Harriet. In spite of a 24-MPH wind, Harriet was the first of the four woman aviators to offer to fly. But a moment after she climbed aboard her plane, Dr. Henry W. Walden, completing a cross-country flight, attempted to undercut a third plane flown by Lee Hammond. Walden hit the ground tail first, no more than 12 feet from Harriet, and somersaulted nearly into her lap but emerged unhurt. Unfazed by the incident, Harriet took off and circled the field several times. By now she had established her image as the beautiful woman clad in purple and, her hood thrown back, she waved and smiled down at her cheering admirers in the stands below. Shortly after, Matilde also took off and entertained the crowd by flying with her friend. But she refused to race with her because she was adamantly opposed to flying for a cash prize.

On Sunday, the second day of the meet, all four women were listed in the program as contestants in the women's events. But only one actually participated. Blanche Scott was ruled ineligible because she did not yet have a flying license, which she had intended to try for during the meet. Quimby, like the Wright brothers, refused to fly on Sundays. And, most disappointing of all for the record crowd and the promoters, was the absence of Hélène Dutrieu, who already held three world records for women—distance, time in flight, and altitude with a passenger. The Frenchwoman had arrived in the United States on the French liner *La Provence* only the day before, too late to have the plane designed for her by Henry Farman assembled in time for the day's events.

Of the four highly publicized women, this left Matilde as the one to save the day for promoter Woodruff. Although she would not fly for money she had no objection to flying on Sundays. And, as the sole contestant in the women's altitude contest, she took off in her 50-hp Moisant monoplane, winning the applause of the crowd and the bronze Rodman Wanamaker trophy for ascending to 1,200 feet.

Woodruff soon found he faced even worse problems than the possibility of losing all his feminine flying stars. Episcopal bishop of Long Island Frederick Burgess and other ecclesiastical dignitaries called on Nassau County sheriff Charles F. De Mott to stop all Sunday flights, claiming they violated a law banning all sports events for profit on the Sabbath. Facing the possibility of arrest, the promoter managed to conciliate the sheriff temporarily by announcing that no prize money would be given that day and even canceling a scheduled race between an automobile and an airplane. Despite the protest the meet continued with all entered flyers participating, each one secretly convinced the prize money would reach him some way or other.

Woodruff had been counting on Dutrieu to be the big draw on Monday, which had been especially set aside for competition among the women. He even worried she might not appear because the French star had been arguing with meet organizers ever since her arrival, claiming they had been "very impertinent" and that their conditions guaranteed "a sure loss."

Apparently changing her mind overnight, however, Dutrieu showed up at the field on Monday, climbing into the seat of her Farman for takeoff. Matilde and Blanche Scott, who was hoping to be tested for her license the next day, were watching nearby when Dr. Charles B. Clark, a noted bicyclist but unlicensed to fly, took off in a plane of Ovington's against the latter's orders. They saw Clark try to turn to the right while climbing, then plunge to the ground in a fatal crash, landing less than 50 feet from where Dutrieu was sitting. Pale with fright and shock, the French woman retreated to her hangar and did not reappear for the rest of the day.

Chaos erupted on the field as spectators rushed from their grandstand seats toward the downed plane and Woodruff screamed at the police, "Drive them back! Drive them back!" Photographers fought with guards and each other to take pictures of the plane. Stadium guards drove them back and smashed their cameras, except for one man who slipped to the ground between mounted police but managed to take one picture before passing his camera to a friend who made off with it. Enraged at the thought the photograph might appear in the newspapers, Woodruff shouted to the guards, "Tomorrow I shall have you armed with guns and if the photographers don't keep away I want you to shoot them!"

Woodruff's troubles continued. Spectators who had paid five dollars for a parking place complained that guards charged them another dollar or more if they left their cars for refreshments. By Tuesday attendance had fallen to 2,000 and the weather deteriorated into lowering clouds and rain. Matilde decided not to fly, Scott couldn't fly because she still had no license, and Harriet abandoned the meet to fly for an interstate fair in Trenton, New Jersey. That left Dutrieu, who made only one flight, a brief one. But she justified her worldwide reputation on Thursday with a flight of 37 minutes, 22$\frac{2}{5}$ seconds, a new American endurance record. For this she won the Ives de Villiers prize of $500, probably a fraction of the prize money she had expected.

All four women were interviewed at length by reporters who were frequently more interested in what they wore than in their aviation skill or experience. Both Harriet and Matilde conveyed the image of alert and decisive but well-mannered young women acceptable to conventional society in spite of their odd vocation.

Matilde was portrayed variously as "a slim, slip of a girl, [a] dashing and dimpling little brunette" more likely to be met at "afternoon teas than an airfield," and as a novice pilot who had been licensed less than two months, had never even driven an automobile, and whose "most exciting experience was when I flew suddenly into a thick cloud."

Harriet was pictured as tall and slim, with a velvet manner that concealed courage and determination, an advocate of cross-country flying to advance aviation. When she declined to give her age, which was 36, one reporter wrote that she couldn't be more than 25. She also thought planes and flying lessons were too expensive for the average woman "but society people can afford it and they'll take to it like ducks to water."

Scott, who never did get her flying license, was described as "in a class by herself," a woman who loved flying herself but disapproved of other women doing so. Not nearly as modest as her two countrywomen, she told newsmen she had engaged in outdoor sports since childhood, piloting a motorboat and driving her own car across the country. "I have an unusual muscle development," she said. "I can make my muscles obey my thought instantly. Most women cannot."

Dutrieu, a foreigner, although recognized as a woman champion and the only true professional among them, was subjected by the press to a more critical and chauvinistic point of view. A typical reaction was that of one reporter who described the Frenchwoman's costume as a Norfolk jacket with "long trousers, ugly, dangling and flapping over white spats, so different from flexible boots encasing the ankles of American girls." Knowing it would no doubt shock most of his readers, he quoted Dutrieu as saying she never wore a corset when she flew, thus guaranteeing herself "freedom of movement and lessen[ing] the danger . . . of a fall." He added that neither Moisant nor Quimby took this precaution and did not find it necessary to mention that neither Harriet nor Matilde would ever even think of discussing such a thing with the press. Dutrieu also said aviation "is the best sport for those who wish to die young," probably the truth but again something not suitable for a young woman of that time to say.

All flights were rained out on Friday but an audience of 10,000 braved the wind and cold on Saturday to watch Quimby challenge Dutrieu in a cross-country contest. The $600 prize went to Quimby when her Moisant monoplane quickly outdistanced her opponent's Farman, a feather in Alfred's cap as a plane builder. Dutrieu stayed aloft, however, in an effort to better the previous endurance record she had set on Thursday, which she did, flying for 1 hour, 4 minutes, and 57 seconds. Other winners that day included Claude Grahame-White, who broke six records in a single flight, and a young Signal Corps lieutenant, H. H. Arnold, who won the altitude endurance contest for flying highest and longest with a passenger and would be known years later as "Hap" Arnold, chief of the U.S. Army Air Forces.

Even after the Nassau meet ended on October 1, Nassau County sheriff Charles De Mott continued his efforts to stop Sunday flying. And when a temporary injunction banning interference with the meet was vacated, De Mott interpreted this as permission for him to arrest all Sunday flyers and appointed twenty-two deputies to patrol the Nassau Boulevard field, stationing one at every three hangars and every entrance gate.

Five hundred people were at the field Sunday, October 9, to watch Earle Ovington take off on another air-mail delivery flight, this one to the West Coast. With the sheriff's men threatening to arrest him, Ovington argued that as a licensed mail carrier he was protected by the federal government and could fly when and where he pleased so long as no admission fee was charged to see him. He took off, but engine trouble forced him to return to Nassau. Eluding the sheriff's men, he hid the mail in a hangar and gave up any effort at a second attempt in favor of a train ride into Manhattan.

Meanwhile, Matilde, Dutrieu, Grahame-White, and Arnold were joined by T.O.M. Sopwith, an Englishman who had won $20,000 for making the longest flight from England to the Continent in 1910 and would later design the Sopwith Camel, famed World War I fighter plane. They all wanted to fly but were undecided on whether to heed or ignore the deputies' warning. Alfred Moisant had no trouble deciding. Furious at the sheriff's interference, he ordered Houpert to take off, which he did, circling the field briefly before landing and also escaping on foot.

Moments later Alfred told his sister to take off and fly to his own field at Mineola where he would meet her, reminding the deputies they could not legally arrest her until she had actually left the ground. This touched off a wild chase through Westbury and Meadowbrook, with Matilde in the air followed by three deputies in a police car heading a long procession of other cars occupied by Matilde's friends and others who had come to see Ovington.

When Matilde landed at Mineola two of the deputies tried to seize her, but were then challenged by the angry crowd which responded with fists and canes. Matilde's hands and face were scratched and her flying suit torn during the ensuing tussle before the Moisant chauffeur, René Porsch, came to her rescue, driving up and pushing her into the car. He was forced to a stop, however, when two deputies jumped on the running board and pummeled him with their nightsticks while a friend of Alfred's, Richard Sinclair, hustled Matilde into another car and drove off the field. This touched off yet another chase by lawmen, which ended only after their police car broke down and Sinclair's glasses blew off, forcing him to stop and recover them. While he was doing so, Matilde changed her mind and asked him to take her back to the field to face the deputies.

Alfred was waiting for her and warned her pursuers that they were on private property without a warrant. To the angry crowd that again threatened the deputies until they left, Alfred complained, "Had my sister been a murderess she could not have been handled more roughly than she was by those deputies" and said he would bring legal action against them for damages.

Years later Matilde claimed, "I was just so happy that I was flying that I never thought about the officers on the field any more, never thought that I was making a scene of any kind." But for all of Alfred's huffing and puffing and Matilde's demure denials, it is clear they were both delighted at the scene she had created. Only Louise was upset. "Now your picture will be in the paper," she grumbled. "You've disgraced the family."

The next day every New York newspaper carried the story, one with a cartoon that Matilde described as "a picture of the cutest little witch you ever saw sitting on a broom, waving to the officers." And she apologized to her sister, saying, "Lou, I didn't disgrace you too much, did I?" Considering herself still a novice pilot, Matilde asked Sopwith to give her a lesson on "how to act if your engine stops dead," an occurrence she had fortunately not yet experienced. She may have been thinking of her late colleague Frisbie when she explained,

I know my limitations, and I am not going to risk my life by trying to do just a little bit more than I realize that I am able to—neither to please myself nor the public. The spectators at aviation meets want stunts, one of the things in flying most likely to cause accidents and loss of life. An aviator has to know when not to go up as well as to know how to fly; and the person who will not let the hoots and jeers of a crowd make him leave the ground hasn't got "cold feet." He has good sense.

The following Sunday, however, in defiance of both the sheriff and her own cautionary advice, she began a series of practice flights that reached ever nearer to the outer limits of safety. On October 16, when friends from Central America and France gathered to watch her, she frightened them by performing a number of sensational dives, pulling up just short of the ground in maneuvers reminiscent of her brother John.

And 10 days later, after Alfred had forbidden her taking up a woman passenger because of strong winds, Matilde took off alone, rising to 1,200 feet as darkness fell and she could no longer see the field. A worried Alfred ordered gasoline to be poured on the grass in the shape of a horseshoe and set aflame to guide her landing. Her descent in dead center of the fiery horseshoe was captured by the American Press Association and distributed to newspapers throughout the country.

Alfred had erred in assuming the Nassau meet offered his two women neophytes the best chance to show their mettle. Show it they did. But not until after the meet did they really surpass themselves—Harriet at fairs at Staten Island and Trenton and Matilde during her flight from the sheriff's deputies and the aerobatics she performed over her home base at Mineola.

20
MATILDE AT THE CONTROLS

On November 1, 1911, Matilde Moisant and Harriet Quimby watched their steamer trunks laden with party frocks and flying costumes being moved into adjoining staterooms on the steamship *Lampasas,* which was about to sail for the Mexican port of Vera Cruz. From the passenger deck rail moments later they waved goodbye to Alfred, who was pacing the dock below, eager to return to his Broadway office. His sister and her friend were to be the featured flyers in his latest drive to sell aircraft, this time to the government of Mexico.

In mid-October Mexican government representative Vic Roumagnac offered Alfred $100,000 in gold to put on a week-long series of air shows as part of the inauguration celebration for President-elect Francisco Madero. Half the purse was to be paid by the government, the other half by leading merchants in Mexico City. A week later Alfred signed a contract for five Moisant aviators to fly for 10 days at Mexico City's Valbuena military airport. The Mexicans, he told the press, also wanted him to open a new military aviation school and to consider leaving two of his pilots and three of his monoplanes there when the air show ended.

In addition to Matilde, Harriet, and André Houpert, Alfred hired two more pilots, George Dyott and his partner, Capt. Patrick Donald Hamilton. Dyott flew a two-passenger monoplane designed by Frenchman Louis Bechereau and produced by Armond Deperdussin. The two men had been using the Deperdussin at Nassau Field to demonstrate night flying with Dyott as pilot and Hamilton manipulating a portable light for takeoffs and landings.

Alfred also attempted to arrange a biplane-monoplane competition by inviting three Curtiss men, J.A.D. McCurdy, Charles F. Willard, and C. F. Walsh, to assist his team in a joint exhibition of both types of aircraft. It was never explained why he encouraged participation by such formidable opposition.

Dyott and Hamilton also sailed on the *Lampasas* as escorts for Harriet, Matilde, her sister Louise, and Matilde's friend Miss M. C. Long. Houpert left by train with five mechanics and two carloads of planes, and Alfred took another, faster train, arriving in Mexico City before the others.

Interviewing them on arrival a reporter for the English-language *Mexican Herald* described both Matilde and Harriet as "cultured, frank and intelligent." Harriet displayed her intelligence but was something less than frank when she said air shows were "really social affairs more than anything else." As a writer for New York society's *Leslie's Weekly,* she knew it wiser to appeal to the Mexican elite than to say anything so crass as she and her friend were actually flying for money. The photographs accompanying the interview showed Harriet in a fashionable beribboned frock and large hat, a dainty parasol clasped in one hand, while Matilde, dressed in her flying suit, rested a demure hand on the propeller of her plane.

Both women were invited to a number of parties at Chapultepec Castle, official residence of the new president. One morning Matilde bought flowers at the market and told Louise she planned to drop the bouquet with a thank-you note to Madero on a large patio of the residence. "Well, I guess I can't stop you," Louise grumbled on their way to the airfield. There

Houpert helped her tie a large rock to the flowers, and, after asking for directions in Spanish from a Mexican Indian standing nearby, Matilde took off for Chapultepec.

As she was to relate the incident years later, Matilde said, "I flew directly over it, and as I passed over it I dropped my flowers. I looked back and I could see it going down and I thought, 'Oh, boy. I'll hit the palace now.'"

The next day President Madero said, "Miss Moisant, I got your flowers. Now if that had been a bomb I wouldn't be here today because it dropped right on the patio."

With that flight Matilde Moisant became the first woman to fly in Mexico. A few days later, Harriet would become the second.

Visiting Mexico more than 30 years later, Matilde went back to see the patio and wrote, "The place has changed so much I had to ask to be shown where it was. I wondered while looking over the grounds if I would have the nerve today to do it over again—quien sabe?"

Although the high altitude prevented both Houpert and Willard from getting off the ground earlier that day, atmospheric conditions on November 16 improved by 5 P.M. when Quimby opened the Mexico City show with a six-minute flight. Unable to climb higher than 250 feet, she said on landing it was "the hardest flight in terms of air conditions" that she had ever made. Dyott made a similar brief flight 15 minutes later. The day's limited show ended only minutes later when Willard tried to take off but was stopped by 300 or 400 spectators who broke through the fences and police lines shouting "Viva Madero!" and "Viva los aeroplanes!" as they scrambled to inspect the aircraft.

Ascribing it to many weather delays and a total flying time of less than a half hour, the *Mexican Herald* reported that attendance was "not large but good for the first day."

Rain washed out the next day of the Moisant show. But the same newspaper reported that on the third day "a laughing girl in a bat-winged, long-tailed monoplane . . . drove her way straight into the hearts of the crowd." It was Harriet Quimby, who flew so far out over Lake Xochimilco that Dyott, followed by a fleet of cars, was sent out to search for her while smudge fires were lighted to guide her down to a landing. She found her way back alone after more than a half-hour aloft.

Quimby didn't fly the fourth day because it was a Sunday. But the rest of the Moisant crew all did. This time Matilde was the star, bringing 2,000 cheering onlookers to their feet with her aerobatics.

The show closed early November 25 with Dyott taking up popular toreador Rodolfo Gaona as a passenger and Harriet and Matilde flying together. But much as the two women were admired they could not salvage the meet, which ended up a financial failure, the crowds dwindling daily until only 200 showed up for the finale. Ticket-buyers complained about the frequent weather delays and that, of the seven flyers and five planes advertised, only three pilots and two planes were flown regularly. Actually, the two women, Houpert, and Dyott had flown almost daily in a number of Moisant monoplanes and the Deperdussins. But the Curtiss men, McCurdy and Walsh, never did appear, nor did Willard after the opening day when he tried to take off but failed.

Aero magazine attributed the poor attendance to "a confused political situation," perhaps better described as political chaos during which Madero's various opponents, each with his own army, were challenging his rule. Even before the meet was over three of them, Emilio Vasquez Gomez, Bernardo Reyes, and Emiliano Zapata, were rumored to be forming an alliance, one that soon ended with each man turning against the other two.

Besides the bad weather and even worse political climate, Alfred was faced at the end of the meet with the desertion of four of his flyers, Willard, Dyott, Hamilton, and Quimby. Willard teamed up with McCurdy for a separate tour of Mexican towns, demonstrating Curtiss biplanes instead of Moisant Blériots. Right after a smiling Alfred helped Madero into Dyott's Deperdussin to become "the first ruler of a nation to be airborne," Dyott and his partner Hamilton announced they were staying on in Mexico City to exhibit the French monoplanes they apparently considered superior to the Moisant aircraft. And Quimby left for New York where she hired a new manager,

A. Leo Stevens, a well-known aeronaut and air-show organizer. By mid-January she was on the Twentieth Century Limited to Chicago for the annual meeting of the publishers of *Leslie's Weekly*. After being flung across the aisle from one seat to another when the train crashed into a string of empty coaches just outside Chicago's La Salle Street Station, Quimby said that given her choice between a plane or a train wreck "I'd rather take a chance in my airship."

However, Alfred did get an order from Madero for five Moisant Blériots and prepaid tuition for five Mexican army men who would go to his Hempstead Plains aviation school for flight instruction. If he also collected the promised $100,000 for the Mexico City show he said nothing about it to the press. Returning to New York, Alfred left Matilde and Houpert to complete the shows he had already booked in six other Mexican cities. The older brother and substitute father, who only four months before had forbidden his little sister to fly for money, returned to New York, leaving Matilde behind as chief of his depleted air troupe in a dangerously unstable country.

Accompanied by Houpert and his mechanics, Matilde left the capital on December 4 and arrived in Guadalajara less than a week after government soldiers fought and won a major victory over the rebel troops of Bernardo Reyes. For two days flights were canceled because of chilling winds, but on the third, a Sunday, Matilde attempted to fly in the only plane available, one that had already been down once with motor trouble. She barely got off the ground before the motor stopped dead and the aircraft dropped, shattering into a pile of wreckage out of which Matilde crawled unharmed.

Determined to fly, Matilde made another attempt six days later in the repaired aircraft despite Houpert's warning of dangerous air currents. The worried Frenchman could only shrug his shoulders and sigh, "I have no power to say you can't," as she walked to her plane.

Houpert was right. Matilde did have the power. She also had the will. The woman who had been brought up to defer to men in a patriarchal society was ready to take the lead. A flight had been promised ticketholders and a flight would be given.

"I started to go up," she said,

and I'd gotten maybe sixty feet from the ground when the wind caught the tail of my machine and it nosed right down. It was just like a rowboat out in a heavy sea. Well, the last [wind current] that caught me just nosed my machine down like that, and I came right down like that. The propeller went into the ground. The crankshaft and motor went right in and the tail stuck up like that. I thought, "If that comes on top of me it's goodby," but I threw myself back in the machine and I had just enough weight to throw the tail back. That's the only thing that saved me.

During that first week in Guadalajara the dangers of flying in treacherous wind currents were secondary to those of the anarchy spreading across Mexico. Heavy fighting all around them made it impossible for the Moisant group to get to San Luis Potosi, Puebla, Hermosilla, Vera Cruz, and Monterrey, the remaining cities on their schedule. But Matilde did manage to arrange shows at Guanajusta and Silao, east of Guadalajara.

As the fighting spread throughout Mexico Matilde and the others were on a train en route to Chihuahua when it was pulled off and stopped on a side track at Torreon, 340 miles north of Guadalajara. "It was but a few days until the city was surrounded and we were totally isolated," she said. The train was stranded there as rebel troops laid siege to the city. Federal troops broke the siege for one day, just long enough to enable a trainload of 170 refugees, mostly Americans and foreign diplomats, to reach the Texas border. The next day, however, the rebels cut the rail line again.

Matilde and her crew remained trapped as rebel and federal troops battled throughout the state of Chihuahua. From the train they could hear Mauser fire across the Rio Naces. And they learned that trains crossing Chihuahua had been held up and the haciendas of friends where they had planned to stop had been sacked.

For almost two weeks, Matilde, Houpert, and the mechanics were stranded in Torreon and lived inside the Pullman car attached to the freight car with its five airplanes. As the sole speaker of Spanish, Matilde took charge of buying food and water as well as their basic sanitation needs.

After government troops finally broke the siege and cleared the tracks long enough for their train to escape, Matilde called the trip across Chihuahua to Laredo, Texas, a ride she would never forget.

"Not one of us disrobed that night for we expected the train to be held up," she said. "All through the night we could see through our car windows the bivouac fires of the rebel army and when our train would halt at the station armed soldiers would put their faces up to the windows of the Pullman car."

On February 27 their train finally arrived in New Orleans, where Houpert credited their salvation to Matilde. "Few men could have managed our affairs as well in Mexico," he said "and had it not been for the cool-headedness of our little woman manager we would have gotten into serious complications at the city of Torreon."

Houpert also commended Matilde's courage.

At Guadalajara, while in the air, Miss Moisant again showed her wonderful nerve, for in all my experience I have never found such air currents as those in Guadalajara, Guanajusta and Silao. There few men would have attempted to fly but Miss Moisant, with true nerve, took her machine up where it was risking one's life. In nerve she is equally as strong as was poor old Johnny.

Obviously, inside Matilde there was more than one woman. The gentle Victorian lady who ran her brother's household coexisted with a masterful supervisor who guided her crew safely through war and rebellion. Not to mention an intrepid aviator who could handle a plane with the same skill, nerve, and courage as her "poor old Johnny."

2 1
MATILDE'S FINALE

Any thoughts Matilde may have had of resting up after her Mexican ordeal ended when she learned on arriving in New Orleans that she would be going on the road again. Encouraged by the sudden spurt of aircraft sales and Madero's interest in his aviation school, Alfred was bent on keeping his planes and his aviators in the public eye.

With this in mind he booked his sister and Houpert for two months of exhibition flights in Louisiana and Texas starting just 10 days after their return to the States. The show would begin in New Orleans and continue through cities such as Shreveport, Dallas, and Wichita Falls. Alfred sent Francisco Alvarez, a young Mexican graduate of the Moisant school who had been licensed on December 13, to join them in New Orleans as a replacement for Quimby. He also added to the group an assistant for Matilde, Richmond Pease, who would work with local committees on ticket sales and field accommodations.

After receiving Alfred's instructions Matilde learned that somewhere between Laredo and New Orleans thieves had broken into the railroad car carrying her planes and stolen most of the mechanics' tools. Complicating matters even further, the airplane car with the planes was stuck outside the city and could

177

not be moved to the airfield until a damaged bridge was repaired, delaying the opening show to March 9.

Matilde and Houpert took advantage of the extra time to publicize the show and attract ticket-buyers. The Frenchman made a flight over the city that brought business and traffic to a standstill, just as John Moisant had done 14 months earlier. Matilde, accompanied by Louise, was photographed and interviewed by the press at a ceremony during which John's old friend Gen. Francisco Altschul presented her with an engraved silver cup honoring John and commissioned by the Central American community of New Orleans. Expressing her thanks, Matilde said the Moisants were especially grateful because the freight-car thieves had also stolen most of John's remaining mementos, making "this cup . . . about the only thing we have left that was originally intended for him."

Matilde's misfortunes resumed when high winds forced a 24-hour cancellation of the opening show, for which 200 people had waited from 2:30 to 6 P.M. before being sent home with rainchecks or refunds. But the next day, Sunday, March 9, the weather cleared and Matilde evoked in the audience vivid memories of her handsome brother John, both on the ground and in the air.

When Matilde walked out onto the field wearing a long grey coat, her flying cap in one hand and goggles in the other, the crowd cheered and photographers ran to her. Smiling for them, she removed the coat and revealed a tiny, trim figure in a blouse and knickerbocker trousers of olive-green corduroy worn with high-laced tan boots. Here was the quintessential "girl flyer"— beautiful and daring.

Her flight proved just as stunning. As one paper reported, "Matilde Moisant flew her great Blériot over the same ground as her brother had. . . . Several thousand people at the city park race track were thrilled by her skill and daring maneuvers." For a grand finale she flew a duet with Houpert, which the paper called "a beautiful sight."

Matilde also resembled her brother John in holding firm opinions and not being afraid to express them. Asked to comment on inventor Thomas Alva Edison's statement that women had only limited brains and it would be at least 2,500 years before they became the intellectual equals of men, she called it "not correct" and explained that "in some things they are sharper than men and there are plenty of women who run their husband's businesses without ever leaving their homes—maybe more than you'd think."

In this, as in all of her published statements, Matilde was typical of her generation of middle-class women who were pioneer homemakers, whether migrating to the American west or El Salvador. Like most of them, she maintained a careful balance between a strong belief in her own ability and a public acquiescence to a patriarchal society. She affirmed this when a reporter called her "as womanly a woman as ever lived . . . , attractive, beautiful, demure yet vivacious and highly entertaining." He also noted that Louise was equally attractive and the two traveled together wherever they went, although Louise disapproved of Matilde's flying and never watched her in the air.

When they arrived in Shreveport in pouring rain, Matilde commented wryly, "They call us birds but we're not ducks." But she hastened to add that she would fly as high as people wanted her to, saying, "We'll give as good an exhibition as we possibly can. It all depends on the wind and weather."

When the rain stopped two days later she gave spectators even more excitement than she had promised. Using a golf course as an improvised airfield, Matilde saw what she thought was a good spot to land but it turned out to be a hilly stretch of wet grass and a sand trap. "Well," she said, "it looked perfectly level [but] when I came down I saw some of this slope and I thought, 'Oh, boy, I don't think I can escape that.'" She didn't. Only one wheel of her plane struck the ground, flipping it back some 25 feet into the air before landing upside down in the bunker.

Everyone assumed Matilde had been crushed. But the heavy engine and crankshaft were suspended just inches above her, held there by the iron supports still attached to the shattered wing. As she later recalled, "I crawled out from underneath there like a little worm." Jumping to her feet she assured Houpert and others who had run to help her that she was not hurt, then ran to reassure Louise who as usual had been sitting in a car but not watching. Meantime, ignoring warnings from mechanics and the police that the plane might explode, people clambered into the sand trap, snatching propeller and wing fragments as souvenirs.

A week later in Dallas, Matilde, Houpert, and Alvarez were joined by Harold Kantner, the handsome young man who the previous summer had given Alfred his last $500 for the lessons he took with Matilde and Harriet. Kantner had been exhibit-flying Moisant Blériots around the country but presumably Alfred decided that Dallas was a large-enough city to warrant a fourth aviator.

To advertise the show Matilde and Houpert arranged a parade through the city with band, banners, and a horse-drawn carriage. But the several hundred people who showed up saw nothing in the air on opening day. The ground was so soggy that mud clinging to the wheels made takeoffs impossible.

The next day Matilde retreated from the field in the face of high winds, only to return a short time later after consulting with Houpert. Posing for photographers in a purple outfit she joined the already airborne Kantner in an aerobatic duet before heading north over the city. She explained later that she changed her mind because "I felt very much disappointed, [knowing that] the people would think I was faking." But as she flew over the city she looked down and wondered if the people knew how frightened she was.

There was no flying on the third day although Matilde stayed at the park until dark, hoping the winds would die down but giving up after again conferring with Houpert. "You know," she told reporters, "it was just such a day as this that Mr. Frisbie who was formerly with our company was killed. I know from the nice way that Dallas people have treated me that they wouldn't care to see me killed, however much they may like to see me fly."

A woman reporter in Dallas echoed her counterpart in Shreveport, writing that Matilde was "a girl you would like to ride horseback with or get up early for tennis. I can even imagine her," she gushed, "embroidering lingerie frou-frou on the gallery in the hot afternoon." Matilde explained that she and Louise were inseparable, even though vacations "always entail a sacrifice for one [since] I want to go to the woods with a tent and fish and hunt . . . and she longs for the veranda of a fashionable hotel." And yet, the admiring reporter wrote, this same woman enjoyed card parties and teas and loved to sew and cook, "this woman who makes $5,000 for 25 minutes of flying."

That week, at the very time Matilde was gaining widespread recognition as a pilot, she startled the aviation world and her admirers by announcing that she intended to retire. "My relatives have been urging me to quit," she explained, "and when I learned of the death of Cal Rodgers I made up my mind." Less than two weeks earlier Rogers, the first person to cross the country (in 84 days and 70 crashes) by plane, had crashed to his death during an exhibition flight after running into a flock of seagulls off the coast of California. "Rogers," she added, "was probably the most careful aviator this country has ever seen. He took every precaution, yet it got to him. It gets everyone who stays with it long enough and I'm going to stop."

When Matilde said "relatives" she really meant Louise, not Alfred, for only a week earlier *Aero* magazine published, with her photograph, a full-column biography of Matilde stating she could be booked exclusively through the Moisant International Aviators. If Matilde had been frightened by the deaths of John, Frisbie, and Rogers and the memories of her own four crashes, Louise was even more terrified, waiting without watching every time her sister flew. Louise had been constantly urging her to retire and Matilde could no longer deny her. She promised Louise she would fly for the last time at Wichita Falls.

Months later Matilde was quoted in *Good Housekeeping* magazine as saying she might in fact fly again, but only for her own amusement. "I have the air intoxication," she explained, "and only a flier knows what that means."

At six o'clock on a windy April 14 the patient spectators who had waited all afternoon watched what was announced as Miss

Moisant's last public appearance. As she climbed up on the seat of her Blériot the crowd cheered and pressed close against the enclosure cables patrolled by police. After barely clearing the wire netting at the top of the park fence on takeoff, Matilde flew for 10 minutes until a sputtering motor forced her down outside the park. Told it would need only minor repairs, she overruled Houpert's warning that it was too windy to fly and decided to go up again. "This is my last flight," she said, "and I want it to be my best."

She took off again but this time as she tried to land her approach was blocked by spectators, most of whom had never seen an airplane before.

They were right in line with the way the wind was. When they saw me coming down they thought that the minute my wheels touched I was going to stay there. Well, the plane didn't do that.

So, I saw the line [of people] right in front of me and I thought, "If I don't do something, I'm going to mow right in there." So I just nosed my plane down so that the tail didn't go over, put on a spark, and I let the wheels touch, and I brought it right back up, but it wouldn't go—only took me over the crowd—and then it burst into flame.

She cleared the crowd but when her plane slammed into the ground nose-first, propeller fragments sliced into the gas tanks, causing fuel to spew over the red-hot exhaust pipe and igniting the wreckage. "They [the tanks] burst their moorings and away we went," Matilde recalled. "The tank went down this way and the gas and oil exploded and got over me."

Houpert, who had quickly realized she was going to crash, reached the wreckage just as the flames enveloped it and, with the aid of a hotel employee, pulled Matilde to safety. "My hair had come out from under my cap," she said, "and my gloves were kind of burnt, but it was nothing."

Putting an end to the pyrotechnics of the day, a Dallas cow-puncher, R. E. Marlow, rode up to the burning wreckage and lassoed the engine, pulling it out of the flames.

Matilde assured Houpert she was uninjured and asked him to telephone the hotel immediately and tell Louise she was safe. Her coat having burned in the crash, she apologized for having to appear in a soiled and torn flying suit. Then the woman who never learned to drive a car because she considered automobiles too dangerous refused numerous offers of a ride back into town, saying she had come to the park by streetcar and intended to return the same way.

Ever the lady, Moisant walked away from her last flight.

22

THE CROSSING

In early 1912, while Matilde and Houpert struggled to keep their engagements in war-torn Mexico, Harriet Quimby was back in New York arranging a new stage in her aviation career—one without Alfred Moisant. As shrewd as she was beautiful, the pilot-writer was preparing to upgrade her reputation and her income by becoming the first woman to make a solo flight across the English Channel. Her first move was to sever her affiliation with Alfred Moisant, hiring in his place her own manager, A. Leo Stevens, a former record-setting balloonist who had taught flying and aerostat maintenance in the U.S. Signal Corps. A handsome and charming man of 50, Stevens was a member of the Aero Club of America with a wide circle of influential friends in the aviation business.

For the channel flight, which she had first conceived in Mexico, Quimby secured a letter of introduction to Louis Blériot because she wanted an airplane like those manufactured by Alfred, one she was familiar with and already knew how to fly. As editor of the newly established aviation section in *Leslie's Weekly,* she had already gained approval of her flight from her employers with their promise that she could return to that position at the magazine after the flight.

On March 7 Quimby sailed for England on the Hamburg-American liner *Amerika,* her identity concealed by the alias "Miss Craig" on the ship's register. On arriving in London she immediately called on the editor of the *London Daily Mirror,* offering him exclusive rights to the story in England if the newspaper would sponsor her. The editor agreed and gave her "a handsome inducement," although she did not disclose the exact figure in a subsequent magazine article.

This done, Quimby went to Paris to meet Blériot and order a 75-hp passenger airplane that she intended to send back to the United States. She also borrowed from him a 50-hp Blériot in which she planned to cross the channel from Dover, England, to Calais on the French coast. Blériot arranged for the borrowed plane to be shipped from his factory to his summer home where he had a hangar in the town of Hardelot, 25 miles south of Calais. Quimby intended to make her trial flights there in seclusion so as to avoid any premature revelation of her plans to the *Mirror*'s competitors.

After a circuitous and difficult train ride from Paris she arrived in Hardelot only to find that the sole hotel was closed, the alternative being a dismal room above a small café. She spent several days there waiting for relentless gale-force winds to abate so that she could try out her borrowed plane. But, realizing that "time was flying—even if I was not," she finally had to abandon the thought of any trial flights. She ordered the plane shipped secretly to her starting point in England, a Dover Heights airfield three miles inland, then took the ferry from Calais back to Dover after wiring the *Mirror* editor to have his photographers and reporters meet her at Dover's Hotel Lord Worden.

There English flyer Gustav Hamel, who had flown a woman passenger across the channel only a few days before, test-flew her plane, fine-tuned the engine, taught Quimby how to use a compass, and, she wrote later, made "an extraordinary offer." He suggested that he "dress up in my costume, which by the way is mauve satin, and make the flight, land at an unfrequented spot and sneak off, and everyone would think I had done it!"

On April 14 the skies cleared, presenting a perfect day for the crossing to France but it was a Sunday and Quimby refused to fly. By then rumors regarding an unknown woman's plan to cross the channel were circulating, bringing a number of reporters from the *Mirror*'s competitors to the area. When one such group happened upon a team of movie photographers filming Hamel tuning Quimby's plane, they mistakenly assumed it was a set for a motion picture and drifted away. The group filming was actually a crew sent by Gaumont Cinematographic Company of London in collaboration with the *Mirror* to film Quimby's takeoff.

Sunday's perfect flying weather changed to gale-force winds by Monday, but on Tuesday morning Quimby was awakened at 3:30 and told there was no wind. She drove with Hamel to the airfield, where the Englishman made a brief test flight in the Blériot before Quimby herself mounted the seat. With her mauve flying ensemble, she wore two sets of long silk underwear beneath it and two coats—one woolen and one raincoat—above. For further protection friends draped a sealskin stole around her shoulders and strapped a hot-water bottle to her waist.

Immediately after takeoff she headed straight for Dover Castle where she had been told a tug carrying press and film crews from the *Mirror* and Gaumont would be waiting to capture her flight. "In an instant I was beyond the cliffs and over the channel," she wrote. "Far beneath me I saw the *Mirror*'s tug with its stream of black smoke. It was trying to keep ahead of me but I passed it in a jiffy. Then the thickening fog obscured my view. Calais was out of sight. I could not see ahead of me at all nor could I see the water below. There was only one thing for me to do and that was keep my eyes fixed on the compass."

Flying by compass at 60 MPH and in fog so thick that her goggles were useless, Harriet did some hasty calculations as to when she might reach land. "The distance," she said, "straight across from Dover to Calais is only 22 miles and I knew that land must be in sight if I could only get below the fog and see it."

When she dropped to 1,000 feet the French shoreline came

into view and she cruised along it, searching for Calais but was unable to find it. Her plane battered by increasingly strong wind gusts, she eventually gave up and landed on a hard, sandy beach only two miles from Hardelot. Including her climbs and descents, the search for Calais and the long spiral down to the beach, she had been airborne almost an hour for the 22-mile crossing.

Within minutes, men, women, and children who had been fishing nearby came running to the plane. One youth set off for Hardelot with Quimby's hastily written message for the *Mirror* while a man at a nearby lifesaving station telephoned the news to Boulogne. A group of French fishermen, charmed by this beautiful woman in purple who flew just like their own beloved Blériot, warned Quimby of the rising tide and hauled her plane first to higher ground and later to the Blériot hangar two miles away. Soon townspeople from Hardelot itself began to arrive, among whom were two women Quimby had met during her previous visit. Ecstatic over the successful flight, they lifted her onto their shoulders and, in their ankle-length gowns, carried her across the wet sand. Following a lengthy session of champagne toasts, interviews, and photographs of the flyer and her aircraft, Quimby left by car for Calais, where she caught a train for Paris, arriving at seven that evening "a very tired but a very happy woman."

She was not happy for long. Just 12 hours later the conqueror of the channel was greeted by blaring headlines of the greatest sea disaster in history, the sinking of the *Titanic* in the North Atlantic. Newspapers in France and around the world all but ignored Quimby's historic flight as the first detailed accounts began to arrive of the tragedy that claimed 1,513 lives. Column after column was devoted to the stories from survivors picked up by the SS *Carpathia,* accounts that began to flood the desks of frantic news editors. In that flood Quimby watched her own story being swept away, a story she had expected would enhance her career, increase her income, and bring her worldwide acclaim.

Two weeks passed before Quimby was accorded a modicum of the attention she would have received if it hadn't been for the

Titanic. The Society of American Women in London gave a luncheon in her honor, and the Hamburg-American line invited her to Stuttgart for a ride in their new dirigible.

When news of Quimby's accomplishment reached California, the *Alameda Daily Argus* quoted Matilde as saying, "Nothing has pleased me more than to hear of Miss Quimby's achievement." The extent of her pleasure was left open to question, however, by adding, "although I had my eye on doing the same thing."

Not until years later did Amelia Earhart comment that Quimby's flight, performed "without any of the modern instruments, in a plane which was hardly more than a winged skeleton with a motor, and one with which she was totally unfamiliar, required more bravery and skill than to cross the Atlantic today. Always we must think of that in thinking of America's first great woman flier's accomplishments."

When Quimby sailed home from London her new two-passenger Blériot with its 75-hp Gnôme engine was in the ship's hold. She told newsmen she was pleased with the borrowed Blériot she had used for her channel crossing. But she did Alfred Moisant no favor by adding, "I had been using a copy of this machine in America since I first started to fly. I decided that an original would be better than a copy and when in Paris placed an order with Mr. Blériot for a special machine."

Quimby returned to Alfred's field at Mineola to practice flying her new plane. Its balance proved so sensitive during her first flight that she had to put a 170-pound bag of sand in the back seat just to keep the craft level. And when she took her former fellow student S. S. Jerwan, who was now chief pilot at the Moisant school, as a passenger he, too, noticed the problem and warned her the plane had a definite tendency to nose over. Although observers at the field noticed Quimby was having difficulty handling the powerful new machine, she continued to practice flying it with passengers and finally appeared to have mastered it. At least she was capable enough to keep the plane on an even keel long enough for her passenger, student pilot Walter Bonner, to crawl out of his seat and retrieve her silk coat which had blown out of her seat and become flattened against the tail!

Quimby was practicing for an appearance at the third annual Harvard-Boston air meet scheduled for June 19 to July 7. The Aero Club of America refused to sanction the meet because its promoters, headed by meet manager William A. P. Willard, were unable to guarantee prize money. When Willard went ahead with the meet, the Aero Club temporarily suspended the licenses of six of his supporting flyers, including Charles Hamilton and Glenn Martin, for the rest of the year.

Rightfully claiming that his client was the world's most famous woman aviator, Leo Stevens struck a bargain with Willard for Quimby to fly, too. He also arranged for his client to fly a bag of U.S. mail from Boston to New York on July 7.

On the evening of July 1, Quimby decided to fly a test run across Dorchester Bay between Squantum's Harvard Field and Boston Light, the route on which she hoped to break Grahame-White's speed record the next day. Willard and his son flipped a coin for the privilege of being Quimby's partner and the senior Willard won. As he climbed onto the rear seat of the white Blériot he was heard to remark jokingly that his weight of almost 200 pounds might be a danger to their takeoff. Quimby sat in the front seat, the wings of the plane extending just below her, while Willard was three feet behind so that his weight would keep the tail from rising.

Once aloft Quimby circled the field before heading east toward Boston Light some eight miles out in the harbor. Her friend Helen Vanderbilt and manager Stevens watched together at Harvard Field as they spotted her return at about 3,000 feet and begin her descent at some 85 MPH. At 2,500 feet she leveled out over the field and then, in a steep descent with her motor wide open, turned sharply to come in for a landing.

Suddenly the tail of the Blériot shot up, standing the machine almost on end and catapulting Willard over the nose of the aircraft. Quimby righted the plane momentarily but the tail shot up again. This time the plane turned over completely, flinging her out as well. Five thousand spectators witnessed the two bodies hurtling down, turning over and over, until they struck the water about 300 feet from shore and sank into the mud five feet beneath the low-tide surface. Ironically. with both its passengers gone, the plane righted itself and glided down after them until its wheels touched the water and it flipped over.

A hush fell over the crowd, followed by screams as a man shouted, "My God, they're killed." Harry Willard and others rushed into the water to recover the bodies, crushed inside their torn and mud-covered clothing. Stevens collapsed at the sight. Blanche Scott, who was airborne at 500 feet when the accident occurred, was so upset she circled the field twice before getting up the nerve to land. When she did she fainted in the seat and had to be lifted from the plane by her friends.

The cause of Quimby's and Willard's death was recorded as "accidental fall from an aeroplane [causing] multiple internal injuries . . . fractures [and] shock resulting in immediate death."

But the cause of the accident was never conclusively determined. Stevens speculated that Willard, always an excitable man anyway, was so exultant over the speed of the flight that, forgetting the inherent danger, he leaned forward to congratulate Quimby, thus upsetting the aircraft's balance. Flyer Earle Ovington examined the wreckage and found tangled control wires which he said indicated a defect in the plane's construction. Aviator Paul Peck guessed that Quimby herself caused the crash by attempting to *vol plane* down with her engine wide open. Glenn Martin blamed her for coming in too steeply and too rapidly and turning sharply after making only a half circle of the airfield. Quimby's mechanic agreed with Martin but added that similar accidents had occurred with Blériots before. In fact the *Boston Globe* reported that the planes had been grounded in France for a government investigation of just such accidents.

Quimby's body was taken to New York but not before vandals in Boston had stripped it of her satin flying suit and jewelry. The funeral service was held at night at Campbell's Funeral Home in Manhattan so that working friends could attend, among them members of three aviation clubs. Quimby's colleague journalist Elizabeth Hiatt Gregory wrote that the flyer lay in an open casket, clad in the long white gown she had planned to wear at a reception in her honor after the Boston meet. Each person attending dropped a rose into the casket as they passed before the brief service. The body was placed in a burglar-proof vault at Woodlawn Cemetery pending its removal for final burial at Valhalla in upstate New York. Ironically, the woman who gambled with death for more than a year had confided in her mother that she feared her body would be stolen for medical experiments.

The career of Harriet Quimby, beautiful pilot in purple and the first woman flyer to be licensed in America, lasted just 15 months, 10 months longer than that of Matilde's brother John. Given a few more years and a few more records, she might well have achieved the same worldwide popularity later granted to Amelia Earhart.

23

THE BOTTOM LINE

The death of Harriet Quimby in 1912 marked the end of the Moisant International Aviators. John Moisant, John Frisbie, and St. Croix Johnstone were dead. Matilde had renounced exhibition flying for good. Hamilton and Seymour had severed ties with Alfred to fly on their own or for others as, indeed, had the original foreign contingent of Garros, Simon, Barrier, and Audemars, all of whom had left the United States for more lucrative flying fields elsewhere. Sponsored by Willis McCornick of the Queens Aviation Company, the four Frenchmen and the Swiss toured Argentina before group leader Garros returned to France in time for the Circuit d'Anjou on June 16–17, 1912. Garros won first place and 75,000 francs to launch a career of cross-country flying. Even the steadfast Houpert returned to France the day after Matilde's last disastrous accident in Wichita Falls.

Alfred's flyers were drawn away from the United States by more than just the increasing number of well-organized air competitions with their higher level of prize money. The growing interest in flying abroad led to more than generous prizes. It also resulted in advances in aircraft design and production, which in turn stimulated the growth of air devotees and willing, knowledgeable investors. As aviation interest prospered in Europe and England, the American public was indifferent, focusing its attention on the automobile. If France's hero was Blériot, America's was Henry Ford.

Alfred Moisant, air-show impresario and self-appointed director of a one-man campaign to make the United States the world's leader in aviation, could not or would not admit this. But he was forced to curtail his free-spending visionary activities by introducing at least some practical measures simply to avoid bankruptcy. His existing assets—the airfield, the school, and the factory—all had to be fully utilized if he were to remain in the aviation business.

Just as he had once done in El Salvador, Alfred relied first on real estate, the land east of Mineola that his Hempstead Plains Aviation Company had leased for a new airfield. He had already put up five concrete hangars there, but not the new office, factory, grandstand, and clubhouse he had originally planned. His opportunity to complete development of the Hempstead Plains field with minimal investment came when the Nassau Boulevard field closed in August.

Moving his school from Mineola to Hempstead Plains, Alfred leased a small factory at nearby Winfield and rented out three of his five hangars. The Aero Club of America rented one for its new headquarters and several pilots moved their wooden hangars from Nassau. The Aero Club brought over the grandstands it had used at the previous Nassau air meet after Alfred agreed to lay out a five-kilometer course properly marked by pylons and a 500-meter course for pilot testing. But he proposed that a five-dollar fee be levied on pilots each time they took a passenger up on a paid flight and a tax of $50 a pupil on any new school using the field.

Alfred staffed his enterprises with former Moisant students who had been licensed and were willing to work for a pittance compared to the salaries he had paid his International Aviators. With George H. Arnold now working as his assistant, chief pilot S. S. "Dude" Jerwan introduced a more demanding preparatory course in mechanics and theory of flight. He also amused the students by bringing along a Boston bull named Mono, fully rigged out with admittance badge, helmet, and occasionally a cigar in his mouth.

To escape Long Island's cold and blustery weather, the popular school was moved to the U.S. Army's aviation camp in Augusta, Georgia, for the winter months, and by year's end the Moisant school had eleven licensed pilots for that year, ranking third in the nation behind Glenn Curtiss's thirty-one and Max Lillie's thirteen.

Alfred hired two more graduates, Alfred Bolognesi and Mortimer Bates, to work in his factory and replaced the International Fliers with other former students, dispatching two of them to give one-man exhibition shows as early as December 1911. The first to go was Jesse Seligman, who showed "true grit with a strong wind" at Kingston, Jamaica, and drew 30,000 spectators at San Juan, Puerto Rico, during a tour of the Caribbean. The other was Francisco Alvarez, who had been sent to New Orleans to meet Matilde and continue her tour with Houpert.

Still another graduate, J. Hector Worden, toured for Alfred in Texas, Missouri, and Illinois. Once assured of their abilities, Alfred assigned Alvarez and Worden to deliver two of the Moisant aircraft President Madero had ordered for the Mexican army. Alvarez flew a 50-hp single-seater and Wordon a 100-hp two-seater. They not only delivered the aircraft; they both joined the Mexican army in its continuing war against insurgents.

Soon appointed training officer for the neophyte Mexican air force, Alvarez returned to Hempstead Plains with two young military officers, Alberto and Gustavo Salinas, to be enrolled in the Moisant aviation school. The brothers, nephews of the governor of Coahuila, Venusliano Carranza, were apt pupils, beginning their lessons in July, getting their licenses in September, and flying scouting missions for the Mexican army a month later.

Even more important to Alfred was the Salinas brothers' recommendation on their return to Mexico that more of their colleagues be sent to the Moisant school for flight training. As a result, another set of brothers, Eduardo and Pablo Aldasoro, trained at the winter field in Augusta and were licensed by early 1913. And before they finished they were joined by two more army officers, Horacio Ruiz and Luis Salazar.

While Alvarez and Worden brought about increased school enrollment and plane sales, an earlier graduate, Harold Kantner, was making himself essential to Moisant's business. With no formal education in either engineering or design, the young man who had built an airplane from a magazine drawing even before entering the Moisant school possessed an inherent talent for aeronautical design. In Tampa his monoplane, the first to be seen in that area, was kept inside a tent where people were charged 10 cents each to "look the oddball thing over."

Before being ordered to join Matilde in Dallas, Kantner had been demonstrating Moisant planes in Florida, Louisiana, and Alabama. In Jacksonville on February 20 he and Wright pilot Max Lillie flew up to join Robert C. Fowler who was just about to complete the first west-to-east flight across the country. "There was no hurry [to meet him]," Kantner said, "as the old Wright wasn't moving from west to east very fast . . . forty miles an hour, I guess. The papers were there and the cameras. We all posed in front of the old Wright plane."

Always eager to augment the small salary he was getting from Alfred, Kantner agreed to distribute advertising handbills while making a demonstration flight over Montgomery, Alabama. Clutching the leaflets between his knees he ascended to 800 feet before noticing "a couple of things flying around in the cockpit, pieces of paper. Then more. Then more" until they finally choked the fuel mixing valve just above the rudder bar and the motor stalled out completely. He crashed, damaging one wing and his landing gear. But, embarrassed to admit what had happened, he "quickly jumped out and started cleaning out that cockpit of those handbills in a hurry" before anyone arrived. The crash ended "a remarkable record of graduating from the [Moisant Aviation] School without a single breakage [and] never meeting with the slightest mishap in more than six months of flying."

After flying with Matilde in Dallas Kantner continued his solo exhibition tour for another seven months before returning to Hempstead Plains in September. Alfred soon asked him to demonstrate a Moisant plane at the Army Signal Corps training field in College Park, Maryland. He was accompanied by Bernetta Adams Miller, another Moisant graduate licensed on September 25. Alfred selected College Park because it was the nearest army training center and only a short auto ride from Capitol Hill, where funds for military planes originated.

He may have chosen Bernetta to illustrate the popular adage among most male pilots that "if a woman can fly it, anyone can fly it."

However, Kantner's initial effort to interest the head of the Signal Corps in the standard 50-hp Gnôme-Blériot being produced at the Moisant factory was met with scorn. "We don't want any part of a foreign plane in the Signal Corps," the officer said. "Furthermore we don't like the rotary [engine]."

Although there seemed little prospect of a sale, Kantner was assigned a hangar and began to make daily exhibition flights. Dubious about women flyers, including Matilde and Harriet, Kantner allowed Bernetta to make one short 10-mile flight but ordered her to "stick right over the railroad tracks and just turn around and come back."

In spite of the Army snub, Kantner flew to Washington on October 16, following the railroad tracks to Union Station, circling the Capitol dome at 1,500 feet, and continuing over the mall to the Washington Monument. But when even this half-hour flight failed to elicit any Signal Corps interest, Kantner returned to Hempstead Plains where he reported to Alfred that the Moisant Blériot simply was no longer good enough. It was outmoded, he said, just as its French prototype had been overtaken by newer, faster aircraft fashioned with stronger body frames of steel tubing instead of light wood. The last major contest to be won by a Blériot was Garros's victory at the Circuit d'Anjou the previous June. And Garros had flown the plane out of loyalty to its maker, pitting it against better aircraft and winning by sheer courage and skill. Not only was the aircraft outclassed in performance but in March 1912 the French army temporarily suspended the use of all monoplanes following a report from Blériot himself that discussed weakness in the top bracing.

Alfred responded to the young flyer's advice by telling him to "go down to the factory and see what you can do." So "I went down and for the next 30 days . . . did nothing but sketch and formulate ideas," Kantner said. The ideas culminated in the Kantner-Moisant, a two-seater monoplane with a 50-hp Gnôme rotary engine. Kantner called the new plane the "Bluebird," he explained, "because I had decided for the sake of camouflage to cover the wings with pure white muslin of good quality, but pure white which I dyed a very light blue."

Kantner spent the winter months building the Bluebird and by June he was ready to test-fly it. He recalled that there were some 150 people around when

the moment of truth finally arrived. . . . Well, she was beautiful in the air, perfectly balanced and I probably started capering around in my usual straight and conservative way. But I got up to maybe a thousand feet and shut the old engine off, which was about the only way to come down. . . . They all came running in to congratulate me. She was good enough for me.

It was good enough for Alfred, too, who set up the Bluebird's first overland flight as a contest between train and plane. At 4:30 the morning of August 8, 1913, C. Marvin Wood, who had replaced Jerwan as new chief pilot, took off from Hempstead Plains to race a train from Manhattan's Pennsylvania Station to Fort Myer in Arlington, Virginia, near the nation's capital. There he was to demonstrate the plane for Army Chief of Staff Gen. Leonard Wood and senior staff officers before flying back to Hempstead on the same day.

Pilot Wood beat the train, setting a record of 239 miles in five hours and one minute. But a forced landing at Gaithersburg, Maryland, to adjust a misfiring engine kept General Wood waiting at Fort Myer. The demonstration flight was finally made before the Bluebird was shipped back to New York by train. No orders for it came from the Army.

In a later demonstration for the commander of the Brooklyn Navy Yard, Kantner and two assistants dismantled the wings from the Bluebird and reattached them in 2½ minutes. "The load wires all slipped into their own fittings and were spring-shaped so they would come out whether they were loose or tight," Kantner said. "I pulled hard on that upper plate until that hole lined up and shoved it in and cotter-pinned the thing and it was in the air in seven minutes. [But] that didn't impress Uncle Sam, either."

The U.S. military had already issued its requirements for a two-man scout plane. It must have protective armor around the motor and body, and a radio, tachometer, compass, aneroid barometer, barograph, map holder, pad, pencil holder, clock, and angle of incidence indicator, all within reach of both pilot and observer. Additionally, the radio must have a trailing antenna and the motor would have to run six hours on a testing block to record its horsepower, speed, and fuel consumption.

Although a remarkably good aircraft for its time, the Bluebird, put together by Kantner and ten men in Moisant's Winfield factory, could not meet all these requirements.

Despite the U.S. military's lack of interest, the Aero Club of America invited Kantner to fly the Bluebird as the American entry in the fifth Gordon Bennett cup race at Rheims on September 29. But the arrangements were so sketchy and depended on so many contingencies that the race was finally contested by only three Frenchmen and a Belgian, all flying French aircraft. However Kantner had other things than the cup race in mind. He had been sent there with Alfred Moisant's blessings and instructions to gather all the new information he could on airplane design. He was particularly impressed by the work being done at the Deperdussin factory, recalling, "My mouth watered looking at the beautiful polish on those smooth monocoupe hulls . . . and, ready for racing, they were just a beautiful polished piece of wood."

In October Kantner resumed work on two Bluebirds for Mexico and a special order from President Manuel Estrada Cabrera of Guatemala who had asked for a two-seater with a 70-hp, six-cylinder radial Anzoni engine instead of the customary Gnôme. To make sure he would have a pilot capable of flying it, Cabrera had already enrolled Dante Nannini in the Moisant Aviation School. After graduation Nannini would become Central America's first aviator and director of air training in his own country. Kantner finished the plane on New Year's Day of 1914 and tested it at Hempstead with two feet of snow on the ground, recalling later, "The photographs show me all bundled up but I always remember how sweet that motor ran . . . even more powerful" than the Gnômes he had been installing on the other aircraft.

While Kantner built Bluebirds Alfred continually looked for other ways to bolster his Hempstead Plains investment. To attract business he converted one of his concrete hangars into the Moisant Clubhouse for the convenience of students, visitors, and reporters. One newsman described the conversion as having "an open-air living room" furnished with wicker rockers, tables, and grass rugs. Another praised the clubhouse view of 500 acres of runway, flag staffs flying silk weather pennants, and the adjoining property of the American Auto Polo Society "where little skeleton autos careen madly." Alfred also replaced both his sales manager and Adolph Wupperman, his long-time partner, secretary, and general manager. *Aircraft* magazine said Wupperman's replacement, Charles de Peloggio, was "untiring" in his efforts to stimulate business for the company, even going so far as to organize a private Bluebird exhibition for the foreign minister of Brazil.

No orders came from Brazil, however, and Alfred was dealt a stunning setback when the Mexican government unexpectedly sent thirty-one air trainees to a Blériot school in France and ordered twenty two-seater Blériots with 80-hp Gnôme engines not from Moisant but from his rival Louis Blériot.

By the end of 1913 Alfred could no longer escape the fact that he had to produce and sell more and better airplanes if the Hempstead Aviation Company were to survive. Once again he turned to Kantner for salvation, sending a telegram asking how long it would take him to turn out a machine that could fly in an inverted loop. This then-considered suicidal maneuver, turning a complete somersault while flying upside down, astounded the aviation world when Frenchman Adolph Pégoud performed it in public at Juvisy on September 21, 1913, in a 50-hp Gnôme-engine Blériot. The "loop the loop," as it came to be known, had actually first been flown 12 days earlier at Kiev by Russian Lt. Peter Nicholaivich Nesteroff who was promptly placed under house arrest for a month for endangering government property.

Having witnessed the Pégoud flight in France, Kantner was encouraged when the Moisant people in New York offered to "sidetrack" one plane from an order then under production for Mexico for him to adapt to aviation's new requirements. When he returned to the States Kantner discovered that Charles H. Niles, a former Curtiss pilot who had come to the Moisant field to learn to fly a monoplane, had been nagging Alfred to build a "looper." Another Curtiss flyer, Lincoln Beachey, had already looped the loop on November 25 at Coronado, California, in a small Curtiss biplane, but Niles wanted to prove it could be done in a monoplane as well.

So did Kantner, who took a Bluebird from the line at the factory in Winfield and moved it to one of the Moisant hangars at Hempstead. There he installed extra bracing and a 50-hp gyro engine, testing it, even with passengers, before turning it over to Niles. On February 2 Niles looped in it at Hempstead Field but not without considerable difficulty and luck. At 3,000 feet he put the aircraft into a 500-foot dive, then pulled up in the first part of the loop. But just as he reached the top, the motor cut out because the fuel could no longer reach the engine. After a tail slide of 1,000 feet, followed by a nose dive of another 1,000, Niles regained control of the aircraft and landed safely after a display of upside-down flying.

As soon as Kantner solved the stalling problem by modifying the fuel system for both vertical and upside-down flight, Alfred placed a full-page advertisement in *Aircraft* magazine with a drawing of the new plane captioned "C. F. Niles flying upside down." This resulted in Niles demonstrating the new Kantner-

Moisant Bluebird for General Venusliano Carranza, who had given up his post as governor of Coahuila State to join in another of Mexico's insurrections. The demonstration was so successful that Carranza, who already had one Moisant plane, bought the Bluebird on the spot and ordered another for delivery on completion. But unfortunately for Alfred the transactions were aborted when Washington embargoed the sale of planes to any of the combatants in Mexico.

The Mexican revolution aroused the War Department's interest in the airplane as a weapon, but this too benefited his competitors rather than Alfred. First Washington asked the Wright Company to speed up construction of two biplanes already on order for the Army. Then, when the American Atlantic fleet in early May took control of the port of Vera Cruz because of the arrest of some U.S. soldiers in Tampico, one of the ships turned out to be carrying three Glenn Curtiss flying boats and their pilots.

That May Alfred had Niles demonstrate the Bluebird again for Army officers at Governor's Island, where he did side slips, loops, head dives, tail drops, and rolls before concluding with an upside-down flight over Broadway past the Woolworth building. In July Kantner piloted a Bluebird to victory in a race from Governor's Island to the Coney Island Yacht Club and back. And in August Niles gave several shows at Coney Island, in one of which he horrified spectators with a stunt in which he dropped a dummy from the plane. The Bluebird demonstrations had deteriorated to the air-circus level of stunt flying which neither sold planes nor made money. Just as Alfred had predicted in 1910, the military use of aircraft had already begun. But, as he had never planned or expected, his own country's military passed him over for the last time.

Alfred's last efforts to promote the Bluebird were probably too late anyway, because by June he had already moved his office from prestigious Times Square to 58th Street and Broadway. His new stationery no longer listed the names of his International Aviators.

Instead it read "Makers of Moisant Aeroplanes of All Types" and bore the true but by now somewhat outdated claim that "the Moisant monoplane secured more records in 1911 than any other American-made aeroplane." A month later he moved the office again, this time to the factory. Ostensibly the move was made "in order to have the executive offices in close touch with their plant at Winfield." But a more likely explanation is that high-rent Manhattan office space was no longer within the Moisant means.

One by one, Alfred's assistants were leaving him. Chief pilot Wood was hired by the government of Guatemala to train flyers. Niles was recruited by Gustavo Salinas to fly for the Carranza revolution in Mexico. The Moisant Aviation School closed and Jerwan followed Wood to Guatemala. Last to leave and by far the greatest loss was Harold Kantner, hired by another plane builder, Howard Huntington. Huntington had taken over three of Moisant's hangars and put Kantner to work in one of them, designing and constructing biplanes.

That Alfred's business was failing was apparent by September when an association of plane makers at Hempstead Plains revealed plans for a series of meets designed "to bring forcibly to the attention of the American public the uses and value of the aeroplane." John E. Sloane of the Sloane Aviation Company was president of the newly formed Week-End Meets Association and Alfred was vice-president. But the board included all five of his competitors at Hempstead—Albert Henrich, Maximillian Schmitt, Howard Huntington, Sidney Beckwith, and Sloane. And at their first meet Kantner flew a Schmitt monoplane.

By January 1914 Alfred's name had disappeared from the pages of aircraft publications. When it reappeared more than two years later it was on the classified advertising page of *Aerial Age* magazine, close to a want ad placed by "a young man 22 years old and of good habits" looking for a starting position in aviation. Alfred had filed for bankruptcy and the notice read:

FOR SALE—MOISANT MONOPLANES
Tractors, Pushers and famous "loop the loop" machines, imported motors, a few secondhand at bargain prices. Imported Gnome piston

rings, brand new. The Moisant-Peloggio Corporation, 1600 Broadway, New York City, N.Y.

The Moisant saga had ended. But among all their colleagues and competitors few had been so doggedly determined that humans were destined to fly. And fewer still had fought so stubbornly and consistently to turn the dream of flight into reality. The names of Alfred, John, and Matilde Moisant typify that band of illustrious though largely unknown pioneers who—often with more courage than common sense but always with conviction—soared bravely into uncharted territory to challenge and subdue the strange new world of flight.

EPILOGUE

The remainder of the Moisant saga is both colorful and tragic.

On January 13, 1946, John Bevins Moisant was honored in New Orleans with the opening of a new airport named after him—the Moisant International Airport. The guest of honor at a two-day celebration and formal dedication was Congressional Medal of Honor winner Lt. Gen. Jimmy Doolittle, a fitting choice. The man who led the first B-25 bombing raid on Tokyo was as daring and dashing as John himself had been in his day. And the new $5,000,000 field with its four-mile-long runways was the largest commercial airport in the United States at the time, on scale with John's own most splendid prophecies.

But the restoration of John's fame was a fleeting thing. Seventeen years later the field was expanded and renamed the New Orleans International Airport, the Moisant name now diminished to a memorial tablet at the new terminal entrance reading,

In commemoration of a pioneer in aviation, John Bevins Moisant, who lost his life in an airplane accident near this site, December 31, 1910. He was the first to carry a passenger across the English Channel, inventor of an early all-metal airplane, a man of lovable character whose tragic death was a great loss to aviation.

John's son, Stanlie John Moisant, followed in his father's foot-steps and became a pilot. The boy who had been kidnapped by his father and brought to Santa Emilia, then sent to California to live with his aunt and uncle, had been a student at Hitchcock Military Academy when his father died. He completed his stud-ies there and earned an undergraduate degree from the Univer-sity of California at Davis. In 1918 he took his flight training at Mineola on the field once leased by his uncle Alfred but now a training center for the Army Signal Corps.

Stanlie was commissioned a second lieutenant and posted to Rockwell Field in San Diego as an Army instructor. By January 1919 he had logged 365 hours of flying time. Mustered out that year he went to El Salvador to assess some property left to him by his father and to see if he could interest the Salvadorans in aviation. While at Santa Emilia a few months later he con-tracted yellow fever, died there on May 12, 1920, and was buried at his uncle's hacienda. He was only 26.

Alfred Moisant never recouped the fortune he had lost in the aviation business. After selling off his planes and motors, he re-mained in New York where he married Virmedella, commonly known as Vera, a widow with one daughter. Like John, though much less successful at it, Alfred turned to inventing and devel-oped a number of devices, including a water-cooler system, on which he never took out any patents. In 1923 he hired a young assistant, J. L. Miles, who was to recall years later that their ef-forts were so unsuccessful that after one year of working to-gether, they had between them only 50 cents for a shared lunch.

Miles also recalled that, bereft as Alfred was of his former en-trepreneurial success, he was still as charming and ebullient as ever. "As you know," he wrote, "he was not prosperous by then [1924]. Some people quite considered that his feet were too far above the ground. Nevertheless, he possessed that sort of genius and spirit that seems lost today."

Alfred and Vera left New York for El Salvador after receiving the news that his brothers George and Edward had died of pneumonia within six weeks of each other—George on December 15, 1927, and Edward on January 21, 1928. They had been managing the main property at Santa Emilia since Alfred's departure and during his absence had acquired seven coffee *fincas*.

In no time at all, Santa Emilia was as crowded as it had been more than 20 years earlier when Don Alfredo and the Moisant family played constant host to luminaries of the area. Alfred and Vera were soon joined by Ann Moisant Weyl and her 14-year-old son John from Los Angeles; George's daughter Melida and her husband Louis Hockwald from San Francisco; and Edward's son Bertin with his wife Elizabeth and Edward's daughter Gladys with her husband Alfred Malcolmson.

Ann's son John remembers Alfred at that time as a vigorous, white-haired man of 67, sturdy, but not fat, always wearing a jacket over his shirt but tieless, a large Stetson hat on his head and a .38-caliber revolver at his waist. He also remembers the rising atmosphere of tension at Santa Emilia as the children of George and Edward realized they would inherit much less than they had expected from the Santa Emilia estate since Alfred had incorporated it years before and was the majority shareholder.

"All the adult males wore .38 revolvers or .45 automatics at the plantation," John said. "It was quite unpleasant at that time. There was a lot of electricity in the air, and I clearly remember coming back with Uncle Fred as we called him from being out in the fields just before lunch time, coming into the walkway and up onto the porch in front of the house when a shot came through the floor. It missed us. Louis Hockwald said his gun went off accidentally, but it didn't."

Before the spring of 1929 all of the family members except Alfred and Vera had left the plantation. Ann and John had returned to Los Angeles and the others were either in Sonsonate or elsewhere in El Salvador. On April 4 that year Vera drove Alfred to Sonsonate in his big Chandler touring car, accompanied by a bodyguard and a hacienda employee in the back. They had an appointment with a lawyer named Martinez to discuss Alfred's claims to the plantation which had become entangled in the Salvadoran court system. After conferring with Martinez at the Santa Emilia Company's Green House that George had used

as both office and residence, they started back home with Vera
again at the wheel, Alfred beside her, and the bodyguard and
worker in the back seat. They were on a dirt road outside Sonsonate when a shot rang out. As Vera described it in a letter to
Ann:

Just off the cobblestones after turning the corner from town towards
Santa Emilia, there is a short incline downwards in front of the Martinez place on the right side of a once-was house and I noticed some
stones in the road in such a position that I had to swerve all the way
across the road to the right to pass. We know now that those stones
had been placed there purposely as the man in ambush was hidden in
this wrecked house on the right. I swerved to [the] right and heard a
crack almost at my right elbow, and turned to say, "More tire trouble"
as we had had a flat the day before, when I saw a stream of red down
Fred's shirt front. Then I knew that it must have been a shot.

Alfred died within seconds.

In the capital of San Salvador, the newspaper *El Dio* reported
the death of "Alfredo Moisant" as "an unsolved mystery," possibly a case of revenge "coldly premeditated and executed with
frightening serenity, considering that Mr. Moisant was not loved
in the country." He was, the paper said, a well-known North
American and "a founder of the National Bank of sad memory," undoubtedly a reference to Alfred's lengthy defiance of his
competitors who, with government backing, attempted to destroy his bank by having it officially declared insolvent.

The paper said Alfred had also founded a grain company for
buying and selling cereals and, more recently, entered the ce-
ramics industry, amassing a great fortune as well as being co-
owner of Santa Emilia.

However, the official government paper, *Diario del Sol*, differed with *El Dio*, calling Alfred's death a tragedy and describing him as "a gentleman well-known in the country and . . .
held in high esteem." The paper added that Alfred's body was
taken to the city where a "cortadas" (i.e. dumdum, or expanding) bullet that had entered his chest above the right nipple was
extracted and he was buried the next day at Santa Emilia.

Although the Salvadoran police investigation never uncovered the murderer there is no doubt that both Edward's son Bertin and George's son-in-law Louis Hockwald were determined to acquire part or all of Santa Emilia. Subsequent events strongly suggest that one or the other of them, if not both of them in collusion, were involved in the killing. The bitter rivalry between them smoldered for some two years before erupting into a gunfight aboard the railroad car from Acajutla to Santa Emilia in which Bertin killed Louis.

Bertin's victory, if such it was, was a Pyrrhic one at best. Some time later, while he was in San Salvador on business and registering at the Hotel Nuevo Monde, Louis's widow Melida walked across the lobby, drew a pistol from her purse, and shot him to death. She was arrested and jailed but never brought to trial. Subsequently rumored to be the mistress of the chief of police, she eventually left El Salvador to live in New Orleans.

In the decade following the deaths of Louis and Bertin Santa Emilia was managed intermittently by the women of the family with Louise assuming much of the responsibility. From 1938 until 1941 Matilde and Louise lived there together until their nephew John Weyl, by then a lawyer, negotiated a final settlement for all the heirs to the estate.

When Matilde was not at Santa Emilia she lived with Louise, first in an apartment in Los Angeles and later in two different houses in La Crescenta, California. For a brief time in the early 1930s Louise was married to, then divorced from Dr. John D. Utley of La Crescenta.

Matilde never flew an airplane again, nor did she ever learn to drive.

Always an ardent patriot, as early as 1917 she offered to serve in France with General Pershing's American Expeditionary Force. When the offer was refused she became a Red Cross volunteer instead. She never did make it to France during that first world war but designed and patented a Red Cross doll and continued to work for that organization for many years. At the age of 61 she wrote a pilot friend after Japan attacked Pearl Harbor,

"Isn't this war terrible? I wish I were 20 years younger. I would love to take a shot at a few of those old birds, wouldn't you?"

Matilde maintained an avid interest in aviation and sought acknowledgment of the contributions she and her brothers had made to its advancement. She joined the Early Birds, an association of pioneer pilots, and lobbied to have her brother John listed posthumously as a member. She failed in that request but succeeded in getting the Aero Club of America to search its records to verify the time she had spent taking flying lessons. It turned out to be 32 minutes (between July 13 and August 13, 1911), the shortest in licensing history, her nearest rival having trained for 1 hour and 57 seconds.

Matilde and Louise led an active social life. Except for the period of Louise's short marriage, she and Matilde remained constant companions, briefly sharing a house in Los Angeles before moving into a larger one in La Crescenta to be close to their older sister Ann Weyl and her family. The two were recognizable figures in the area, always traveling together, Louise always behind the wheel of the automobile because her older sister, who had loved and lived with planes, still considered cars a menace.

In 1957 Matilde suffered a double loss in the death of both her sisters—Louise in April just two weeks short of her 74th birthday, and Ann the day after Christmas. With her lifelong companion gone, Tillie—or Tudy, as she was known to her family and friends—moved into a small apartment. Her nephew John, who considered her his "second mother," called frequently and took over as chauffeur.

Matilde died peacefully in 1964 at the age of 86. Numerous Early Bird members came to the memorial service to eulogize her. All were impressed by her aviation achievements but at least one was impressed by the woman as well, noting that "rarely have we had one of our members more deserving of public praise and acclaim, yet so retiring and self-effacing."

The Moisant family is separated in death as it never was in life. Matilde and Louise are buried in a single grave at the Portal of the Folded Wings in North Hollywood, California. Next to them is the grave of their brother John, whose body was removed from the vault in New Orleans. Alfred, who never flew but contributed as much as his siblings to their shared vision of aviation, lies at Santa Emilia ignored and unhonored some 2,200 miles away. This despite the fact that his predictions of only 20 years back—scheduled flights between cities, transatlantic crossings, and air delivery of mail and freight—had already been made reality. On the very day he died, Mayor James J. Walker, speaking of Floyd Bennett Field then under construction, said, "New York must have several airports in the near future"; Hugo Eckener announced that the Graf Zeppelin that year would make two Atlantic crossings, and the Aeronautics Branch of the U.S. Commerce Department reported that planes in the U.S. had flown more than 70 million miles in 1928, more than in any other nation.

Like so many of early aviation's true pioneers, the Moisants expected too much too soon. Gambling against the odds, they all lost. John lost his life. Alfred his fortune. And Matilde the two men she most loved. But they never faltered in their stubborn convictions, their farsighted predictions, and their wholehearted dedication to flying and to each other.

NOTES

Four reliable sources provided and/or confirmed information on the family of Medore Moisant during the period between 1858 and Medore's death in 1887. They are: Verna Drake, research chairman of the Iroquois County Genealogical Society, Watseka, Ill.; Norma Meier, CGRS (Certified Genealogical Records Specialist); Ray S. Fearing, director, Family History Center, Bourbonnais, Ill.; and John A. Weyl, nephew of Alfred, John, and Matilde Moisant. Hereafter these persons shall be cited simply as Drake, Meier, Fearing, and Weyl, with the person named having provided the major material.

Documents used by one or more of the above include: U.S. Census, 1860 and 1880; the 1884 Atlas of Iroquois County, Illinois; *Iroquois County Original Land Purchases, 1831–1882,* a research project of the Iroquois County Historical Society by Ralph D. and Virginia M. Moore; *Translation, Abstraction and Compilation of St. John the Baptist Catholic Church, L'Erable, Illinois, Record Book One, 1856–1879, Baptisms, Marriages, Burials, Confirmations,* by Norma Meier. Copyright 1980 Norma Meier. McDowell Publications, Owensboro, Kentucky.

Material on Moisant family activities in Central America—such as dispatches, cables, letters, and affidavits—is in the National Archives in Washington, D.C. It is filed under Record Group 84, Records of Foreign Service Posts, El Salvador and Nicaragua. In chapter notes it is designated NA (for National Archives), the box or volume number and, where available, the date of the document.

Chapter 1. The Surrogate Father

1 Josephine was 21: Drake, Meier, and Fearing.
   The Moisant family name appears frequently . . . : Drake.
2 Marriage of Edwin Booth and Mary McVickers: Emmett Dedmon, *Fabulous Chicago* (New York: Random House, 1953), 88.
   Land Medore purchased: Drake.
   System of drainage tiles: Harold T. Drake, agriculturalist, interview with author, Watseka, Ill., Aug. 22, 1994.
3 Birth of Joseph Georges: Drake.
   Move to Clifton: Meier.
   Birth of Joseph Jean Baptiste: A family genealogical note that shows John Bevins as being born April 25, 1873, in Kankakee, Ill., is obviously in error. John's passport application states he was born April 25, 1870, in Chicago; the 1880 Federal census records him as as being 10 years old that year, and records from the Notre Dame Church show he was baptized there on May 29, 1870. (Josephine Moisant was a devout Catholic and all of her children were baptized.)
   Hardware store account: Meier.
4 Birth of Ann Marguerite: Fearing.
   Birth of Matilde Josephine: Weyl.
   Manteno census of 1880: Fearing.
5 Clannishness of rural French immigrant families: Drake.
   "Boss City": Dedmon, *Fabulous Chicago,* 119, 134.
   Alfred's claim as general manager: Alfred Moisant, press release from the Moisant Scrapbooks at National Air and Space Museum, Smithsonian Institution (hereafter NASM Scrapbooks).
   "Mikado Ball": Dedmon, *Fabulous Chicago,* 119–34.
6 1888 Alameda city directory: *Oakland, Alameda, Berkeley City Directory,* F. M. Husted, Publisher, 604 Merchant Street, San Francisco.
   Park Street in Alameda: Woodruff C. Minor, *Historic Commercial Buildings of Alameda* (Alameda, Calif.: Historical Advisory Board, 1993).
   Alameda's growth: City of Alameda Planning Department, *City of Alameda Historic Preservation Element* (May 6, 1980).

6 Newspaper carrier's complaints: *Alameda Daily Argus,* Jan. 25, 1888.

7 "splendid farm in Alameda": *New Orleans Picayune,* Jan. 1, 1911. City records show no evidence of Alfred's ownership. But the *Alameda Daily Argus* of Feb. 11, 1983, lists his brother John as delinquent in payment of taxes on lands adjacent to Encinal, lot 4, plot 2, to be sold on Feb. 28 by the city tax collector if the debt was not paid.
Moisants in the social column: *Argus,* March 15, April 5, and July 2, 1890.

8 Coffee plantations: *Argus,* Aug. 5, 1891.
Property in El Salvador, Mexico, Nicaragua, and Honduras: Press releases, Jan. 17 and 25, 1911, NASM Scrapbooks.
"watchfulness and seizing opportunities": *New Orleans Picayune,* Jan. 1, 1911.
"as much as a horse and buggy to ride in fashion": *Argus,* July 25, 1888.
John's marriage to Edith F. Stanle: Weyl. Copy of marriage license and notice in the *Alameda Argus,* Feb. 7, 1895.

9 Birth of Stanlie: *Alameda Daily Argus,* Nov. 25, 1895.
Beauty of El Salvador: John A. Weyl, interview with author, La Cañada Flintridge, Calif., April 1994 (hereafter Weyl interview).
Move to Santa Emilia: Ann spent almost eight months (Jan. 29 to Sept. 11) at Santa Emilia in 1897 before enrolling at the University of California at Berkeley. Twenty-year-old Matilde became a virtual commuter, going back and forth from high school, spending longer and longer periods each time. When Alfred brought his mother to Santa Emilia in 1900, only George's wife, Mary, their children, and Ann were left in Alameda, and even they became yearly visitors.
"a hacienda": Letter, June 10, 1907, Box 87.5, "Participation in the Escalon Revolution in El Salvador," 1907, NA.

10 Third largest quota in El Salvador: Weyl.

11 "Green House": Ibid.
Co-owners of the salt works: Letter, July 19, 1907, Box 87.5, NA.
Owning coffee plantations: Letter, July 1, 1907, in "Dispatches to the Department of State" (hereafter "Dispatches"), Box 87.5, NA.
Selling Banco Nacional stock: "Dispatches," 1907. Dodge, Frazier, Heimke, July 28, 1909, c8.3. vol. 4, NA.

11 Partnership with Perez, Moisant & Co.: Letter, May 1, 1907, Box 87.5, NA.
12 Shipwreck off Acajutla: "General Letters Sent," May 9, 1904, 1904–1905–1906, c8.3, vol. 2, NA.

Chapter 2. The Buccaneer

14 "No hero of romance": *New York Times,* Aug. 18, 1910, in NASM Scrapbooks.
    "That night, in the teeth of the gale . . .": Ibid. (The newspaper, as well as many others, misspelled John's Christian name throughout, a common press error of the times.)
15 "dried fish . . .": Percy F. Martin, FRGS, *Salvador of the Twentieth Century* (London: Edward Arnold, 1911), 290–93.
    Edith at Santa Emilia: *Alameda Daily Argus,* Jan. 26, 1901.
16 Divorce records: Ibid., Feb. 14, 1901.
    John leaving with Stanlie: Ibid., April 23 and 24, 1901.
17 "Stanlie's sword and air gun": "General Letters Received," Jan.–June 1908 and others from 1900 to July 1907, Sept. 4, 1902, c8.8, NA.
18 Stanlie's return: 1905 San Francisco City Directory, Bancroft Library, University of California at Berkeley.
    Stanlie at boarding school: Weyl interview.
    Central American Federation: Martin, *Salvador of the Twentieth Century,* 290–93.
19 Figueroa and Alfred: Enclosure no. 3, June 10, 1907, Box 87.5, NA.
    "not acceptable": "Dispatches," April 3, 1907, c8.3, NA.
    "subversive language . . . ": Enclosure no. 3, June 10, 1907, Box 87.5, NA.
    George and Alfred leaving the country: "Dispatches," April 4 and May 12, 1907, c8.3, NA.
20 George's arrest and release: Ibid., April 27 and May 12, 1907.
    "If you think that hostile . . . ": Ibid., April 27, 1907.
    George and Edward arrested: "Dispatches," May 30, 1907, Box 87.5, NA.
21 Merry's descriptions of the Moisants: Merry to Secretary of State Elihu Root, June 1, 1907, Box 87.5, NA.
22 Moisants' release: Enclosure 2, June 10, 1907, Box 87.5, NA.
    Losses to forces: John Moisant was not the only foreign soldier

of fortune with the invasion forces. Francisco Altschul, a reported German army deserter, supervised the occupying troops in Acajutla while Moisant took the main contingent to Sonsonate. He later served as Nicaraguan Consul at New Orleans. American Legation Managua, Miscellaneous correspondence 1908, letter, Oct. 19, 1908, c8.4, vol. 3, NA.

22 Wager's account of the invasion: Wager, letter to AmConGen, San Salvador, June 12, 1907, c8.2, vol. 3, NA.

23 Figueroa on his way to Sonsonate: Martin, *Salvador of the Twentieth Century,* 63–64.

24 Evacuating Santa Emilia: "Dispatches," June 20, 1907, Box 87.5, NA.
Scott's arrest and release: Ibid., June 23, 1907.
Protecting Santa Emilia: Ibid., June 15, 20, 30, and July 1, 1907.
Keeping the plantation operating: Ibid.
"wipe the slate": Ibid., June 26, 1907.

25 Occupying the salt works: Ibid., Sept. 3, 1907.
"things would go easier": Affidavit of George Moisant, Sept. 3, 1907, Box 87.5, NA.
"without being threatened with torture . . .": Affidavit of Andrew J. Leonard, Sept. 3, 1907, Box 87.5, NA.
Supporting the coup attempt: Letter, July 20, 1907, c8.3, vol. 3, NA.
George contesting mayoral race: Ibid., July 21, 1907.

26 "Permit the people of Salvador . . . ": Ibid., Undated letter from William L. Merry, American Minister San Salvador.
George and Edward's trial: Ibid., "Dispatches," Oct. 12 and 15, Nov. 16 and 19, 1907.
"he would have done as much damage . . . ": Ibid., Oct. 2 and 5, 1907.

27 "swooped down upon the port . . . ": *Alameda Daily Argus,* Nov. 21, 1907.
John on Nicaragua: Ibid.

Chapter 3. A Troubled Paradise

28 Moisants' claim of indemnity: Jan. 1, 1908, c8.6, vol. 5, NA.

29 Conspiracy of General Potencia Escalon: June 14, 1908, c8.3, vol. 3, NA.
"immediate expulsion of any Americans": Ibid., March 14, 1908.

30   Bribing the captain: Ibid., March 24, 1908.
      " . . . the evidence is not conclusive": Ibid.
      Retreat to Managua: Ibid., May 26, 1908.
      Suarez's refusal to come ashore: Ibid., Sept. 30, 1908.
31   "protected as they seem to be . . .": Ibid., Dec. 19, 1908.
      SS *Acapulco:* Dec. 14, 1908, c 8.4, vol. 3, NA.
      "a great naval fight": *Evening Times-Star,* Jan. 4, 1909.
      Loading weapons: Dec. 14, 1908, vol. 3, c 8.4, NA.
      Invasion: c 8.3, Vols. 4, 5, and 6, NA.
32   Planning another invasion: April 8 and May 1, 1909, vol. 7,
      American Legation, Managua, "Dispatches," 1908–9, NA.
33   Facing possible trial in the States: *Alameda Evening Times-Star,*
      July 6, 1909.
      Alfred's appeals in Washington: Jan. 14, 1908, vol. 3, c 8.3,
      NA.
34   Run on the bank: Oct. 7, 1909, vol. 4, c 8.3, NA.
      "personal friends": April 7, 1910, vol. 5, c 8.3, NA.
      "he was making more money than he could utilize": Ibid.

Chapter 4. The Aviator

35   "They're ugly on the ground . . .": "The Reminiscences of
      Matilde Moisant," Oral History Research Office, Columbia
      University, New York, 1960.
36   John would fly: Ibid.
37   John's first airplane: *La Revue Aérienne,* Feb. 1, 1910, 49–50.
      John's description of plane: *Alameda Times-Star,* Feb. 18, 1910.
38   The Aluminoplane crashed: A. J. Moisant press release, Jan. 25,
      1911, NASM Scrapbooks.
      Description of first flight: *San Antonio Light,* Jan. 31, 1911.
      "No man should build an aeroplane . . .": *Air-Scout,* January
      1911, 9.
      Design of *Le Corbeau: Aero,* Jan. 19, 1910; correspondence to
      author from Wesley R. Smith, Dec. 28, 1993.
39   Blériot's schools: *Aero,* Nov. 19, 1910, 23, and April 12, 1910,
      288.
40   American license: Henry Serrano Villard, *Contact! The Story of
      the Early Birds,* rev. ed. (Washington, D.C.: Smithsonian Insti-
      tution Press, 1987), 260.
      Description of Blériot XI: *Aircraft,* Jan. 19, 1911, 439; Maj.

James F. Sunderman, USAF, *Early Air Pioneers, 1862–1935* (New York: Franklin Watts, 1962), 70–72.

40 World's first long-distance air race: Villard, *Contact!,* 98.

41 "Paris, which usually stays abed . . .": G. F. Campbell Wood, "A Month in France," *Aircraft* (October 1910): 282–84.

Garros flying Demoiselle: *Temple* (Texas) *Daily Telegram,* Jan. 24, 1911.

Moisant flying from Paris to Issy: AJM press release, Jan. 25, 1911.

"Whilst the excitement was at its height . . .": Wood, "A Month in France," 282–84.

42 " . . . perhaps helped my reputation a little": Richard Ryland, "John B. Moisant: The Man Who Flew Up the Ladder of Fame," *Air-Scout* (February 1911): 17–19, 44.

Easier ways to commit suicide: Ibid.

Hubert Latham: Curtis Prendergast, *The First Aviators* (Alexandria, Va.: Time-Life Books, 1980), 68.

Flying with Filieux: AJM press release, Jan. 25, 1911.

43 His critics giving up on John Moisant: *AAHS Journal* (Spring 1963): 5.

Landing at Calais: *New York Times,* Aug. 18, 1910.

Chapter 5. World Record

44 Takeoff: *New York Times,* Aug. 18, 1910.

46 Interview with *London Daily Mail: London Daily Mail,* Aug. 18, 1910.

Triple record: AJM press release, Jan. 25, 1911.

Narrowly missing the mouth . . .: *New York Times,* Aug. 18, 1910.

47 "in an awkward position . . .": *Montreal Star,* Aug. 18, 1910.

Splintered propeller: *New York Times,* Aug. 18, 1910.

Wiring for new propeller: *London Morning Advertiser,* Aug. 19, 1910.

"like a marble . . .": *London Evening Star,* Aug. 18, 1910.

Paree-Londres: *Montreal Star,* Aug. 18, 1910.

"What an airman he is": *New York Times,* Aug. 18, 1910.

Grahame-White and Drexel: *London Daily Mirror,* Aug. 19, 1910.

47   "Then charge them sixpence each . . .": *London Daily Mirror,*
      Aug. 22, 1910.
48   Still 18 miles from London: *Flight* magazine, Aug. 27, 1910;
      New York Times, Aug. 22, 1910; *London Daily Mirror,* Aug.
      23, 1910.
      Sending mechanic and workers to England: *London Daily Mir-
      ror,* Aug. 24, 1919.
      "I can't fly yet": *New York Times,* Aug. 19, 1910. Louis Paul-
      han was a popular French aviation pioneer.
49   Events at the repair site: *London Daily Express,* Aug. 27, 1910.
      Fourth crash: *London Daily Mail,* Aug. 29, 1910; *London
      Morning Leader,* Aug. 29, 1910.
      "Dear Sir . . .": *London Penny Illustrated,* Sept. 3, 1910.
      Waiting for winds to die down: *Kent Courier,* Sept. 10, 1910.
50   Reaching London: *Yorkshire Evening News,* Sept. 6, 1910.
      "I have done what I set out to do . . .": *Northern Daily Mail,*
      Sept. 10, 1910.
      Family in New York: "Reminiscences of Matilde Moisant."
      At Folkestone: *The Graphic,* Sept. 20, 1910.
51   "the recklessness of the crowd": *Morning Advertiser,* Sept. 23,
      1910.
      The French couldn't help it: *Brooklyn Eagle,* Oct. 9, 1910.
52   Photo opportunities: *Baltimore News,* Oct. 12, 1910; *Grand
      Rapids Press,* Oct. 17, 1910.
      "In five years time . . .": *Somerset County Gazette,* Sept. 9,
      1910.
      Hotel Astor: *Brooklyn Eagle,* Oct. 9, 1910.
      Day interview: *Air-Scout,* November, 1910.

Chapter 6. For America!

54   World's most prestigious air tournament: *New York Press* and
      New York Morning Sun, Oct. 19, 1910.
      Curtiss winning trophy: Villard, *Contact!,* 79–82.
55   Blériot test flight: *New York Herald,* Oct. 20, 1920.
56   "I simply forgot . . .": *New York Telegram,* Oct. 21, 1910;
      New York Sun, Oct. 21, 1910.
      Repairing plane: *New York Herald,* Oct. 21, 1910.
      "King of the Air": *New York City Review,* Oct. 22, 1910.

57   Belmont meet: *Brooklyn Eagle,* Oct. 23, 1910.

58   "a mariner's feat in midair": *New York City World,* Oct. 23, 1910.
      "the most marvelous aviator . . .": *Dallas Times-Union,* Oct. 23, 1910.
      "How he ever found his way back . . .": *Aircraft,* December 1910.
      Grahame-White's wreck: *Aero,* Oct. 29, 1910, 7–8.

59   Moisant's wreck: Sherwood Harris, *The First to Fly: Aviation's Pioneer Days* (New York: Simon and Schuster, 1970), 205–6.
      "a death trap": *New York American,* Oct. 24, 1910.
      Course too dangerous: *Brooklyn Standard-Union,* Oct. 24, 1910.
      Moisant's complaints about show: *New York American,* Oct. 24, 1910.
      Lost in the fog: *New York Herald,* Oct. 26, 1910.

60   Saving the Blériot: *Brooklyn Standard Union,* Oct. 27, 1910.
      "so angry he sputtered . . .": *Boston Post,* Oct. 27, 1910.
      Team members: *Washington* (D.C.) *Times,* Oct. 28, 1910.

61   "It was like hitting the pipe . . .": *New York Telegraph,* Oct. 29, 1910.
      Racing aircraft: *Aircraft,* December 1910.
      Leblanc's crash: *New York American,* Oct. 30, 1910.

62   "I had started over . . .": Harris, *First to Fly,* 205–6.
      "I am going to throw . . .": *Springfield* (Mass.) *Union,* Oct. 30, 1910.
      Moisant's flight: *Portland Oregonian,* Oct. 30, 1910.
      "The cup will not remain . . .": *New York Times,* Oct. 30, 1910.

63   "Here's to America—next year!": *Springfield* (Mass.) *Union,* Oct. 30, 1910.
      The next race: Norman E. Borden, "The Remarkable John B. Moisant," *American Aviation Historical Society Journal* (Spring 1963): 8.

Chapter 7. "The Greatest Race of Modern Times"

64   "*before* a bad accident . . .": *Aircraft,* December 1910, 355.
65   Attendees from the social register: *New York Herald,* Oct. 31, 1910.

65 Costumes: *New York Morning Sun,* Oct. 31, 1910.
Moisant's wreck: AJM press release, Jan. 10, 1911.
Alfred's reaction to wreck: *New York Herald,* Jan. 31, 1910.

66 Buying Leblanc's plane: AJM press release, Jan. 18, 1911.

67 "The great crowd watched . . .": *New York Herald,* Oct. 31, 1910.
Flights of de Lesseps and Grahame-White: *New York American,* Oct. 31, 1910; *New York Tribune,* Oct. 31, 1910; *New York Sun,* Oct. 31, 1910.
"to rise steadily . . .": Clipping provided by his nephew, John A. Weyl, of bylined article written by John B. Moisant from otherwise unidentified newspaper. Graham-White's official time was actually 35:21:30, a half-minute slower than Moisant had been told.

68 Moisant's return flight: *New York Telegram,* Oct. 31, 1910; *New York Tribune,* Oct. 31, 1910.
"He's won! He's won!": *Baltimore Sun,* Oct. 31, 1910.
American celebrations: *New York Telegram,* Oct. 31, 1910.
Winning time: Moisant's official time was 34:38.34 versus Graham-White's 35:21.30.
Average speed for flight: Borden, "Remarkable John B. Moisant," 8.
Average speed for return flight: AJM press release, March 3, 1911.
Alfred's celebration: *Baltimore Sun,* Oct. 31, 1910.

69 Grahame-White's protest: *Baltimore Sun,* Oct. 31, 1910, and *New York Times,* Oct. 31, 1910.
Drexel's protest: 22. *New York American,* Nov. 1, 1910.
"a demonstration that has never been equaled . . .": *New York Herald,* Oct. 31, 1910.
"the greatest race . . .": *New York World,* Oct. 31, 1910.

70 Justin's interview with Matilde and Louise: *New York Mail,* Oct. 31, 1910.
"as well as I know English": *New York Globe,* Nov. 12, 1910.
Carew's interview with John: *New York American,* Nov. 6, 1910.
Paree-Londres in the news: *New York City Telegram,* Oct. 29, 1910; *New York Mail,* Oct. 26, 1910.

71 "My cat's gone! . . .": *New York American,* Nov. 2, 1910.
"like agate set in balls of ivory": *New York American,* Nov. 6, 1910.

Chapter 8. The Moisant Bird Men

72 "none but the biggest . . .": Article submitted by AJM to *Billboard* magazine, March 2, 1911.

73 "When an aviator actually got up . . .": "Jack" Sterns Gray, *"Up": A True Story of Aviation* (Strasburg, Va.: Shenandoah Publishing House, 1931).

74 Editorial: *Aero,* June 21, 1910.
Future of the airplane: AJM press release, March 2, 1911.
Moisant International Aviators, Inc.: *New York Times,* Nov. 2, 1910.
Garros: Villard, *Contact!,* 37; *Aero* magazine, Aug. 19, 1911. A pilot in the First World War, Garros escaped from a German prisoner-of-war camp and was made a Chevalier of the Legion of Honor. He died a month before the war ended in a fight with a group of German Fokkers. The sports stadium in Paris where the French Open tennis matches are played was named in his honor.

75 Simon: *Aero* magazine, Aug. 19, 1911.
Audemars: *Aircraft,* December, 1910.
Hamilton: Harris, *First to Fly,* 179; *New York Times,* Nov. 5, 1910.

76 "the only really Irish aviator": AJM press release, Sept. 2, 1911.
Seymour: Ibid.
Pilot salaries: *New York Times,* Nov. 21, 1910.

77 Daily expenses: Ibid.
"The flyers' corner . . .": *New York Sun,* Nov. 21, 1910.
Bookings: *New York Times,* Nov. 21, 1910.

Chapter 9. Beginners' Luck

78 Hamilton, Simon, Barrier, and Garros were all in the air . . .: *Richmond News Dealer,* Oct. 23, 1910.
Frisbie's biplane needed repairs . . .: *Aero,* Dec. 3, 1910.

79 Complimentary tickets: *Richmond Leader,* Nov. 24, 1910.
Friday and Saturday shows: *Richmond Times-Dispatch,* Nov. 26, 1910.

80 Although attendance was poor . . . : *Aero,* Dec. 3, 1910.

80   Show in Chattanooga: *Chattanooga News,* Nov. 29, 1910;
      Chattanooga Times, Nov. 29, 1910.
81   Daly's accusation: *Aero,* Dec. 10, 1910.
      "Our men are not grass-cutters": *Memphis Commercial Ap-
      peal,* Dec. 1, 1910.
82   "the kind of crowd pleasing . . .": *Aero,* Dec. 10, 1910, 13;
      Memphis Scimitar, Dec. 2, 1910; Harris, *First to Fly,* 227.
      "The program said . . .": Harris, *First to Fly,* 227.
      Second and third days: *Memphis Scimitar,* Dec. 3, 1910; *Aero,*
      Dec. 10, 1910.
      Garros's crash: *Memphis Scimitar,* Dec. 4, 1910.
83   Eleven days of flights: *Memphis Commercial Appeal,* Dec. 8,
      1910.
      John's altitude attempt: *Aero,* Dec. 24, 1910.
      One of Moisant's stunts . . .: *Memphis Commercial Appeal,*
      Dec. 10, 1910.
      John's reckless turn: *New Orleans Picayune,* Dec. 16, 1910.
84   "to drop a detonating explosive . . .": *Galveston* (Texas) *News,*
      Dec. 9, 1910.
      John on war: "The Moisant International Aviators," pamphlet
      issued by AJM, 1911.
      Accidents and near accidents: *Memphis Commercial Appeal,*
      Dec. 11, 1910.
85   Memphis show held over: *Aero,* Dec. 25, 1910.
      Promise to promoter: *New Orleans Picayune,* Jan. 1, 1911.
      John's last landing: *New Orleans Picayune,* Dec. 21, 1910.

Chapter 10. When It's Wintertime Down South

87   Meeting in St. Charles Hotel lobby: *New Orleans States,* Dec.
      22, 1910.
88   "limousine monoplane": *New Orleans Times-Democrat,* Dec.
      15, 1910.
      Passenger load: *New Orleans Picayune,* Dec. 17, 1910.
      "John Moisant's funny little plane . . .": Kantner tapes, cassette
      1-A (provided by son Richard D. Kantner), Oct. 18, 1993;
      Aero, Sept. 12, 1910.
      "where today there is one aeroplane . . .": *New Orleans Times-
      Democrat,* Dec. 18, 1910.

89   Morning flight over New Orleans: *New Orleans Item,* Dec. 24, 1910; *New Orleans States,* Dec. 25, 1910.
90   Opening show: *Aero,* Dec. 31, 1910.
91   Christmas show: *New Orleans Picayune,* Dec. 26, 1910; *Boston Morning Globe,* Dec. 26, 1910.
      "so that we may enjoy life": *New Orleans Picayune,* Jan. 2, 1911.
      John's altitude attempt: *New York Herald,* Dec. 29, 1910; *Aero,* Jan. 7, 1911.
92   Caught in a gale: *New Orleans Picayune,* Dec. 30, 1910.
      The crowd was "delirious": *New Orleans Picayune,* Dec. 31, 1910.
      Tabuteau's time: Villard, *Contact!*
      Dinner with the Ellises: *New Orleans Picayune,* Jan. 1, 1911.

Chapter 11. More Than Any Man

94   Preparation, flight, and crash: *New Orleans Picayune,* Jan. 2, 1911.
96   "as if he had been shot from a gun": *New Orleans Picayune,* Jan. 1, 1911.
      "He's dead!": *San Antonio Light,* Jan. 1, 1911.
      But his smile was a grimace . . .: *New Orleans Picayune,* Jan. 2, 1911.
      On the flat car: Ibid.
      "No use flying up there . . .": Harris, *First to Fly,* 218–19.
97   The family learns of John's death: *New Orleans Picayune,* Jan. 2, 1911; *Oakland Tribune,* Jan. 1, 1911; *San Antonio Light,* Jan. 1, 1911.
      "There's another good man gone . . .": *San Antonio Light,* Jan. 1, 1911.
98   Hoxsey's death: *Aero,* Dec. 31, 1910.
      Viewing: *New Orleans Picayune,* Jan. 1, 1911.
99   Eulogies: *Fort Worth Record,* Jan. 1, 1911.
      Funeral: *New Orleans Picayune,* Jan. 1 and 2, 1911; *Fort Worth Record,* Jan. 2, 1911.
100   Leaving for Jacksonville: *New Orleans Picayune,* Jan. 2, 1911; *La Luca* (Havana), Jan. 6, 1911.
101   "Two centuries ago . . .": *Air-Scout,* January 1911.

101 "abandon all idea . . .": *Aero,* Jan. 7, 1911.
   Reasons for crash: *New Orleans Picayune,* Jan. 2, 1911; *Aero,* Jan. 7, 1911.
102 "No air machine . . .": *Oakland Tribune,* Jan. 1, 1911.
   "He was due . . .": *New Orleans Picayune,* Jan. 2, 1911.
   "He did more than any man . . .": Ibid.

Chapter 12. Circus Soldiers

103 Preserving John's memory: *Aircraft,* Jan. 17, 1911.
   "a limousine monoplane . . .": *Dallas Morning News,* Dec. 21, 1910.
   McGarvie's boasts: Ibid.
104 Simon's crash: Ibid., Jan. 7, 1911; *Elmira* (N.Y.) *Advertiser,* July 20, 1911.
   Other mishaps: *Fort Worth Record and Register,* Jan. 7, 1911.
   Crowds on January 8: *Galveston News,* Jan. 9, 1911; *New York Times,* Jan. 9, 1911.
   Colquit: *Aero,* Jan. 21, 1911; *Waco Daily Times-Herald,* Jan. 10, 1911.
105 Fort Worth: *Fort Worth Telegram,* Jan. 12, 1911; *Fort Worth Record,* Jan. 13 and 14, 1911.
   Waco shows: *Waco Times-Herald,* Jan. 21 and 23, 1911; *San Antonio Light,* Jan. 24, 1911.
106 Other Texas dates: *Temple Mirror,* Jan. 22 and 29, 1911; *Houston Chronicle,* Jan. 25 and Feb. 1, 1911.
   "Then . . . ": *New York Globe,* Jan. 28, 1911.
   "tame, tractable aeroplanes": *Binghamton* (N.Y.) *Herald,* Jan. 28, 1911.
   Garros's perfect landing: *Houston Chronicle,* Jan. 28, 1911.
107 Garros in the prairie: Ibid., Jan. 30, 1911.
   January 31 competition: *Dallas News,* Feb. 1, 1911.
   Arrangements for Cuba: *La Luca,* Jan. 6, 1911; *Aircraft,* May 1911.
108 "the present aerial equipment . . .": *Aero,* Jan. 21, 1911.
   "neither of whom . . .": *Aeronautics,* February 1911, 66.
   Hempstead Aviation Company and board: *Aero,* Dec. 31, 1910, and March 4, 1911.
109 Hiring Lovelace: Ibid., Feb. 11, 1911.

109 Bombing maneuvers: *San Antonio Light,* Feb. 5, 1911; *Aero,*
Feb. 25, 1911, n.p.
110 Garros's rough landing: *San Antonio Express,* Feb. 6, 1911.
Aero cover story: *Aero,* Feb. 25, 1911.
111 Reconnaissance mission: *Shreveport* (La.) *Times,* Feb. 7, 1911.
Press release: AJM press release, Feb. 4, 1911.
"would be taken into consideration": *Wheeling* (W.V.) *Intelli-gencer,* Feb. 9, 1911.
Press reports: *San Antonio Light,* Feb. 5, 1911.
112 Taft's opinion: *Wheeling* (W.V.) *Intelligencer,* Feb. 9, 1911.
Hamilton's flight to Mexico: *Aero,* Feb. 25, 1911; *New York World,* Feb. 12, 1911; *El Paso Times,* Feb. 11, 1911.
113 Borrowing: From its owner, Robert J. Collier.
"It is rather a feather . . .": *Aero,* March 4, 1911.

Chapter 13. Show and Sell

114 Staging Mexican air shows: *New York Evening Sun,* Feb. 15, 1911.
"a howling success": *Monterrey News,* Feb. 20, 1911.
115 The second day in Monterrey: *Mexican Herald,* Feb. 22, 1911.
Hamilton's lawsuits: AJM press release, March 25, 1911; *New York Times,* Aug. 2, 1910.
116 Hamilton's arrest: NASM Scrapbooks.
"do not waste lead . . .": *New Haven Journal,* March 26, 1911.
117 First day of Mexico City show: *Mexican Herald,* Feb. 25, 1911; letter from Albert LeVino, *Aircraft,* April 1911.
"the elite society . . .": *Mexican Herald,* Feb. 26, 1911.
National Railway record: *Mexico City Record,* March 2, 1911.
118 Formal opening of show: Ibid., Feb. 25 and March 2, 1911; *New Orleans Picayune,* April 8, 1911.
"The road was inches deep . . .": *Mexico City Herald,* March 1, 1911.
"the International Aviators . . .": *Aero,* March 4, 1911.
Garros's record: LeVino, letter to Carl Dienstbach, March 15, 1911, NASM Scrapbooks.
Bombing exhibition: *New Orleans Picayune,* March 4, 1911.
119 "greatly benefitted": *Aero,* March 18, 1911.

119 Diplomatic corps of China and Chile: *Mexico City Record,*
March 2, 1911.
Alfred's expenses: Article by AJM, *Billboard* magazine, March
2, 1911; *Mexican Herald,* Feb. 23, 1911.
"not be a financial success . . .": *Aero,* March 4, 1911.

120 Johnstone: AJM press release, June 2, 1911, NASM Scrapbooks.
Cuba shows: Ibid.
"had to chase cows . . .": Harris, *First to Fly,* 226–27.
McCurdy: Henry A. Wise Wood, "The Havana Meet," *Aircraft,* May 1911.
Barrier competes: *Aircraft,* May 1911; *New York Herald,* May
11, 1911.

121 Johnstone's flight and crash: *Aircraft,* May 1911.
Other crashes: Ibid.
Prize money: *Aero,* March 22, 1911.

122 Garros's crash: Ibid.
"rather a disappointment . . .": *Aero,* April 8, 1911.

Chapter 14. A New St. Emilia

123 Statue of Liberty race: *New York Times,* March 15, 1911;
Aero, March 18, 1911.
John's watch: *Aero,* April 1, 1911.
John's estate: *New York Herald,* April 2, 1911.

124 Monument: *New York Sun,* April 2, 1911.
Pilot contracts: *Aero,* May 6, 1911.
"except for the surface . . .": AJM press release, March 27,
1911.

125 Moisant Juniors: *Aircraft,* May 1911.
Delay at docks: *New York Tribune,* April 17, 1911; *New York
Times,* April 17, 1911.
Aviation complex: *Aero,* March 6, 1911.

126 Complex's boundaries: Lygia M. Ionnitiu, "The Mineola Air
Field," *Harriet Quimby Research Conference Journal* 1 (1995),
ed. Giacinta Bradley Koontz. Moisant's land was renamed
Hazelhurst Field in 1917, Curtiss Field in 1921, and Roosevelt
Field in 1929. In 1951 developers took over the whole area for
residential and commercial buildings.

126 Other aviation schools: *Aero,* March 6, 1911.
Aircraft factory: AJM press release, March 8, 1911.

127 "limousine-bodied tourabouts": AJM press release, March 27, 1911.
"John's funny little plane": Kantner tapes, cassette 1-A, transcript p. 25 (hereafter, e.g., Kantner, 1-A, 25).
First monoplane: AJM pamphlet, n.d., NASM Scrapbooks.
School opening: *New York Herald,* April 24, 1911.

128 Hangars, instructors, and new planes: *Brooklyn Eagle,* May 4, 1911; *Aeronautics,* May 1911; AJM pamphlet, n.d., NASM Scrapbooks.
Promotional pamphlet: AJM pamphlet, n.d., NASM Scrapbooks.
Moisant Aviation School: *Brooklyn Eagle,* May 4, 1911; AJM press release, May 5, 1911; Kantner, 1-A, 36–40.

Chapter 15. Angels in the Air

129 "Rain and fog . . . ": Undated news clipping, S. S. Jerwan Scrapbook, NASM.
Harriet Quimby: "Reminiscences of Matilde Moisant," 1.
"When Moisant landed . . .": Unidentified news clipping, May 21, 1911, NASM Scrapbooks.

130 Quimby's series of articles: Ed Y. Hall, *Harriet Quimby: America's First Lady of the Air* (Spartansburg, S.C.: Honoribus Press, 1990), ed. with an introduction by Ed Y. Hall, 37; *Leslie's Illustrated Weekly,* Jan. 26, 1911.
"tall and willowy": "Reminiscences of Matilde Moisant."
Quimby's costume: *New York Times,* May 10, 1911; Hall, *Harriet Quimby,* 41.
Alfred on plane safety: AJM to Harriet Quimby, May 12, 1911, NASM Scrapbook.

131 "grass-cutting": *Leslie's Illustrated Weekly,* May 25, 1911.
"deceptively easy . . .": George Weston, "Beauty and the Blériot: The Story of Harriet Quimby, Pioneer Aviatrix," *Aviation Quarterly* 6, no. 1 (Spring 1980): 59.
Houpert's methods: Harriet Quimby, "How A Woman Learns to Fly," *Leslie's Illustrated Weekly,* May 25, 1911.

131 "about 4:30 . . .": Unidentified news clipping, May 21, 1911, NASM Scrapbook.

132 "absolutely refuse . . .": *New York American,* May 14, 1911.
Bessica Raîche: *New York Times,* May 10, 1911.
Marvingt's record: 45 kilometers in 53 minutes.
Dutrieu's records: Villard, *Contact!*
Jerwan: Unidentified news clipping, Jerwan Scrapbook.
Kantner: Kantner, 3-A, 37, 39; "Reminiscences of Matilde Moisant," 35.

133 Runaway plane: *New York Times,* June 25, 1911.
Matilde's interest in flying: "Reminiscences of Matilde Moisant," 2.

134 Matilde's first lesson: Ibid., 35–36.

135 "I could have had my license first . . .": Ibid., 33–34.
"a flying machine was safer . . .": *Washington Post,* May 7, 1911.
Kruckman's comments: *New York American,* May 14 and July 18, 1911.
"are temperamentally unfitted . . .": *New York American-Examiner,* September 1911.

136 Quimby's license: *Leslie's Illustrated Weekly,* Aug. 24, 1911; *Flight,* September 1911.
"control their nerves": *New York Evening Telegram,* Aug. 2, 1911.
Quimby's background: Hall, *Harriet Quimby,* 202–27; San Francisco City Directories, 1901–3, Bancroft Library, University of California–Berkeley.
Matilde on women flying: *Chicago Daily News,* Aug. 15, 1911.

Chapter 16. Mixed Reviews for a Box Office Flop

139 "Ze man . . .": *Hutchison News,* April 17, 1911.
Pueblo shows: *Pueblo Chieftain,* April 5 and 19, 1911; *Aero,* April 29, 1911, 96; *Denver News,* April 17, 1911.
"more skillful and graceful": *Aero,* April 29, 1911.

140 "wobbled to the ground . . .": *Omaha World-Herald,* May 12, 1911.
Topeka: *Topeka Daily Capital,* April 30, 1911.

140 St. Joseph: *St. Joseph Gazette,* May 8, 1911.
Sarah Bernhardt: *Los Angeles Examiner,* May 24, 1911; *San Francisco Post,* May 26, 1911.

141 Crashes: *Memphis Commercial Appeal,* May 7, 1911; *Wichita Beacon,* April 27, 1911.

142 Arrests: *St. Joseph Gazette,* May 6, 1911.
Unserviceable planes: *Aero,* May 6, 1911.
Young's deal: *Omaha World-Herald,* May 12, 1911.
Needed overhauls: *Chicago Examiner,* May 23, 1911; *Detroit Times,* May 29, 1911.
Shows in Ottumwa: *Clinton* (Iowa) *Advertiser,* June 8, 1911; *Des Moines Tribune,* June 9, 1911.
In Davenport: *Dubuque* (Iowa) *Times,* June 13, 1911.
In Galesburg: *Macomb* (Ill.) *Journal,* June 14, 1911; *Galesburg Mail,* June 14, 1911.
In Terre Haute: *Terre Haute Star,* June 19, 1911.
In Logansport and Marion: *Indianapolis Sun,* June 28, 1911; *Logansport Journal,* June 29, 1911; *Marion News-Tribune,* June 29, 1911; *Richmond Item,* June 30, 1911.
Collegiate Aviation meet: *Detroit News,* May 1 and 12, 1911; *Detroit Free Press,* May 3, 1911; *Detroit Journal,* June 6, 1911; *Petosky* (Michigan) *News,* May 31, 1911.

143 Dinner at the Hotel Pontchartrain: *Petosky* (Michigan) *News,* May 31, 1911; *Detroit Times,* July 1, 1911.
Detroit crashes: *Detroit Journal,* July 4, 1911.

144 Financial situation: Ibid.; *Detroit News,* July 2 and 8, 1911; *Dover* (N.H.) *Democrat,* July 2, 1911.
"The World's Greatest Aggregation of Airmen": *Aero,* July 1, 1911.

Chapter 17. Big Plans and Bad Luck

146 Alfred's costs: *Kankakee Daily Republican,* Aug. 17, 1911.
Company directorate: Official brochure of Moisant International Aviators, Inc., June 28, 1911. The other directors were listed as H. W. Jacobs, assistant director of motive power, Atchison, Topeka and Santa Fe Railroad; Edwin E. Bush, assistant general traffic manager, American Express Company;

James S. Herrman, trustee, Union Dime Savings Bank, New York; Christopher J. Lake, vice-president, Lake Torpedo Boat Company, and W. J. Taylor, capitalist.

147 *Aero* ads: *Aero,* Aug. 12, 1911.

Expansion: Research by Vincent F. Seyfried, cited in July 29, 1997, letter to author from aviation historian Frank Strnad.

European trophies: *Elmira* (N.Y.) *Advertiser,* July 21, 1911.

Cross-country prizes: *Aero,* July 27, 1911.

148 International air meet: *Chicago Daily Tribune,* Aug. 12, 1911.

Simon's protest and Johnstone's crash: Ibid.

149 "risking his own neck . . .": *Chicago Post,* Aug. 14, 1911.

Frisbie's flight: *New York World,* Aug. 14, 1911.

"sorry to see . . .": Letter from Otto to Gus Baysdorfer, Historical Society of Douglas County, Library/Archives Center, Omaha, Nebraska.

Simon on the lake: *Seattle Times,* Sept. 2, 1911; *Chicago Tribune,* Aug. 15, 1911.

150 Johnstone's accident: *Chicago Interocean,* Aug. 16, 1911.

151 Alfred's comments about Johnstone: *Kankakee Daily Republican,* Aug. 16, 1911.

"they cheerfully paid . . .": G. F. Campbell Wood, "Impressions of the Big Meet," *Aircraft,* September 1911.

Barrier's departure: *Chicago Record-Herald,* Aug. 22, 1911; *Brooklyn Eagle,* Aug. 22, 1911.

152 "In ten months here . . .": *Chicago Record-Herald,* Aug. 15, 1911.

Chapter 18. Resigning, Regrouping, Replacing

153 Going to Kankakee: *Kankakee Daily Republican,* Aug. 17, 1911.

Economizing: *Joliet News,* Aug. 27, 1911.

154 In Joliet: *Joliet Herald,* Aug. 27, 1911.

Frisbie's departure: *South Bend* (Ind.) *Tribune,* Sept. 2, 1911.

Heegel's crash: *Rockford Republican,* Aug. 31, 1911; *Freeport Bulletin,* Sept. 1, 1911.

Selling the plane: *Freeport Journal,* Sept. 1, 1911.

Frisbie's crash: *New York Herald,* Sept. 2, 1911.

155 "was not flying . . .": *Kankakee Daily Republican,* Sept. 2, 1911.

155 Alfred's promises: Ibid., Sept. 5, 1911.
Kankakee shows: *Kankakee Daily Republican,* Sept. 5 and 6, 1911; *New York Tribune,* Sept. 9, 1911.
At South Bend: *South Bend Times,* Sept. 11, 1911.

156 Simon's departure: *Aero,* Oct. 7, 1911; *New York Daily Mail,* Oct. 12, 1911.
Seligman's flights: *Canton Repository,* Sept. 28 and 29, 1911.

157 Aviation school: *Aero,* Sept. 29, 1911.
Announcing move: *Aircraft Magazine,* October 1911.
Lake's resignation: *Bridgeport* (Conn.) *Telegram,* Sept. 12, 1911.
Passenger-carrying biplane: *Aeronautics* magazine, October 1911.

158 Matilde's flying: *Brooklyn Eagle,* Aug. 17, 1911; *New York Sun,* Aug. 27, 1911.
"born to the sport": *New York Evening World,* Sept. 18, 1911.
Hensingmuller's article: *Mobile* (Ala.) *Register,* Sept. 3, 1911.

159 "I have taught many women . . .": Ibid.
Quimby's exhibition flight: *St. Louis Globe-Democrat,* Sept. 3, 1911; *Brighton Long Island Star,* Sept. 9, 1911; *New York Sun,* Sept. 3, 1911.
Quimby's first contract: *New York Tribune,* Sept. 5, 1911; *St. Louis Globe-Democrat,* Sept. 5, 1911.

160 Matilde's flight: *New York Times,* Sept. 10, 1911; *New York Telegram,* Sept. 10, 1911; *Miami Herald,* Sept. 16, 1911.

Chapter 19. Rising Stars

161 Nassau meet: *Aircraft* magazine, October 1911.

162 Opening day: *Pittsburgh Gazette-Times,* Sept. 24, 1911; *St. Paul Pioneer Press,* Sept. 24, 1911.
Air scouts: The flyers were Claude Grahame-White and Thomas O. M. Sopwith of England, and J.A.D. McCurdy, George W. Beatty, and Eugene B. Ely of the United States.
Air-mail delivery: *Boston Journal,* Sept. 24, 1911.
Harriet and Matilde's flights: *New York Times,* Sept. 24, 1911; *Boston Journal,* Sept. 24, 1911.

163 Women not flying on Sunday: Villard, *Contact,* 248. Marie-Josèphe de Beauregard, *Femmes de l'air: Chronique d'une con-*

quête (Paris: Éditions France-Empire, 1993); *New York Herald,*
Sept. 29, 1911.
163 Matilde's flight: *New York Herald,* Sept. 29, 1911.
Sunday prize money: Ibid.; *New York Times.* Sept. 25, 1911.
164 "very impertinent": *New York Times,* Sept. 26, 1911.
Monday's events: Ibid.
Rest of meet: *Brooklyn Eagle,* Sept. 28, 1911; *New York
Times,* Sept. 26 and 27, 1911; *Aircraft* magazine, November
1911.
165 Descriptions of Matilde: *New York Press,* Oct. 1, 1911; *Dallas
Herald,* Oct. 1, 1911.
Descriptions of Quimby, Scott, and Dutrieu: *New York Press,*
Oct. 1, 1911; *Dallas Herald,* Oct. 1, 1911.
166 "is the best sport . . .": *Brooklyn Eagle,* Oct. 1, 1911.
Saturday records: *Aero,* Oct. 7, 1911; *New York Times,* Oct. 1,
1911.
168 Sunday flights: *New York Tribune,* Oct. 9, 1911.
"I was just so happy . . .": "Reminiscences of Matilde
Moisant," 49.
Louise's disapproval: Ibid., 49–50.
"I know my limitations . . .": *New York Evening Sun,* Oct. 3,
1911.
Matilde's stunts: *San Francisco Call,* Oct. 17, 1911; *Alameda
Times-Star,* Oct. 25, 1911.

Chapter 20. Matilde at the Controls

170 Air shows in Mexico City: Pat Fry, education coordinator, San
Diego Aerospace Museum, letter to author, Oct. 29, 1996.
171 Two new pilots: *New York Tribune,* Oct. 27, 1911; *Aero,* Oct.
23, 1911.
Curtiss team: *Aero,* Nov. 25, 1911.
Traveling to Mexico: *New York Evening World,* Nov. 2, 1911;
Aero, Nov. 25, 1911; *New York Times,* Nov. 2, 1911.
"really social affairs . . .": *Mexican Herald,* Nov. 12, 1911.
172 Flying over Chapultepec Castle: "Reminiscences of Matilde
Moisant," 16–17; Matilde Moisant, letter to the Early Birds,
April 11, 1947.

172 First day's show: *Mexican Herald,* Nov. 17, 1911; *Aero,* Dec. 2, 1911.

Third day: *Mexican Herald,* Nov. 19, 1911.

173 Sunday flights: Ibid., Nov. 20, 1911.

Close of show: Ibid., Nov. 25, 1911; *Aero,* Dec. 2, 1912.

Flyers' departures: *Aero,* Dec. 9 and 23, 1911; *Mexican Herald,* Dec. 1, 1911, and Jan. 18, 1912; *Aero,* Dec. 9, 1911; Hall, *Harriet Quimby,* 102.

174 Madero's order: Fry, letter to author, Oct. 29, 1996.

175 Matilde's flights in Guadalajara: *Mexican Herald,* Dec. 11, 1911; "Reminiscences of Matilde Moisant," 21–22.

Other shows in Mexico: *Joliet News,* n.d., NASM Scrapbooks.

176 Trapped on the train: Ibid.; *San Antonio Light,* Feb. 16 and 17, 1911; *Joliet News,* n.d.

Chapter 21. Matilde's Finale

177 New hires: *Aero and Hydro,* April 24, 1913.

178 Delays: *New Orleans Picayune,* March 7, 1912.

"this cup . . .": Ibid.

Cancellation: *New Orleans Statesman,* March 10, 1912.

Opening day: *New Orleans Picayune,* March 11, 1912.

179 "not correct": *New Orleans Item,* March 11, 1912.

"as womanly a woman . . .": *Shreveport Times,* March 15, 1912.

"They call us birds . . .": Ibid.

Matilde's crash: "Reminiscences of Matilde Moisant," 19; *Shreveport Journal,* March 18, 1912.

180 Dallas shows: Kantner, 3-B, 50; *Dallas Morning News,* March 25, 26, and 27, 1912; *Dallas Dispatch,* March 22, 1912.

181 Retirement announcement: *Alameda Times-Star,* April 10, 1912.

Advertising Matilde: *Aero,* April 6, 1912.

"I have the air intoxication . . .": *Good Housekeeping,* September 1912.

182 Last flight: *Wichita Falls Daily Times,* April 15, 1912; "Reminiscences of Matilde Moisant," 20–21.

Chapter 22. The Crossing

184 A. Leo Stevens: *Aircraft,* April 1910.
Introduction to Blériot: Hall, *Harriet Quimby,* 102.
Approval from employers: Ibid., 92.

185 Exclusive British rights to story: Harriet Quimby, "An American Girl's Daring Exploit," *Leslie's Illustrated Weekly,* May 16, 1912.
Arrangements for plane: Ibid.
Hamel's offer: Elizabeth Hiatt Gregory, "Woman's Record in Aviation," *Good Housekeeping,* September 1912. In 1914 Hamel, who made many channel flights the year before and had recently completed a nonstop flight from Dover to Cologne, started across it from France to England and was never seen again.

186 Quimby's flight: *Leslie's Illustrated Weekly,* May 16, 1912.

187 "a very tired . . .": Ibid.

188 Society of American Women in London luncheon: *Christian Science Monitor,* May 2, 1912.
"Nothing has pleased me . . .": *Alameda Daily Argus,* April 23, 1912.
Earhart's comment: Weston, "Beauty and the Blériot," 56.
"I had been using a copy . . .": *Aero,* June 1, 1912.
Problems with new plane: *Sportsman Pilot,* December 1938; *Aero and Hydro,* July 6, 1912.

189 Harvard-Boston air meet: *Aircraft,* August 1912.
Flying the mail: *New York Times,* July 2, 1912.
Quimby's final flight: Hall, *Harriet Quimby,* 127, 128; *New York Times,* July 2, 1912; *Boston Globe,* July 2, 1912.

190 "accidental fall . . .": The Commonwealth of Massachusetts Standard Certificate of Death, City of Quincy.
Speculations on cause of accident: *Aeronautics,* August 1912; *Aircraft,* August 1912; *Boston Globe,* July 3, 1912.

191 Funeral: *Boston Globe,* July 3, 1912; Elizabeth Hiatt Gregory, *Show Window of Life* (Wayside Press, 1944), 70; *New York Times,* July 5, 1912; *Daily Courier* (Coldwater, Mich.), July 6, 1912.

Chapter 23. The Bottom Line

192 Garros's victory: Villard, *Contact!*, 148–51.
Houpert returns to France: *Wichita Falls Daily Times*, April 15, 1912.

193 Leasing factory: *Aero*, April 28 and May 5, 1912.
Chief pilot Jerwan: Jerwan Scrapbook, NASM.

194 Aviation school: *Augusta* (Ga.) *Herald*, Dec. 1, 1912; *Aero and Hydro*, Dec. 21, 1912.
Seligman's exhibition: *Kingston* (Jamaica) *Gleaner*, Dec. 21, 1911; *Aero*, Feb. 10, 1912.
Deliveries for Mexican army: *Aero and Hydro*, Aug. 10 and Sept. 10, 1912; *Aircraft*, September 1912.
Salinas brothers: Jerwan letter, Aug. 17, 1912, Jerwan Scrapbook; *Aero and Hydro*, July 27, Aug. 20, and 31, 1912.

195 Aldasoro brothers, Ruiz, and brothers: *Augusta Herald*, Dec. 1, 1912; *Aero and Hydro*, Oct. 26, 1912, and April 20, 1913.
Kantner's contributions: Kantner, 3-A, 41, 42; B-3, 44–45; *Aero and Hydro*, April 6, 1912.

196 Kanter's demonstrations to Signal Corps: Kantner, 3-B, 51, 53.
Phasing out monoplane: Villard, *Contact!*, 152.

197 Kantner-Moisant plane: Kantner, B-4, 56.
Testing the Bluebird: *Aircraft*, July 1913; Kantner, 4-B, 58.
Demonstrating the Bluebird: *Aeronautics*, August 1913.

198 "The load wires all slipped . . .": Kantner, 2-B, 15.
Two-man scout plane: *Aerial Age*, February 1912.
Gordon Bennett cup race: Villard, *Contact!*, 188–91.

199 Kantner on new plane design: Kantner, 2-B, 18; 4-B, 61.
Building Bluebirds: *Aircraft*, October 1913 and February 1914; Kantner, 4-B, 58.
Moisant Clubhouse: *Aircraft*, June 1913; *Motography*, Sept. 9, 1913.
Alfred's telegram: Kantner, 4-A, 68.

200 "loop the loop": Villard, *Contact!*, 193–94.
Building a looper: Kantner, 4-A, 68, 70; Harris, *First to Fly*, 288–89.
Flying the looper: *Aero and Hydro*, Feb. 14, 1914. S. S. Jerwan, "Flying as It Was," *Sportsman Pilot* (Dec. 15, 1938): 18–19, 30–32.

200 Full-page ad: *Aircraft,* March 1914.
Sale of plane to Mexico: Jerwan, "Flying as It Was," 32.
Smuggling Curtiss planes: *Aero and Hydro,* April 23, 1914.
Bluebird demonstrations: Jerwan, "Flying as It Was," 32; Kantner, A-1, 24; *Aero and Hydro,* Aug. 15, 1914.

202 "the Moisant monoplane . . .": Manuel Estrada Cabrera, letter, July 20, 1914, Jerwan Scrapbook.
Moving the office: *Aircraft,* October 1914.
Assistants leaving: Jerwan, "Flying as It Was," 32; Kantner, 4-A, 70–73.
Association of plane makers: *Aero and Hydro,* Sept. 12, 1914.
Bankruptcy: Research by Vincent F. Seyfried, cited in July 29, 1997, letter to author from aviation historian Frank Strnad.
"FOR SALE": *Aerial Age,* March 13, 1916.

Epilogue

204 Stanlie as pilot: *Alameda Times-Star,* May 13, 1920; aviation historian Ed Leiser, letter to Giacinta Bradley Koontz, Nov. 20, 1995.

205 Alfred's life after aviation: *Alameda Times-Star,* May 13, 1920; letter to author from John Weyl, dated March 4, 1996; J. L. Miles, letter to Paul Edward Garber, Aeronautics Section, Smithsonian Institution, and later director of NASM, Dec. 27, 1935; Miles, letter to Matilde Moisant, Feb. 20, 1935, NASM Scrapbooks.

206 Tension at Santa Emilia: Weyl interview.

207 Alfred's murder: Vera Moisant, letter to Ann Weyl, n.d., John Weyl's papers.
Alfred's obituary: *El Dio,* April 5, 1929; *Diario del Salvador,* April 5, 1929.

208 Gunfight: Weyl interview.
Bertin's murder: John A. Weyl, letter to author, March 4, 1996 (hereafter Weyl letter).
Final settlement: Weyl interview.
Louise's marriage: Weyl interview and letter from John A. Weyl to Dr. B. E. Moisant, March 3, 1981.

209 Matilde's life: Weyl, letter to author; letter, Dec. 30, 1941, from Matilde Moisant, in Matilde Moisant file, NASM; letter to the

Early Birds, Oct. 2, 1961; letter from Matilde Moisant to Aero Club of America, May 24, 1961; "Reminiscences of Matilde Moisant," 40.

"rarely have we had one . . .": Text of eulogy delivered Sept. 13, 1964, by Ivan P. Wheaton, treasurer of the Early Birds of Aviation.

BIBLIOGRAPHY

Borden, Norman E., Jr. "The Remarkable John B. Moisant." *American Aviation Historical Society Journal* (Spring 1963).

Caidin, Martin. *Barnstorming*. New York: Duell, Sloan, and Pearce, 1965.

Crouch, Thomas. *The Bishop's Boys: A Life of Wilbur and Orville Wright*. New York: Norton, 1989.

Dade, George, and Frank Strnad. *A Picture History of Aviation on Long Island, 1908–1938*. New York: Dover, 1989.

Davenport, William Wyatt. *Gyro! The Life and Times of Lawrence Sperry*. New York: Scribner's, 1978.

de Beauregard, Marie Josèphe. *Femmes de l'air: Chronique d'une conquête*. Paris: Editions France-Empire, 1993.

Dedmon, Emmett. *Fabulous Chicago*. New York: Random House, 1953.

DeLear, Frank J. "What Killed Harriet Quimby?" *Yankee Magazine* (September 1979): 113–15, 210–16.

Gray, "Jack" Sterns. *"Up": A True Story of Aviation*. Strasburg, Va.: Shenandoah Publishing House, 1931.

Gregory, Elizabeth Hiatt. "Woman's Record in Aviation." *Good Housekeeping*, September 1912.

Gunn, George C. Curator, Alameda Historical Museum. *Documentation of Victorian and Post-Victorian Residential and Commercial*

Buildings. City of Alameda. 1854 to 1904. Photograph reproductions by Dr. Vernon Rabbach. Cover, Lisa Haderlie Baker. 1985. Revised, 1988.

Gwynn-Jones, Terry. "The Meteoric Rise and Fall of Brash Johnny Moisant." *Smithsonian Magazine* (September 1985): 148.

Hall, Ed. Y. *Harriet Quimby: America's First Lady of the Air.* Spartansburg, S.C.: Honoribus Press, 1990.

Harper, Harry. *The Evolution of the Flying Machine: Balloon, Airship, and Aeroplane.* Philadelphia: David McKay Company, 1930.

Harris, Sherwood. *The First to Fly: Aviation's Pioneer Days.* New York: Simon and Schuster, 1970.

Holden, Henry. *Her Mentor Was an Albatross: The Autobiography of Harriet Quimby.* Mount Freedom, N.J.: Black Hawk Publishing Company, 1993.

Jablonski, Edward. *A Pictorial History of Aviation.* Garden City, N.Y.: Doubleday, 1980.

Jane's. *All the World's Airships, Aeroplanes, and Dirigibles Flying Annual.* London: Sampson-Low Marston & Co., Ltd., 1910.

Jerwan, S. S. "Flying as It Was." *Sportsman Pilot* (December 15, 1938): 18–32.

Klym, Julie Opell. "America's First Flight Academy." *The AOPA Pilot* (October 1979).

Martin, Percy F., FRGS. *Salvador of the Twentieth Century.* London: Edward Arnold, 1911.

Maxim, Hudson, and William J. Hammer. "Chronology of Aviation." Reprinted from *World's Almanac* (1911). (James Means Collection. Smithsonian Institution Langley Aeronautical Library.)

Meier, Norma CGRS. *St. John the Baptist Catholic Church. L'Erable, Illinois. Record Book One.* Owensboro, Ky.: McDowell Publications, 1980.

Moisant, John B. "The Gentle Art of Aviation." *Air Scout* 1, no. 3 (January 1911): 9.

———. "My Paris to London Flight." *Aeronautics* (January 1911): 2.

Moore, Ralph D., and Virginia M. Moore. *Iroquois Original Land Purchases, 1831–1882,* a research project of the Iroquois County Historical Society, 1977.

Oakland, Alameda Berkeley City Directory. San Francisco: F. M. Husted Publisher, 1880–1908.

Peterson, Houston. *See Them Flying: Houston Peterson's Air Age Scrapbook, 1909–1910.* New York: R. W. Baron, 1969.

Prendergast, Curtis. *The First Aviators*. Alexandria, Va.: Time-Life Books, 1980.

Quimby, Harriet. "An American Girl's Daring Exploit." *Leslie's Illustrated Weekly,* May 16, 1912.

———. "American Bird Woman. Aviation as a Feminine Sport." *Good Housekeeping,* September 1912.

———. "How I Won My Aviator's License." *Leslie's Illustrated Weekly,* August 24, 1911.

Sunderman, Maj. James F., USAF. *Early Air Pioneers, 1862–1935.* New York: Franklin Watts, 1962.

Tallman, Frank. *Flying Old Planes*. Garden City, N.Y.: Doubleday, 1973.

Villard, Henry Serrano. *Blue Ribbon of the Air*. Washington, D.C.: Smithsonian Institution Press, 1987.

———. *Contact: The Story of the Early Birds*. Washington, D.C.: Smithsonian Institution Press, 1987.

Weston, George. "Beauty and the Bleriot: The Story of Harriet Quimby, Pioneer Aviatrix." *Aviation Quarterly* 6, no. 1 (Spring 1980): 56.

Whitt, Samuel E. "Miss Harriet Quimby." *National Aeronautics* 1, no. 1 (Spring 1973): 20.

Wohl, Robert. *A Passion for Wings: Aviation and the Western Imagination*. New Haven: Yale University Press, 1994.

INDEX

241